The Passion Parties

GUIDE TO

Great Sex

The Passion Parties

GUIDE TO

Great Sex

SECRETS AND TECHNIQUES TO KEEPING
YOUR RELATIONSHIP RED HOT

Pat Davis

BROADWAY BOOKS

NEW YORK

This book is dedicated to women everywhere who want to explore new possibilities. Whether you are seeking a relationship, are in a short-term or long-term romance, or are happily flying solo, sexual pleasure is your birthright. There is a Passion Diva in you, and she is fabulous! Meet her, embrace her, make her your best friend, and together you will be unstoppable in enjoying life to the fullest.

PUBLISHED BY BROADWAY BOOKS

Published in the United States by Broadway Books, an imprint of The Doubleday Broadway Publishing Group, a division of Random House, Inc., New York.
www.broadwaybooks.com

BROADWAY BOOKS and its logo, a letter B bisected on the diagonal, are trademarks of Random House, Inc.

Book design by Chris Welch

Library of Congress Cataloging-in-Publication Data

Davis, Pat, 1944–
The Passion Parties guide to great sex : secrets and techniques to keeping your relationship red hot / Pat Davis. — 1st ed.
p. cm.
1. Sex instruction for women. I. Title.

HQ46.D36 2007
613.9'6082—dc22

2006025592

ISBN: 978-0-7679-2437-5

PRINTED IN THE UNITED STATES OF AMERICA

7 9 10 8

Contents

Part III
Passionate Partners

The Passion Parties
GUIDE TO
Great Sex

Introduction

Meet Your Passion Diva

My party that Friday night began like every other party: women giggling as I passed around tasty and buzzy things . . . except for one woman. She stood at a distance and didn't participate. I thought she wasn't interested, so I didn't push it by trying to engage her in the fun. After everyone had ordered her products, this woman came back and said she didn't really want anything. I must have looked puzzled because she went on to explain that she had been served with divorce papers that afternoon and had no idea why. I was very young and very new in the business, so I had a tendency to treat all situations with humor. I simply said, "Well, are you ever going to have sex again?" She smiled and said, "I imagine so." So I sent her home with a few of our basic products—a lubricant, a small vibrator, an edible lotion, and a simple game.

At 7 A.M. the next morning I got a phone call from the woman. She asked me where I lived. "My husband wants to talk to you," she said. I wasn't sure how to react. Was he going to chew me out? Was he going to tell me to mind my own business or just shoot me? Well, I'm pretty brave, so I gave her directions and they both arrived by 8 A.M. I stepped outside in my pajamas as she stepped out of the car. To my amazement, this woman looked like a completely different person. She bounced over to me with a big ol' smile, and I bravely asked her if she was there to buy more products. After nodding, she motioned for her husband to get out of the car. Just as I turned around to face him, I looked and saw that he had papers in his hand—their divorce papers. He smiled at me and tore them up right there in my driveway.

That moment excited me, changed me, and matured me. In fact, it changed everything. I realized that by opening lines of communication and by knowing how to encourage intimacy, the romance and passion in virtually any relationship can be rekindled. The moral of the story is that it is never too late to bring sexual pleasure and love into your relationship—even if it seems as though it is.

That's a story I heard from Trudy, one of our full-time Passion Consultants from a small town in Tennessee. In fact, that story has practically become a classic here at Passion Parties International—it expresses so well the work we do and the extraordinary effect it can have.

I've been at Passion Parties for almost a decade now, happily helping this wonderful company reach out to women across the United States and Canada, empowering us all to have better sex, a better sense of our own bodies, and, most important, better relationships. My time at Passion Parties has taught me that we women have at least one thing in common: Whether we are seeking a new relationship, are involved short-term or long-term, or are happily flying solo, we've all got sexual needs. And, at least once in a while, we wonder if there's something more we can do to satisfy ourselves and our partners or even to take it up a notch.

Like the woman whose life changed at Trudy's party, you may have long since given up on finding sexual satisfaction. Or you may feel that things are working fine for you—but you have the nagging feeling that they could still be better. Maybe you've got a terrific sex life but are looking for a few new ideas for how to spice it up. Perhaps you're in a long-term relationship and would like some fresh inspiration. Maybe you've been dating for a while and want some new tips on how to please yourself and your partner. Perhaps you're just starting to date—

or maybe you're just getting back out there. No matter who you are or what your sex life is like, I promise you that we've got a product, a tip, or a technique that will bring something extra into your bedroom. From the basics to the "advanced course" and beyond, Passion Parties can help you explore your sexual needs and find the joy and satisfaction you deserve.

For those of you who've never heard of Passion Parties, let me tell you a little bit about who we are and what we do. We've been in business for more than a decade, distributing products that help women achieve sexual pleasure. We use the business model first made popular by such firms as Tupperware and Mary Kay in which a network of women reaches out to their friends and neighbors, selling our products and spreading our message through in-home presentations.

Our team of tens of thousands of Passion Consultants operates in every region of the United States and Canada—in rural areas, small towns, big cities, and suburbs; among women age eighteen to eighty; for women who are single, married, divorced, separated, or widowed. We reach every type of woman, because let's face it, all of us are looking to enjoy our bodies, our partners, and ourselves.

I've come to realize that the Passion Consultant is a very special person, because it all starts with her. She gets the word out to her friends and neighbors, organizing Passion Parties for ten to fifteen women at a time—maybe friends, maybe strangers, maybe some of both. At these in-home parties, she introduces her guests to our wide range of products: everything from sensual body products and personal lubricants to playful edibles, vibrators, and sex toys. Many of us are a bit uncomfortable with these products at first—after all, our mothers probably never took us aside and showed us how to operate our first vibrator! But our Passion Consultants make it easy to learn more about what these items are and how they can enhance your sex life. Maybe when the evening starts, some of the guests are a little nervous, but by the end of the evening, it's like being at the ultimate "girls' night in"—everyone is laughing, joking, and sharing stories. Most important, everyone is looking forward to getting home and trying out all the new things she's bought! Whether it's Pure Satisfaction UniSEX Enhancement Gel (a clitoral stimulant), White Chocolate Passion Pudding (an edible product made for enhancing foreplay and oral sex), or your first-time Bullet vibrator, you *know* it's going to add something special to your sex life.

Contact us at www.passionparties.com if you'd like to attend a Passion Party. We're growing all the time, and we've probably got something going on right in your neighborhood. And if you think you'd like to become a Passion Consultant, contact us at the same Web address, and we'll be glad to have you: Our consultants are the foundation of our business, and we couldn't do without them. Although earnings vary with effort, we are proud of our Passion Consultants, from the ones who work for "top-up money" of $1,000 a month to the Passion Parties "Million Dollar Club" women who net an income in the high six figures, we empower them all, from the bedroom to the bank. In fact, that empowerment is right at the heart of our mission statement:

> To share the Passion Parties opportunity so that any woman can experience the prosperity of owning her own business; to share the products that will enhance any woman's relationship; and to share the philosophy of women helping women.

If you'd like to be part of the Passion Parties experience, we'll welcome you with open arms. But you can also treat this book as your own personal Passion Party—a chance to find out about all the wonderful products we offer, to learn or review "Sex 101," and to hear about some great new ideas that can bring a whole new level of magic into your bedroom. (Hey, why stop there? Why not make some magic in your living room, your bathtub, and—if you've got a nice, high fence—your backyard!)

I can't wait to share with you the Passion Parties secrets that can make your relationship red hot. But before we get started, I'd like to tell you a little bit about myself. When I tell people what I do, I must admit that I get a lot of surprised looks. When people who've never met me invite me to speak or arrange an interview, they usually expect a Playboy Bunny, some twenty-year-old sex kitten in a size-four negligee. Imagine their surprise when *I* show up—a full-figured businesswoman proudly in her sixties, with photos of my grandchildren in my wallet (and, yes, some lacy silken lingerie beneath my black suit!). I've been married to the same wonderful man since I was seventeen—but I'm here to tell you, ladies, we still have great sex. That's how I know that all those Hollywood images are simply not true. You don't need to look like Angelina Jolie or Halle Berry to have a great sex life—and your partner doesn't need to look like George Clooney, either. The two of you can bring each other all kinds of ecstasy, from your first date to your fiftieth anniversary, but you do have to work at it.

Of course, you also have to *play* at it. Relationships may be a lot of work, but never forget: Sex itself is a lot of fun! At least, it can be—that's what Passion Parties, and this book, are all about.

So how did a mother of two, a grandmother, and a housewife married to her high school sweetheart become the CEO of the world's largest sensual party planning company? Perhaps it all began on the day I was born—February 14th, Valentine's Day. Or it might have been on an ordinary winter day in 1959. I was an outgoing fourteen-year-old just two weeks shy of my fifteenth birthday, living in Portsmouth, Virginia, with my widowed mother and younger sister. In those days, my mother was dating the produce manager of a local grocery store. He was a large, heavyset German man whose biggest claim to fame in my mind was that he managed a team of very cute male produce clerks. The cutest one was Gerald, an Italian boy with curly black hair. Whenever I shopped at the store, I would hang around the tomatoes, hoping to catch the eye of my Italian fantasy.

One day, it happened. Out of the blue, Gerald rang me up and asked if I was busy. I was, but I quickly threw those plans out the window and told him I was free. Then he said the words that no girl wants to hear from her first crush: "I have this friend who would like to go out with you Saturday night."

My heart sank, but as calmly as I could, I asked, "Who is it?"

"My friend Ollie," he replied.

I had seen Ollie, a handsome Marine, because I used to baby-sit for some of his neighbors. I always thought he looked very cute in his dress blues, but he was a little shy, and I had never thought of dating him. Well, it was a bit awkward at first, but by the end of the evening, the sparks were flying, and soon we were going out on a regular basis. We were married five months before my eighteenth birthday and three months from his twenty-first. How young we were—but so much in love!

Looking back on it, it's a wonder we ever figured out how to make each other so happy. Remember, this was the fifties, and I was just a teenager. The only sex education I ever got was from my mother, on my wedding night. "Now, Pat," she told me, her face flushed with embarrassment, "you know there's going to be stuff he'll expect."

That was it. Like most girls back then, that was all the information anyone saw fit to give me. I know my mom was doing the best she could, but come on—"stuff he'll expect"? How sad is that? (And my mother, mind you, was eventually married four times!) But that's what a lot of girls were told. The guy's sexual satisfaction was all that mattered. If you were lucky enough to enjoy any of the sexual encounter, more power to you—but you sure weren't going to get much help.

Yes, it was an Ozzie and Harriet world when I was growing up. Ozzie worked, while Harriet stayed home and kept house. The man was responsible for bringing home the bacon and for making sure his sexual needs were fulfilled. If he wanted to, and if he knew how, maybe his wife would get some sexual pleasure, too, but if he couldn't or didn't want to provide that little service, then she was flat out of luck.

Happily, things have changed a whole lot since then. We've evolved, and I'm happy to say that I evolved, too. As a woman who started dating in the fifties and then lived through the sixties, seventies, and beyond, I've seen women facing a whole range of expectations and choices. As the times changed, I changed with them, which has put me in a terrific position to understand the many different hopes, fears, and dreams that women of all ages and backgrounds bring to our parties.

These days, of course, women work both inside and outside the home. And we don't just share in the financial responsibilities of our households. We expect to share in the sexual pleasure, too. After all, fair is fair, whether we're talking about the bank account or the bedroom. Like our husbands, we bring home the bucks—and, like them, we want to enjoy all the pleasures that sex has to offer.

So if we're being fair, we can no longer expect the man to take full responsibility for our sexual experience. It's up to us to know what makes us happy, what turns us on (and off), what sounds like an adventure we might want to try or a fantasy we might like to explore. It's up to us to initiate sex once in a while, to make it clear that we are not passive maidens submitting to our partners, but active and vital women with our own sexual needs and desires.

When I figured this out, I came up with a notion that has served Passion Parties well—the concept of the Passion Diva. As I see it, every woman has one, that lusty, sexy, sparkling creature who lives inside us and is just waiting to be let out. Your Passion Diva knows all about the kind of sex that will make your toes curl and your breath come more quickly. She knows what will get you tingling with anticipation and what will leave you glowing with pleasure. She's the expert on which parts of your body like to be caressed and kissed, when you like it sweet and gentle, and when you're looking for fiery and intense. Plus she knows all sorts of things that will turn your man on and leave him panting with desire—and more than happy to satisfy you.

You may be best friends with your Passion Diva already—or you may not even have realized that she was there. Either way, she is what Passion Parties are all about. By the time you're through with this book, you and your Passion Diva will be on the best of terms—and you'll both know a whole lot more things you can do to fire up the passion between you and your partner.

Meanwhile, though, let's get back to me and Ollie. Like many young couples, we began our marriage by learning about each other sexually.

Neither one of us had gotten all that much help in knowing what to expect, but we always loved each other, liked each other, and respected each other, and that went a long way toward helping us figure out the sexual part of things. Right from the beginning, I looked forward to waking up with Ollie each morning. I felt that I belonged with him—that when I was with him, I was home. I still love to go to sleep beside him and to wake up to his touch. But as with any marriage, between that first date and our forty-fifth anniversary last September came a whole set of unexpected challenges.

For one thing, we had children. Now I love my children dearly, and I wouldn't trade a minute of the time they lived in my home—but as any mother knows, kids are not exactly an aphrodisiac. Figuring out how to keep the passion going, how to find the energy for sex and intimacy in the midst of midnight feedings and dirty diapers and soothing a sick child, could be pretty daunting at times. (If you want to know more about my secrets for keeping the intimacy alive after the kids come along, check out Chapter 5 on RomantaTherapy and learn how to become your own Romanta Therapist.) But I'm here to tell you from my own experience: You *can* keep the romance alive if you know what to do and stay committed to doing it.

Then, too, we both had demanding jobs—Ollie, right from the first; me, after the kids got a bit bigger. Suddenly, it seemed we didn't even have time for a five-minute conversation, let alone for a luxurious evening of foreplay and everything that follows. He was tired, I was tired, and every time we got to where we maybe could have found a little energy, it seemed like one of the kids needed help with his homework or a Band-Aid for her skinned knee or maybe a quiet talk about *her* dating life. For both Ollie and me, learning how to slow down long enough to make time for each other—the kind of intimate time that includes talking, sharing, and cuddling as well as fantastic sex—has been a lifelong challenge. You *can* keep alive the magic in the midst of the madness, but it definitely takes work. (You'll read more about my suggestions for building relationships in Chapters 1 and 2.)

One of the biggest lessons I've learned from my forty-five-year marriage is that soul mates are made, not born. Sure, Ollie and I fell in love early on—and maybe you, too, have a guy who set your heart beating faster from the moment you laid eyes on him. But I know lots of happy couples who grew into intimacy with one another, who found their sexual heat as they got to know each other in more gradual ways. And by the time you've reached your first-year anniversary, take it from me: It doesn't much matter how you started. You've still got to work to keep the magic alive, to stay present to each other, to share your hopes and dreams and daily concerns so that you remain friends and companions in the best sense of those words.

Sex and passion are a big part of that sharing and intimacy, and I feel proud to be part of a company that enhances those experiences for women and their partners. But Passion Parties isn't just about techniques and products—it's also about relationships, communication, and freeing your Passion Diva. In fact, it's what your Passion Diva knows that forms the foundation of the company's philosophy—principles that are the basis of everything you'll read in this book:

Every Passion Diva Knows That . . .
1. Sex is good for you.
2. Soul mates are made, not born.
3. Even if you're a "good girl," you get to have great sex!
4. If you take responsibility for your pleasure, your pleasure will pay you back.
5. Being sexy is in how you feel, not how you look.
6. You need all five senses to make sex great.
7. For sex at night, foreplay starts in the morning.
8. Your most important sex organ is your brain.
9. Your most important sex toy is your tongue (and we're talking about *talking!*).
10. If you want great sex, bring the right woman to the bedroom.

Welcome to the beginning of *your* next passionate journey! But before we continue, I'd like to share with you one more favorite story, this one from Mindy, a part-time Passion Consultant who's also an emergency-room nurse in Washington State.

I decided to give my husband a romantic weekend getaway for his birthday, so I bought tickets to Hawaii and got a hotel right on the beach. I didn't plan for us to spend much time outside, however, and packed the "Passion Parties Lover's Coupon Booklet," the "52 Weeks of Romance" game, some Dirty Dice, and my Body Finger Paints, along with a couple of toys and my favorite lingerie. Now, I knew I shouldn't put these things in my carry-on luggage because I had heard that the X-ray machine would pick them up, and I wasn't exactly crazy about the idea of the security personnel viewing our intimate secrets. So being the savvy person that I am, I packed all our sexy treats in my checked luggage. Turns out I wasn't really all that savvy, however, because believe it or not, I had never heard about random inspections. When we got to the hotel, I opened my bag. Right on top was a typewritten note that said: *This bag has gone through Random Inspection.*

Was I mortified! I started to blush beet red—until I saw the hand-written note underneath. There, in tiny blue letters, someone had written, *Let the games begin.*

I think that says it all, don't you? So come on, ladies! Let the games begin!

Part

I

Freeing Your Passion Diva

Angie was a thirty-five-year-old mother and part-time receptionist living in Little Rock, Arkansas, when she came to her first Passion Party. "I'm not sure this is for me," she told Wanda, her Passion Consultant, with a nervous laugh. "I'm just not the sexy type." Our parties are designed to make women feel comfortable, so like all our Passion Consultants, Wanda started her presentation slowly, beginning with some RomantaTherapy Alluring Body Lotion and Bath & Shower Gel. Soon, though, she was on to Revelation Lubricant; Passion Powder, a white chocolate flavored dusting powder designed to be licked off the body; and finally, the Bullet and the Jelly Osaki, two types of vibrators. Some of the women at her party were shy at first, but soon they were turning the vibrators on and off, feeling the way they tingled in their palms, and smiling at the thought of what else those little machines might do.

All except Angie. As the evening went on, she looked more and more uncomfortable. When it came time for each guest to meet with the Passion Consultant privately, in the hostess's bedroom, she hung back. Finally, when her turn arrived, she entered the private ordering room reluctantly. But then she began to confide in Wanda.

"Look," she said in a low, ashamed voice. "I've never done any of the things you talked about. I've never . . . you know . . . had . . ." Her voice dropped to a whisper—"*Oral sex.* Either way—him to me, and certainly not me to him. I've never even . . . you know." Her whisper got even lower. "*Had an orgasm.*"

Wanda spent time with Angie, explaining how she might use an edible product called D'Lickious to make oral sex more fun, and how a generous helping of Revelation Lubricant plus the right use of the Magic Mushroom vibrator could help her learn how to have an orgasm. Angie left the party looking nervous—but determined.

The next week, Wanda got a call. "Thank you," Angie gushed, her voice filled with gratitude. "Thank you, thank you, *thank you!* I finally see what I've been missing all these years—and well, honey, that's it. Now that I get what's over here on the other side, you *know* I'm never going back!"

Like so many of the women who come to our parties, Angie had just met her Passion Diva—and it was a very pleasant meeting, to say the least! The important thing to remember, though, is that Angie's Passion Diva had been there all along. She was just waiting for Angie to set her free. Like so many of us, Angie had grown up with a "good-girl" philosophy and a couple of anxious parents who had never really given her the message that it was okay to enjoy sex, let alone taught her the ins and outs of how a woman's body works and what she needs. Tips and techniques are important—I'll be the first to admit it!—and don't worry, we'll tell you everything you need to know, starting with the basic biology of you and your guy, and moving on to specific techniques for self-pleasuring, foreplay, intercourse, oral sex, and some even more adventurous choices. Whether you've never tried any of it, or have done it all and want some new ideas—or anything in between—I promise you'll find what you're looking for in these pages.

But before we get to any of the nuts and bolts, so to speak, I want us to start where passion always begins—in the brain and in the heart. I want you to get to know your own personal Passion Diva, because in the end, it's not me or this book or even your Passion Consultant who's going to bring spice and heat and tenderness and joy into your bedroom—it's *you*. Freeing your Passion Diva is the key to every single one of your sexual desires, no matter what you know or don't know about which body part goes where.

Maria, for example, had been married for more than ten years, and she and her husband had done just fine. But when Maria came to her first Passion Party, she learned something she didn't expect:

Maria was a forty-three-year-old claims adjustor living in central Ohio, when she came to Valerie's Passion Party. Maria had had two serious relationships and a number of brief affairs before finally settling down in her early thirties, and she thought of herself as relatively experienced sexually. Her girlfriend had to talk her into coming to a Passion Party, and at first, Maria was reluctant to participate.

As the evening continued, though, Valerie noticed that Maria was becoming more interested. She seemed especially curious about D'Lickious, Sweet Sensations, and Tasty Tease—edible products that can make both male and female oral sex a lot tastier and more satisfying (for more details, see Chapter 8). And she really perked up when Valerie told the group about Gigi, the lifelike sleeve that fits around a man's penis, leaving only the tip exposed. Lots of women have found that Gigi offers an easier and more satisfying approach to giving a man oral sex, one that makes the whole experience much more fun for both parties.

By the time Valerie got out her order book, Maria was grinning from ear to ear. She listed the products she wanted and asked urgently when they would arrive. "You know," she told Valerie as she was about to leave, "my husband and I have been doing just fine, and I'm sure if I hadn't come tonight, we'd have kept on doing fine. But why live with 'fine' when you can have 'fantastic'?" Later, Maria sent Valerie an e-mail: *Everything worked out just great. Yes, all the things I wanted us to do—and all the things he's been wanting us to do—we're doing! Finally! And the best part is, we're both enjoying all of it!"*

Maria's Passion Diva had been alive and well—she just hadn't been allowed to reach her full potential. Like many of us, Maria had always been a bit shy in the bedroom. She'd learned to enjoy lots of things, and even to initiate them, but there'd always been some areas where she'd never quite been comfortable. Her experience at a Passion Party had helped Maria free a portion of her Diva that she'd always kept hidden before—and nobody was happier about it than Maria (unless, maybe, Maria's husband!).

Freeing your Passion Diva goes well beyond what you do in bed. Sometimes it's about being able to talk freely about sex, knowing that it's okay to think about sex and to make your interest in sexual pleasure a significant part of your life. Natalie, for example, found that a Passion Party was the opportunity for her Passion Diva to burst forth in a whole new way:

A bubbly, confident single woman in her twenties, Natalie worked as a buyer for a department store in a Minneapolis suburb. She walked cheerfully into the Passion Party that Diane had organized, and from the very first moment, she was full of stories, questions, and even a few ideas Diane hadn't thought of. Her obvious enthusiasm for all the products was contagious, and Diane found herself taking orders from the other guests that were even larger than usual. Clearly, Natalie's Passion Diva was alive, well, and out for fun, and she was unquestionably the life of the party.

But when Natalie came to place her order, she had tears in her eyes. "Honestly," she whispered to Diane, "I always really, you know, liked sex, but I always felt like kind of a freak. I mean, so many of my girl-friends just didn't want to talk about this stuff. I think they felt kind of embarrassed. Coming to a place where it's *okay* to talk about sex—where someone who knows so much will actually talk about it with you and give you some new ideas, and not make you feel like there's some-thing wrong with you for wanting to know more—well. I just can't tell you how much it means."

Natalie's Passion Diva was happy to play—but sometimes, she wanted company! She needed to know there were other Passion Divas out there who could share her pleasure and pass on some fun things they had learned how to do. If Natalie had never gone to a Passion

Party, her Diva would have been just fine—but maybe a little lonely, and certainly not as well-informed!

So whether your story is more like that of Angie, Maria, or Natalie—or maybe like all of them or none of them—your first step is always to check in with your Passion Diva. What does she want? What does she need? How can you give her even more freedom to make you and your partner happy—maybe even ecstatic? In Part I of this book, we'll help you free your Passion Diva by showing you what she knows (Chapter 1), helping you hear her voice (Chapter 2), giving her a sexy biology lesson (Chapter 3), and reviewing with her the art of self-pleasuring (Chapter 4). And in every chapter, we'll show you how to stock her Passion Pantry with the products and other items that every Diva should keep on hand for maximal sexual pleasure.

So let's get started! Your Passion Diva is rarin' to go!

— 1 —

What Your Passion Diva Knows
The Passion Parties Philosophy

So far, I've been doing an awful lot of the talking in these pages. Now I think it's time to hear from you! Start this chapter by taking the quiz below, and find out just how much your Passion Diva knows. This isn't like one of those quizzes you took in school, where someone's going to grade you on right or wrong answers. It isn't even like one of those quizzes they give you in the women's magazines, where afterward, they rate you. It's just a chance for you to find out some things about your own Passion Diva, things you maybe hadn't even realized yet. That's why, along with the multiple-choice options I've given you, I've also left a blank space after every question, so that you can fill it in with any secret desires of your own.

1. My idea of a sexy evening is . . .
   a. a long, hot bath, a romantic dinner, and a long, slow session of making love.
   b. I introduce a new sex toy into our bedroom, and together, we figure out how to use it.
   c. we find somewhere new to make love and make sure not to get caught!
   d. _____

2. If I could get my partner to try one new thing, it would be . . .

a. He spends at least an hour on the foreplay portion of the evening—he doesn't move on to the next step until I'm ready for him.

b. I've always wanted to try a vibrator—maybe one of those gently vibrating rings that fits around his penis and gives me extra stimulation.

c. We try out a new position, maybe "69," or standing up, or "wheelbarrow" style.

d. _____

3. If I could add one thing to my own sexual repertoire, it would be . . .

a. I'd learn how to get better at communicating what I want.

b. I'd find a way to get more pleasure out of giving him oral sex.

c. I'd have an easier time reaching orgasm during intercourse.

d. _____

4. One new way to put myself in the mood for love might be to . . .

a. start the day wearing sexy lingerie under my work attire, jeans, or even sweats.

b. purchase a flirty little frisky French maid costume to help us act out one of our fantasies.

c. indulge in a sexy or romantic daydream, picturing a scenario that really turns me on.

d. _____

5. One new way to put my guy in the mood for love might be . . .

a. give him a teasing little glimpse of that sexy lingerie I'm wearing, well before we get to the "undressing" part of the evening.

b. leave a sexy note in his briefcase or a sexy message on his cell phone's voice mail. (Lots of businesses monitor the company e-mail, so I won't use that!)

    c. give him a wink of the eye or a pat on the butt as he leaves for work in the morning.

    d. _____

If taking this little quiz has left you bursting with ideas, more power to you! You'll find even more sexy notions—and more details about the ideas in the quiz—throughout this book. In fact, if you want to put the book down and go try out one of these ideas right now, be my guest! I'll be right here when you get back.

And if all of these questions and suggestions make you nervous, intimidate you, or leave you cold, don't worry. Your Passion Diva is in there—she just needs a little encouragement. But I promise you, she's there, right this very minute. You don't need to lose ten pounds or work out at the gym or buy a whole new wardrobe to access your Passion Diva. You don't need to envy Sharon Stone or even that cute little cheerleader you went to high school with. We live in a media culture with *very* unrealistic ideas about women and their bodies—but ladies, take it from me. I've met women all over the country, all ages, shapes, and sizes, from homemaker to CEO, from age eighteen to eighty, from size two to size twenty-two, and I'm here to tell you—they're all having great sex. Maybe none of them would make it onto a TV show or a billboard—and they sure don't all want the same things. But whatever they want, whatever turns them on, whatever makes them purr with pleasure or squeal with delight, they've figured out how to get it as often and as satisfyingly as they want it.

Why? Because they've learned to access their Passion Diva—that sexually self-confident woman who knows she's desirable, who's absolutely certain that she can make her partner gasp with ecstasy, who's figured out how to communicate her needs and get what she wants so that she can reach her own ecstasy as well. I *know* that Diva lives inside every single woman on the face of this earth—and she's there inside you, too.

So if your Passion Diva is already alive and well, give yourself a big

**EXPERIENCES THAT MIGHT HAVE
SCARED OFF YOUR PASSION DIVA**

- Being made fun of
- Being asked to fit somebody *else's* idea of "a sexy woman"
- Being told you are "bad"
- Being told you are "boy-crazy" or "sex-crazy"
- Being called promiscuous or fearing being called promiscuous

Has someone been giving your Passion Diva a hard time? Did your parents, neighbors, religious leaders, high school classmates, or first few boyfriends give you the idea that you weren't supposed to be "too into it," too self-confident, or too ready to initiate sex? Well, now's the time to turn the tables on all that misinformation. Access your Passion Diva, have the kind of sex that makes you happy—and you and your partner will be so blissed-out and satisfied that you won't even be able to remember the names of the people who tried to bring you down.

congratulations! We live in a society that doesn't always make that so easy for women. And if your Diva is a bit shy or is hiding out in your attic—or is hiding out in someone *else's* attic two counties over!—don't worry. I've helped thousands of women access their Passion Divas, and I can help you, too. As you saw from the list on page 9, Passion Divas know the ten secrets of intimacy and great sex. In this chapter, we'll take a look at just what they know, and why you need to know it, too.

1. Sex Is Good for You

If you happened to need one *more* reason to unleash your Passion Diva, here it is: Good sex is good for your health. That's right. Your health. Sexual satisfaction lowers your stress levels, helps you be more focused, fights the aging process, improves your sleep patterns, and provides a host of other benefits.

Of course, good sex also makes you feel good. How many things in life are calorie-free, don't cost a dime, and just plain make you feel terrific? Sex is the ultimate indulgence—better than a shopping spree or a hot-fudge sundae, and better for you, too. (And if you're not yet having the kind of sex that makes you feel that way, don't worry— you will!)

But sex isn't just one of life's great pleasures—it's also one of life's great medicines. Here are ten sexy reasons why:

- **Sex is a fountain of youth.** Tired of buying all those anti-aging lotions and potions? Supplement your beauty regimen with a little sex, which stimulates your adrenal glands to bathe your body in the hormone DHEA (short for *dehydroepiandrosterone,* and don't ask me how to pronounce it!). Your body converts DHEA to other key hormones, including the sex hormones estrogen and testosterone. It's not just men who have testosterone—we women have it, too, and it's a very important support for our vitality and mood. DHEA also helps produce hormones that control fat, stress, and depression; and, according to many medical experts, it helps maintain youthful vigor, a lean body, and a balanced immune system. As if that weren't enough, DHEA helps improve cognition, promotes bone growth, and keeps your skin healthy and supple. So when you're purring like a kitten, your whole brain and body feel like cheering.

- **Sex is a stress reliever.** This isn't just a psychological effect. Your whole circulatory system appreciates a good orgasm, and your brain feels the benefits, too. Like any exercise, sex boosts your heart rate and increases the flow of blood to your brain, organs, and muscles. The blood bathes your body in fresh oxygen and hormones while carrying away the metabolic waste products that can cause discomfort and fatigue. Thus, the physical and emotional release you get from sexual satisfaction reaches your innermost core, melting away the stress from today and leaving you better prepared to cope with the stresses of tomorrow.

- **Sex is a sleep aid.** Before you even think of reaching for that Ambien, I want you to try a little sex! Poor sleep leaves you vulnerable to a host of disorders, including a weakened immune system, a tendency to gain weight, and a greater vulnerability to depression. You'll sleep far more deeply and comfortably after having sex—and your whole body will thank you for it.

- **Sex is a hormone booster.** Experts say that regular sexual activity boosts testosterone and estrogen levels in both men and women. Estrogen, the female hormone, keeps your vaginal tissue supple and may also protect you against heart disease. Testosterone fortifies your bones and muscles while keeping your heart healthy and your "good cholesterol" levels high. And the more testosterone in your system, the more often you'll want to have sex, which will keep your testosterone levels nice and high, so that you keep on wanting to have sex. That's what we call a very positive cycle!

- **Sex is great exercise.** Now here's a statistic that may surprise you: If you have sex three times a week for an entire year, you'll have burned as many calories as if you'd jogged seventy-five miles. And without the shin splints, blisters, or muscle cramps (unless you are having some *very* athletic bedroom romps!). Or maybe you'd rather picture it in the short term: Half an hour's worth of sex burns about 150 calories, which is what you'd do while running 15 minutes on a treadmill or playing a spirited game of squash. So, sex or Pilates— which would *you* rather indulge in?

- **Sex is a pain reliever.** Sexual activity causes your body to secrete the hormone oxytocin, which in turn stimulates the release of endorphins, nature's own pain relievers. Those "feel-good" endorphins— which are stimulated by any kind of aerobic exercise—alleviate the aches and pains associated with arthritis, headaches, and many other conditions.

- **Sex is an antidepressant.** Those endorphins don't only dull physical pain, they're also a powerful natural antidepressant. So are the balanced hormone levels, improved sleep patterns, and stress-relieving exercise that sex provides. Not to mention the way a good orgasm or two can just purely boost your mood!

- **Sex is a flu fighter.** This is an especially nice benefit for those of you with small children: Despite all the obstacles kids pose to sex, they also make it more necessary, because you want to resist all those colds they bring home! Some studies suggest that people who have sex even once or twice a week have a 30 percent higher level of the antibody immunoglobulin A, which is known to boost the immune system, staving off colds and all sorts of infections. Hmmm . . . flu shot or orgasm—which would *you* prefer?

2. Soul Mates Are Made, Not Born

Now I'm not the world's biggest expert on soul mates—but, on the other hand, I have been happily married to mine for the past forty-five years, so I think I know a little bit about the topic, at least enough to assure you that this statement is absolutely true: *Soul mates are made, not born.* Maybe you fell in love at first sight; maybe you had to work your way into it. Maybe your sex was hot and passionate right from the beginning; or maybe that, too, took work. However you got to where you're having a good time with someone, you should always remember—turning your sexy, adorable lover into a long-term soul mate is going to take both work and play. Work, because relationships are work. Play, because often, sex is—or should be—just plain fun.

One of the most-often asked questions at our Passion Parties is whether a B-minus or even a C-plus sexual relationship can make its way up the grading ladder to where it's a tingly, steamy A-plus. My answer—and I know that every one of my tens of thousands of Passion Consultants will agree with me—is a lusty, passionate *YES*. Of course, it might not happen overnight. But if you and your partner like each other, respect each other, and genuinely want to create greater intimacy and passion, you've got more than a fighting shot at turning okay sex into "off the charts" sex. In fact, I'd say that most relationships start off with less-than-stellar sex that only improves as the people involved come to know and trust each other. Certainly it was that way for Ollie and me. Then, if you stay together long enough, you may find that your former heat starts to turn lukewarm, and you've got to make a new effort to heat things up again. In relationships, there's never a dull moment!

Of course, great sex doesn't *always* take work. Maybe right at the beginning, the process of exploring, sharing, and caring is enough to give you that "soul mate" connection, with less focus on your sexual technique and more on just getting to know each other. Maybe further on down the line, you come to appreciate that "old shoe" feeling, where you just feel comfortable together, without having to work at it. You like that your guy is kind, that he makes you laugh, that you never seem to run out of things to talk about. You like the way he brings you a cup of coffee in the morning (that's one of the things I appreciate most about Ollie!). You know he'll be there through thick and thin, that if you or the kids or anyone you care about needs a shoulder to lean on— or to cry on—your man will be there, strong and caring.

But somewhere in the mix of affection, respect, and comfort, whether we're talking about the beginning of a relationship, the two-year mark, or your silver anniversary, I urge you to give some attention to passion. Your soul mate will be that much dearer to you—and you to him—if you can keep on savoring together one of the most joyous activities that we humans are blessed to experience.

Let me share with you one of my own favorite "soul mate" techniques. In fact, I'm not sure Ollie even knows I do this (though I guess he will now!). But every so often, when I feel we're in danger of getting a little bored, I consciously try to fall in love with my husband all over again. "This is the week I'm going to remember why I married him," I tell myself. "This is my time for remembering what I like about him." I ask myself to notice all the little things he does that I appreciate—the way he keeps track of my TV shows and reminds me when they're on or the way he'll suddenly call at the end of a long day and announce that he's made reservations at one of our favorite restaurants. I remember the way he keeps me grounded—sometimes I feel like I'm the kite and he's my string—and yet at the same time, he encourages me to "think outside the box." I notice what I like about him physically—his square features, his strong shoulders, his vigor, his loving smile. I notice how much I like talking to him, about politics and the news and what our grandchildren are up to. I wake up all over again to how much I enjoy his company, whether we're reading the paper together, chatting about the show we saw, or cuddling up to sleep at night.

Because we've worked at communicating, sharing, and being respectful, Ollie and I have managed to make it through all the changes and challenges of marriage *together*. And throughout it all, we've kept our passion alive, even though our sexual needs and tastes have occasionally evolved right along with our bodies. It takes time and care and attention to nurture and maintain an emotional and physical connection. That's why I say soul mates are made, not born.

So if you're looking to make, keep, or find a soul mate relationship, let your Passion Diva guide you toward being the best soul mate *you* can be—sexy, creative, passionate, alive. Let her show you how to express your joy in life with your partner, making every encounter—inside the bedroom and out—a passionate and pleasurable one for you both. You never know what surprises life is going to hand you, but as long as you stay close to your Passion Diva, you can't go wrong.

3. Even If You're a "Good Girl," You Get to Have Great Sex!

In the fifties, when I was growing up, women were firmly divided into two camps: good girls who got married but who didn't necessarily like sex, and bad girls whom no one would marry—but who supposedly had great sex!

Then, in the sixties, everybody wanted to be a bad girl so much that she turned into another type of good girl—the easygoing chick who didn't make too many demands on a guy and didn't expect him to stick around. She maybe had better sex, but she often couldn't stick up for what she wanted, either in bed or in the relationship.

During the seventies, we had the "me" generation and also the rise of feminism, and the mixed messages really started to fly. Women, and people in general, were supposed to figure out what they wanted and go after it—but what if the person you loved wanted something different than you did? Where did "me" end and "us" begin? At what point did being strong and assertive turn into being bossy and demanding? Did we want men to respect our independence, pamper us like old-fashioned girls—or do a little bit of both? And how were the guys supposed to know which role to play and when to switch?

Confusing as the seventies, eighties, and nineties may have been, I think our present generation is even more mixed up. Scantily clad pop singers wear clothes so revealing that even bad girls wouldn't have dressed that way when I was young—but these teenage performers also sign pledges of virginity and suggest that their fans should do the same. Schools are supposed to offer sex education—but only a few years ago, Dr. Joycelyn Elders was fired for suggesting that teaching high school students about self-pleasuring might reduce the rate of teenage pregnancy. The blandest sitcom that airs during family hour features language and topics that even the raciest people I knew growing up would never have allowed in "mixed company." Yet for all our openness, many of us women don't even understand how our bodies work, how to have an orgasm, or how to achieve real emotional intimacy. What's more, despite the sexual revolution, we don't always know how to go about getting that knowledge or making that satisfying sexual connection.

Amidst all the confusion and mixed messages, many of us are still struggling with the "good girl/bad girl" dichotomy. We still fear—and with good reason!—that we'll be branded as "loose" or found unfit for marriage or simply feel "bad" if we openly make sex a priority in our lives and take some responsibility for making it as pleasurable as possible. We still have trouble grasping the simple truth that sex is healthy, natural, and normal—a great way to express your love and intimacy for your partner. We forget that good girls *should* be able to enjoy an activity that is meant to be pleasurable. Wanting orgasms doesn't mean you're "loose" or even a bad girl—your body was *made* to have orgasms, they're good for your health, and you *should* enjoy them!

Of course, you should never do anything in the bedroom that you think is wrong. Your own personal morals are up to you to decide, and nothing in this book should get in the way of that. But if you *know* you're not doing any harm and yet you *feel* worried, anxious, or guilty, maybe it's time to give a little more space to your Passion Diva and a little less space to those critical voices in your head.

Let me help you get started. How many of the following statements do you agree with? How many are you ready to laugh off? And how many do you *know* are incorrect—but you can't help believing them anyway?

- Good girls don't wear sexy lingerie.
- Good girls don't initiate sex.
- Good girls don't think about what they like in bed.
- Good girls don't talk about what they like in bed.
- Good girls don't pleasure themselves.
- Good girls don't pursue orgasms through means other than intercourse—and then only in the missionary position.
- Good girls don't give or receive oral sex (and if they do, they don't enjoy it!).
- Good girls don't use sex toys or sexual products—and they certainly don't initiate using them.
- Good girls do whatever their husbands want in bed, no questions asked.

If you're blushing, don't worry—you're not alone! Many of us have to struggle with these outmoded ideas, so let me suggest some Passion Diva alternatives. Whenever you find yourself making a "good girl" statement to yourself, try replacing it with one of these Passion Diva Proclamations:

- Passion Divas are willing to wear sexy lingerie at least some of the time, if their partners like it—and they'll wear it *all* the time if *they* like it!
- Passion Divas are free to initiate sex, so long as they're respectful to the man in question and to any other people who might be affected.
- Passion Divas spend a fair amount of time thinking about what they like in bed. After all, who else is going to figure this out, if they don't? Even the most loving and experienced partner can only do so much without a Passion Diva to point the way.
- Passion Divas not only think about what they like—they communicate it to their partners, with or without words. Believe me, their partners are *very* happy to know!
- Passion Divas pleasure themselves—sometimes alone, and sometimes with their partners. They know it's healthy, normal, and just plain fun!
- Passion Divas pursue orgasms "through any means necessary"!
- Passion Divas give and receive oral sex if they enjoy it (and if they don't enjoy it, they check out Chapter 8 before writing it off entirely!).
- Passion Divas use sex toys and sexual products if they want to— and they also feel free to introduce these items into sex play with their partners.
- Passion Divas set whatever limits they need to set, whether with a husband, a boyfriend, or a casual relationship.

If there's one gift I could give every woman reading this book, it would be this: *It's okay to look for your Passion Diva.* As long as you're following your own moral code, give yourself permission to play, to enjoy, to try something new. You deserve it—and so does your partner.

4. If You Take Responsibility for Your Pleasure, Your Pleasure Will Pay You Back

"Responsibility" is such a heavy word, and "pleasure" is such a fun one. So how do these two words fit together?

Actually, they kind of depend on each other, because if you *don't* take responsibility for your pleasure, you run the risk of not getting any! Few things are more upsetting, off-putting, or demoralizing than engaging in sexual activity that you don't enjoy—and it's only your own sense of responsibility that can keep that from happening. Responsibility in the bedroom doesn't just refer to safety or protecting yourself from unwanted pregnancy—it's about knowing what turns you on and what satisfies you, and then finding a way to communicate that to your partner. It's a very rare guy who knows right off the bat all the things you like in bed and all the things you need to feel satisfied. Men's bodies are different from ours, and therefore most men need a little education when it comes to getting your motor running. On top of that, every woman has different likes and dislikes, and different techniques that make her happy. Guys will often get in there and do their best, but who can blame them for coming up with less-than-satisfying moves when they're flying blind?

The good news is that you don't have to just sit back and wait and hope that something delicious and exciting happens. You can be proactive—after all, you are half of the party! This might mean experimenting with self-pleasuring to learn how YOU and your body work so that you can share that coveted information with your partner. It might mean being willing to step in and show him exactly where and how something feels good to you. Above all, it means knowing that you play as much of a role in your own pleasure as he does and then putting that knowledge to work in your relationship. Otherwise, you'll get a lot less pleasure out of sex than you deserve—and why put up with that?

Of course, being responsible also means setting limits: You should never let someone else's idea of what you "should" enjoy push you into a place you don't want to go, whether that's a certain technique, a casual relationship, a lifelong marriage, or anything in between. Sex is like anything else in life—a combination of habit, challenge, and adventure—and you may have to experiment a bit before you find the sexual style and bedroom moves that are right for you. But if you take responsibility for your own pleasure, your chances of having a good time in bed go up exponentially. And, once again, your partner is likely to have a better time, too.

5. Being Sexy Is in How You Feel, Not How You Look

So many women are prevented from enjoying sex because they feel bad about how they look, and it is *so* unnecessary. Let me share with you one of my favorite stories, just to prove my point.

Every so often, I drop in on the Passion Consultants in various parts of the country, and one night I was visiting Maddy, who, as luck would have it, also styles hair in a beauty salon in Georgia. I was getting a bite in a roadside diner before going to Maddy's party, and I couldn't help noticing a beautiful blonde in her early twenties sitting with her guy at the counter. She was stunning—big blue eyes, long shapely legs, and a size-two figure—and the guy at her side was just staring at her with this adoring look, like he couldn't believe how lucky he was.

I hadn't seen my husband for a couple of weeks, and besides missing him, I must admit, I felt a bit envious of that lovely young woman. Even when I'd been younger and thinner, I hadn't ever looked quite like *that*.

Well, when I went to the party that night, who should walk in but that gorgeous blond woman I'd seen at the diner! And when it came time for the guests to order their products, and as they were lining up around Maddy, this young woman made her way over to me. Some-how, she got the idea that she could trust me, so she started to talk.

I won't betray her confidence by repeating everything she told me. Suffice it to say that when I heard about the sexual difficulties she and her husband were having and about the fears and frustrations that had brought her to the party, I was reminded all over again that you just never know. Hollywood and the fashion magazines give us the impression that the world is full of beautiful creatures having hot sex, and the rest of us—the ones who look like ordinary people—are just missing out. But it's just not true; in fact, Maddy told me later, the happiest woman at that party was a full-figured woman who'd had a string of passionate boyfriends throughout her twenties and was now celebrating her tenth wedding anniversary with a fabulous guy who adored her.

Of course, it can work the other way, too—you can look terrific *and* have fabulous sex! My point is, there's no way to know. But never fall into the trap of thinking that fame and physical perfection can guarantee anybody happiness, in or out of bed. Reading a few celebrity biographies can help you remember—even the Beautiful People can be starved for love and affection.

As Maddy told me, "I hear so many women tell me that they don't think they are sexy, and the advice I give those women is this: You don't have to be a beautiful woman in order to radiate sexual confidence. When you walk into a room, hold your head high, keep your shoulders back, and meet the eye of the man you're attracted to. You don't have to be a model with a gorgeous figure to have the allure and sensuality that make men take notice. Carry yourself with the confidence and knowledge that you are awesome in bed." (And if you're not right now—you will be by the time you finish this book!)

Think about your best features. What are they? Do you have great eyes? Play them up! Flirt with them! Perhaps you have pretty hands. Use them to slowly brush your hair out of your eyes, or lay a hand on the arm of a guy you're attracted to and let it rest there just a little too long. Give him a hint of what he can expect later on if he takes you up on your implied offer. Dress in bright colors and soft fabrics that you

TRY A LITTLE TV THERAPY

For all of us who watch *Sex and the City,* it's easy to get the impression that if you don't look like Samantha, Miranda, Charlotte, or Carrie, you're never going to be sexually satisfied. If that's how you're feeling, maybe you should change the channel once in a while! There are plenty of examples out there that do a more accurate job of reflecting love in the real world, reminding us that passion comes in all shapes and sizes.

For example, take a look at Frank and Marie Barone, Ray's parents on *Everybody Loves Raymond.* Several episodes on that show make it clear that this elderly, argumentative couple has a terrific sex life, even though he's bald and wrinkled, and she's heavy and pushing seventy. Or what about Hal and Lois, the ordinary-looking couple on *Malcolm in the Middle?* They can barely manage to get out of bed, despite the stresses and strains of raising four rowdy kids. Watch the way Hal looks longingly at Lois, even when she's dragging herself home from work or hugely pregnant with their fifth child, and know that there's a guy out there—or maybe already in your bedroom—who will look at you that way, too.

Maybe you'd get more inspiration from Red and Kitty on *That '70s Show,* a middle-aged couple who dash up the stairs to their bedroom any time they're lucky enough to be home without the kids. Even though Kitty despairs at her low score when she takes a *Cosmo* quiz ("We're only 'moderately passionate'—and that's because I cheated!"), you see them working at making each other happy as well as being sexually playful. And if you're a big woman, you couldn't do better than to imitate the sexual self-confidence of actresses like Queen Latifah, Mo'nique, Kathy Bates, or Liz Torres (the flirtatious, flamboyant Miss Patty on *Gilmore Girls),* all of whom walk, talk, and put themselves out there, knowing there'll be no shortage of men to fall at their feet. TV *is* full of unrealistic images—but thank heavens there are a few alternatives to remind the rest of us that being sexy is in how you feel, not how you look.

enjoy looking at and feeling against your skin, and don't choose big, tentlike dresses that hide your body. Even if you're large, wear clothes that cling to your curves, just like you want him to do. Men are attracted to women who are confident about themselves and who have a healthy attitude about sex. So put that out there, and you'll be surprised at how many offers you get!

I won't say that I don't spend my share of time obsessing about the size of my derrière. But I've learned that my hip size really doesn't have much to do with my happiness—or with my husband's happiness, either.

6. You Need All Five Senses to Make Sex Great

Even though we should know better, many of us fall into a very narrow idea of what's involved in truly great sex. Guys can sometimes be focused on simply getting to the goal—that is, achieving their own orgasm. And we women are sometimes all about getting it over with—lying back and letting the guy do what he has to do. Both sexes may be relying mainly on the basic mechanics of intercourse to give us whatever pleasure we get.

But sex isn't just about penetration and orgasm—at least, not always! At its best, sex can be a whole-body experience, involving much more than just the obvious equipment. As a Passion Diva, you'll want to take advantage of all five of your senses: sight, hearing, smell, and taste as well as touch. The more sensory pleasure you incorporate into your sexual time, the richer and fuller and more exciting the sex is going to be—and the more intense and satisfying the orgasm.

Let's take a look at the following scenarios to get a sense of why each of the five senses is important—and how they can each enhance or detract from your bedroom life. Which of the two following sexual encounters do you think has the best chance of turning both parties on and giving them the best whole-body orgasmic experience?

Sight

Laundry scattered on bedroom floor; unpaid bills piled up beside the bed; harsh light or no light.

Bedroom clean and neat, with no distractions to remind anyone of chores or housework; a scarf thrown over the lamp to create soft, rosy light.

Hearing

The TV is blasting or perhaps you can hear the washing machine running in the distance. When it comes to the sexual act itself, you're pretty quiet and maybe he grunts a few times.

You've created a special space with the use of soft music or perhaps an environmental noise machine conveying the sound of a rushing stream, a gentle rain, or a Brazilian rain forest. During sex, each of you lets your sighs, "oohs" and "aahs," convey just what effect a touch or a kiss is having so you can share in each other's pleasure. Maybe every so often, one of you will murmur, "That feels so good" or "Don't stop!"

Taste

His skin tastes salty after a long day; your skin tastes like moisturizer.

Your nipples are fruit-flavored and tingly with Nipple Nibblers, and your body tastes sweet from the Crèmesicle Massage Cream he has massaged into your skin. Your guy's penis tastes like candy from the Lickety Lube you've applied there.

Smell

Both of you bring a bunch of everyday scents to the bedroom—a little sweat, the smell of dinner cooking—nothing too bad, but nothing that turns you on, either.

A stick of spicy incense is burning in the background, and you've sprayed the sheets with Silky Sheets, so your bed smells fresh and lovely. You've taken a bubble bath, so your skin is wonderfully perfumed. And even your man has a little cologne behind his ears—the same scent he's been wearing since you met, so it reminds you of those heady, early days of falling in love.

Touch

He's in a hurry to watch the 11 o'clock news, and you want to get in another load of laundry, so you both get right to "the main event" with the bare minimum of touching.

You spend a few minutes gently rubbing his shoulders, easing away his stress—but every few minutes, you lightly brush your palms over his nipples, teasing him, tantalizing him. He nuzzles your neck with his whole face, while his hands gently caress your cheeks. Just these few moments of silent touch help bring your focus back to each other and your time together.

See what I mean? Not only do the sensory elements help you focus more fully on the sex and on each other, they also serve as powerful associations that, all by themselves, can turn each of you on. Smell, in particular, is very closely tied in with emotion. So if you can develop close associations between a particular smell and a sexual experience, both of you will get a head start, right out of the box.

Throughout this book, I'll be sharing with you lots of suggestions for waking up your five senses and his, too. Now that you see why senses are such a big part of sex, you can start coming up with your own sensory treats—and invite your partner to think of some as well. You might be surprised at how sensitive and aware he becomes once you introduce this aspect of pleasure into your lovemaking.

7. For Sex at Night, Foreplay Starts in the Morning

Now, ladies, I'm not suggesting that you and your guy get into bed in the morning and don't get up again until the *next* morning (though sometimes, that may be just what the doctor ordered!). I am suggesting that you will have a much better sexual experience—especially when you and your partner live together—if you look at sex as a part of your entire day and not just as the thirty to ninety minutes that comes in at the end.

Let's face it: If you're not very good to each other during the day, you're not going to like each other much when the time for sex finally rolls around. If you've snapped at each other over breakfast, dashed through a hasty dinner while refereeing the kids' fights, and then dragged yourselves through dishwashing and bill-paying and carpool-arranging while shepherding the kids through their baths and bedtime stories, by the time night falls, all you want is to bury yourself in a book or a TV program and forget your spouse exists! Who wants to have sex with someone they've just griped at, hurried along, or basically ignored all day? Even if you have good intentions, you can't necessarily turn on good feelings toward someone you've been annoyed with for the past twelve hours, and he probably won't feel like the world's best lover, either.

If you've set aside some time specifically for intimacy, it's all the more important that you lay the groundwork leading up to that point. I'll never forget one of my friends, who used to have a regular Saturday-

PAMPER YOUR PASSION DIVA

One great way to wake up your senses and to feel good about your body is to pamper your Passion Diva—give her something to remind her that you appreciate her sexy, passionate place in your sometimes stressed-out life. You may already know just what your Passion Diva wants, but here are some suggestions, just in case:

- a manicure or pedicure (*my* personal favorites—I make time for them every other week)
- a facial (I enjoy one once a month)
- a long hot soak in the tub (try throwing in some RomantaTherapy Sensuous Bath Salts or some of your favorite bubble bath)
- a fragrant, stimulating shower (try using some RomantaTherapy Salt Glow Body Scrub and rubbing yourself all over with RomantaTherapy Alluring Body Lotion or Passion Body Dew afterward)
- a special piece of jewelry to commemorate a really special achievement (so that every time you wear it, you'll remember how special you are)
- a silky piece of lingerie (in fact, wear some lovely lingerie every single day, just to keep that pretty, sexy side of you alive)
- a *very* leisurely cup of tea or coffee where you invoke all five senses: *see* the liquid steaming in a lovely cup; *hear* the sounds around you as you sip (perhaps with some favorite music or a soothing sound-effects tape in the background); *smell* the fragrant brew; *feel* the warmth of the cup in your hands and the dampness of the steam on your face; and of course, *taste* the delicious drink you've prepared as you savor every sip . . . mmm-mmmmmmm

What I've noticed about pampering *my* Passion Diva is that every time I do something nice for her, she starts feeling like it's a necessity, and as far as I'm concerned, that's a *good* thing. Before you know it, treating yourself like the sexy, special, sparkling woman that you are has become not a "once in a blue moon" thing, but rather a daily part of your routine. Believe me, your sex life will benefit, and every single person you come in contact with will wonder why you seem so blissed-out and serene!

night arrangement with her husband. "Okay, neighbors," she'd say as dinnertime drew near. "I've got to get home. Tonight is sex night." She never sounded all that happy about it. As far as she was concerned, sex was just another household chore—quicker than grocery shopping, perhaps, but messier than doing the laundry. And she certainly didn't give herself any time to get into a sexy frame of mind. It's tough for anyone to make a transition that easily.

So what I'm suggesting is a paradigm shift, a way of integrating your and your partner's needs for sexual pleasure into your daily life. In this approach—which your Passion Diva will love—foreplay starts in the morning and doesn't stop until the two of you are actually involved in intercourse. Sure, there's a stage where the foreplay gets a bit more physical—but let's not neglect Stage 1. Look at this list of "all-day foreplay" suggestions and see if you think any of them can spice up your relationship with your partner (we'll have more "all-day foreplay" suggestions for the dating woman in Chapter 5).

- Find a point during your morning routine when you smile at him and say something nice—about how he looks, something he's done, or something you've thought about him.

- Before either of you leaves for work, find some sexy or affectionate way to touch him at least once—pat him on the butt, stroke his cheek, run your fingers lightly down his bare arm—just something to remind him that your body likes his body, and vice versa.

- Check in with him at least once that day with some kind of sexy, loving, or affectionate message—a note in his briefcase, a message on his voice mail, a quick call to him at work—just to remind him that you like seeing him and are looking forward to your evening together.

- Find at least one nice thing to do for him before the evening ends. If your partner is cooperative, you might make a deal that each of you will do one nice thing for the other—a few moments of massage, a foot rub, him running a hot tub for you to soak in, you keeping the kids quiet while he watches the news—anything to convey the message that you appreciate each other.

Now, having pictured a day like that, does sex look more likely as you make your way toward the bedroom? And does it seem as though the sex you have will be more tender, more passionate, and a lot more fun? Ideally, you'd have that kind of day *every* day of your relationship, but you'll especially want to start in with the all-day foreplay if you plan on having sex that night. And if your guy seems to want sex more often than you do, talk him through this new game so he can play, too, because if you're both making foreplay an all-day thing, you'll definitely start having sex! Let your Passion Diva entice him with the prospect of getting a little sexual thrill at 8 A.M. and staying turned on for the next twelve hours, until you finally shut the bedroom door. Kindness, courtesy, and consideration can be just as arousing as sexy little gestures—so make sure your "all-day foreplay" includes some of both.

8. Your Most Important Sex Organ Is Your Brain

Does that sound like a radical statement to you? Contrary to what most of us believe, it's not just our physical equipment that leads us to feel hot and tingly—our brains play a very important role. Try this little exercise to see what I mean:

Picture yourself in a beautiful setting—whatever place makes you feel happy and alive. Allow yourself to fully imagine this joyous place with all five of your senses—see its beautiful sights, hear the sounds in the background, feel the sun or rain or wind on your skin, taste the delicious mountain air or the delightful salt tang of the ocean, smell the lovely scents associated with this place. Keep visualizing until you're feeling happy and relaxed.

Now introduce an exciting sexual partner into the scenario. It might be your current guy, or it could be someone you've fantasized about, maybe even a movie star. See this man come over to you. Notice the look on his face as he stares deep into your eyes and whispers the words you'd most like to hear him say. Feel the touch of his hand as he leads you to a quiet, private, comfortable place and slowly, slowly, begins to undress you. . . .

OK, now compare how you feel right this very moment with how you felt before starting to read the previous paragraph. I'm hoping you're experiencing at least a little sexual tingle, or at least imagining the thrill you'd feel if the fantasy continued. If so, you'll be able to recognize that the only sexual organ we actually tantalized was your brain. The inspiration for those feelings was purely in your head—proof of the mind's tremendous power when it comes to feeling sexy and aroused.

I'm not suggesting you substitute fantasy for reality or that you try to pretend your guy is really a movie star (although every so often, that may not be a bad idea!). But how you think about a person and a situation has an enormous effect on your sexual feelings—something that's especially important as you try to build a relationship with someone or rekindle a passion that has started to flicker. Your brain is a very powerful part of your sexual apparatus, so let your Passion Diva help you to think sexy thoughts and put you in the right frame of mind for a pleasurable encounter. All your other sex organs will be grateful if you do!

9. Your Most Important Sex Toy Is Your Tongue (And We're Talking about *Talking!*)

I think communication is such an important part of sex that I've devoted the whole next chapter just to that. So I'm not going to spend a lot of time on it here. I just want to remind you that if you don't speak up and ask for what you want, you can't always expect your partner to know, let alone to give it to you.

Of course, there are lots of ways to communicate your needs, wishes, and desires other than with words—though in many cases, your tongue will still be involved! And in Chapter 2, we'll talk about nonverbal as well as verbal communication. Still, it's your tongue that says, "Thank you," and "That was great," and "What can I do for you now?" both inside and outside the bedroom. And it's communication between the two of you that leads to comfort, intimacy, and closeness, which in turn paves the way for passion to grow. As we've seen, even the smallest words and actions can make a world of difference to your Passion Diva and your partner.

10. If You Want Great Sex, Bring the Right Woman to the Bedroom

This one definitely comes under the "last but not least" category. So what exactly do I mean by the "right woman"? Well, if you're lying there fretting over a quarrel with an office colleague or reminding yourself to pick up the kids' soccer uniforms tomorrow, how can you respond fully to all the sexy things your guy is doing? And if he's just going through the motions, how can you nudge him gently into a more present, generous, and sexy mode if you've checked out due to boredom, frustration, or your to-do list?

Ladies, if you really want to have great sex, you need to bring your inner Passion Diva to the event—that part of you who is fully present, sexually alert, and physically alive. You'll never experience true passion if you're not fully there to participate! So please take to heart the suggestions you'll find throughout this book for bringing the right woman to the bedroom—and everywhere else. It may seem like a lot of work at first, but soon you'll find that it's the best energy you've ever spent.

Now that you know what your Passion Diva knows, you're ready to help that lovely lady find her voice. So let's move on to Chapter 2, which is all about communication.

In Your Passion Pantry

- **Your favorite piece of lingerie.** Wear some lingerie to look sexy for your man—or to feel sexy for yourself.

- **Chocolate.** When you're alone, chocolate reminds you of your sweet, sensuous side, and when you're with a lover, some rich, dark chocolate can operate like an aphrodisiac. (See Chapter 6 for instructions on the Chocolate Kiss.) Mmmmm . . .

- **Beautiful bedding.** Your Passion Diva knows how to prepare her Passion Playground: soft sheets made of silk or of high-thread-count Egyptian cotton (I prefer 600-threads, myself); a luxurious duvet to envelop you; sensuous romantic colors, a sexy red-and-black décor, or maybe soft, inviting pastels . . . Make your bedroom an oasis for pleasure, romance, maybe even love. . . .

- **A feather boa.** Let the soft feathers caress your shoulders while the playful boa brings out your Queen Latifah strut. Hang the boa on your bedpost to let your partner know you're ready to play. Or, if you're really feeling adventurous, greet him at the door wearing your boa and nothing but!

- **Your favorite perfume.** The most evocative of our five senses is the sense of smell. Develop a signature scent that your guy will always associate with you. Or maybe choose a different fragrance for every mood. You know, there's a reason that every major perfume company sells its products by associating its scents with sex.

- **A Do Not Disturb sign.** Use it both during sex and for Passion Diva pampering time!

~ 2 ~
Let Your Passion Diva Speak
Improving Communication for Better Sex

As you may recall from Chapter 1, one of your Passion Diva's key pieces of wisdom is: *Your most important sex toy is your tongue (and we're talking about* talking!*).*

You heard me. Talking. Now, why do I think something as ordinary and as potentially un-sexy as talking is one of the secrets to great sex? It's simple: If your Passion Diva can't find her voice, she loses an enormous amount of her power. But if she knows how to speak up about what she wants—and not just in the bedroom, but in every aspect of her life—her sexual power is multiplied a thousandfold.

Just in case you're still not convinced, let me share with you one of the most moving stories I've ever heard about a Passion Party, this time from our Passion Consultant Jean, an advertising copywriter in Connecticut. Months ago, Jean conducted a party where one of her guests was sixty-eight years old. The woman's daughter had brought her. She was super-quiet but listened intently during the presentation. After the party, she and her daughter came into the confidential ordering room together. The mother was still a bit reluctant, but she quickly warmed up to Jean. With the encouragement of her daughter, the woman purchased a Jelly Osaki toy—a very popular vibrator that provides both vaginal and clitoral stimulation—and some Revelation Lubricant— one of our most popular lubricants, because it feels so much like your own natural lubrication, is clean, and lasts a long time. Then, as she

43

gave Jean her credit-card number, the woman started to talk about what a big deal this was for her and suddenly she became very emotional. She told Jean that her husband had passed away a year ago and that in all the times she'd had sex with him, it had always been for *him*. She said she hadn't known that women could ever enjoy themselves during sex or that they were supposed to expect sexual pleasure.

"I had sex with my husband when he wanted, how he wanted, and how often he wanted," this woman told Jean. She went on to say that she'd never made any decisions regarding their sexuality as a couple, she certainly had never owned a toy, and she had *never ever* had an orgasm. She wiped away her tears and told Jean that she was looking forward to this purchase being all for her.

Later, Jean told me that the whole experience had made her realize how incredibly important being a Passion Consultant is. "I started this business for the extra income," Jean said, "but my eyes have opened to what as a company we are really accomplishing." When I heard this story, I, too, felt proud of our wonderful Passion Consultants, who reach out to so many women in so many ways. It was also a reminder of just how many women were out there who had maybe started out, just as I had, with no knowledge or information about what their bodies and their sexuality were capable of—women who had never spoken with their husbands, boyfriends, or dates about what they wanted, how they felt, or what might make sex better for them.

Sometimes, women have a tendency to interpret a lack of communication in the bedroom to mean that their partner just doesn't care. Well, maybe some men don't. But I believe that the vast majority of them actually *want* to know what will make their partners happy! Most men get a lot of pleasure from knowing that they brought their partners to orgasm, or warmed them up to the boiling point with foreplay, or created that special joy that comes from really satisfying sex.

The problem is that men often don't know how to communicate about what's going on between the sheets. They don't know how to ask you about what you might like, partly because they think they're supposed to know already. And they don't know how to communicate what *they* might enjoy in a way that resonates with us girls. The result is a whole bunch of not-quite-satisfied women and kinda-sorta-puzzled men, all afraid to bring this hot topic out into the open.

So let's get rid of the communication gap once and for all and get this party started with some real connecting. This chapter is all about giving you some easy, comfortable ways to let your man know how he can please you and to find out how you can please him, too. We'll begin with a little quiz that covers all types of communication between couples: daily communication, saying what you want in bed, finding out what he enjoys, "passion chat," and setting limits. Your Passion Diva needs to be able to communicate in all five ways to keep the healthy sparks a-flying.

Making Yourself Clear: The Passion Diva Communication Quiz

1. You've had a really frustrating day at work with your new boss, and now you and your honey are having a quiet dinner together. He says, "So how was work?" You say:
   a. "Oh, my gosh, I *hate* that new boss. I just *hate* her! Let me tell you the twenty-five awful things she did to me, just this afternoon alone!"
   b. "Oh, it was fine."
   c. "Okay, since you asked, I need to blow off a little steam. It's not that serious—nothing to get upset about—but this new boss really is driving me nuts."
   d. "I'd love to tell you, but do me a favor. Let me know when I've been talking for five minutes, and we'll change the subject. This woman is driving me nuts, but I don't want her to spoil our whole evening. Five minutes is all she deserves!"

2. You're in bed together and your partner is squeezing your breast in a way that's more uncomfortable than stimulating. You want him to ease up and go more gently. You say:
   a. "Ouch! I'm not a doorknob, you know!"

    b. "Um . . . would you be willing to . . . go a little softer there? I'm kind of sensitive."

    c. "I love it when you touch my breasts. . . . You know what would be great? . . . If you stroked them really gently, the way you'd pet a kitten."

    d. (*You take his hand and gently guide it the way you'd like it to go, while nibbling on his earlobe and sighing with pleasure.*)

3. You and your partner are making love, but he doesn't seem to be all that into it—just going through the motions. You say:

    a. "Hey, if you've got something more important to do, don't let me stop you!"

    b. "You're not having a very good time, are you?"

    c. "Is there something special you'd like me to do tonight? You make me so happy . . . and I'd love to make you happy, too."

    d. (*You think of something you know he likes—or some new move you read about in a magazine—and see how he responds.*)

4. Your partner has asked you to "talk dirty" to him. You say:

    a. "What am I, a porn star? I don't think so!"

    b. "I'll try, but I don't think I'm very good at it. Can you help me out? What would you like to hear?"

    c. "Okay, let me tell you exactly what I'd like you to do to me. First, I want you to kiss me so passionately and deeply that I start getting wet. . . . Then I want you to trace your finger down my belly and slide your hand inside my panties."

    d. (*You ask him to start making love, and then you start describing what he's doing and how you feel about it.*)

5. Your partner has just tried to use his finger on you for a little back-door entry—something you might be into someday, but definitely not tonight. You say:

    a. "Stop that right now!"

b. "I really wish you wouldn't."

c. "Honey, I'm not saying never, but let's not go there tonight."

d. *(You take his hand, stroke it lovingly, and place it firmly some-where you do want to be touched.)*

Okay, now let's take a closer look at your answers. As with so many things in the sexual arena, it's less about "right" and "wrong" than about getting the results you want. Read on to see how these different responses can affect your relationship and your life beneath the covers.

QUESTION 1: DAILY COMMUNICATION

a. "Oh, my gosh, I hate that new boss. I just hate her! Let me tell you the twenty-five awful things she did to me, just this afternoon alone!"

It's fine to talk to your guy about work. In fact, you should keep him up to date with what's going on in all areas of your life, especially if he asks. Just be careful not to let your frustrations overwhelm the conversation—particularly if you don't want him to worry. Frustration and anger are guaranteed to make you and your partner feel unsexy, even if your anger is directed at a third party. So approach the conversation as a chance to confide and share rather than just spewing venom. How you handle any given situation can either pull your partner closer or push him away.

b. "Oh, it was fine."

On the flip side, there's such a thing as not being expressive enough. "Oh, it was fine" is probably not quite *enough* communication, especially if you ever want him to ask about work again. Your man might take this brief response as a rebuff, when all you really meant was "I don't feel like talking about work *right now*." It's fine not to get into something, especially if you don't want to ruin the mood. Just make sure to be encouraging as you change the subject. "I'd love to talk about that another time. Thanks so much for asking. Will you ask me again later when I have the energy to go into it?"

c. "Okay, since you asked, I need to blow off a little steam. It's not that serious—nothing to get upset about—but this new boss really is driving me nuts."

Now this is a terrific answer. You get to vent, but you've made it clear that your guy doesn't have to do anything other than nod, listen, and say, "She sounds like a piece of work, all right!" You've made it crystal-clear what kind of response you're looking for without putting him on the spot.

d. "I'd love to tell you, but do me a favor. Let me know me when I've been talking for five minutes, and we'll change the subject. This woman is driving me nuts, but I don't want her to spoil our whole evening. Five minutes is all she deserves!"

Another terrific answer, with the added benefit that you've asked him to help you set a boundary. Of course, if you *want* to complain about your boss all evening, go right ahead. We all need to do that once in a while. But think about it. Is that really how you want to spend *all* of your precious date or dinner time with your favorite guy? There's a fine line between keeping him up to date and obsessing, between sharing your problems and simply dumping them on your man. Think about how much energy a problem really deserves before you let it take over your evening. (And if you think *he's* too obsessed about work, his family, or any other topic, ask him to show similar restraint!)

THE *Passion Diva's Guide* TO DAILY COMMUNICATION

- **Say something.** Simply open your mouth and begin. Silence has a way of growing and can quickly become a way of life if you don't nip it in the bud. Just be sure to choose your times wisely: Resist the temptation to introduce heavy topics when he's hassled, harried, or late for a meeting.

- **Pick your battles.** So he doesn't pick up his socks all the time or do the dishes as often as you'd like—is that really worth a huge fight?

You probably do some things that bother him, too, so why not shrug off the little things and save the big talks for things that really matter.

- **Get to the point.** The four words men dread most? "We have to talk." He's no fool. He knows this *really* means, "We've got a problem, I know what it is, and it's all your fault," and so any conversation that follows is sure to be awkward and defensive. Instead, say what you mean, mean what you say, and leave him as little room as possible to wonder about your intentions.

- **Take ownership of what you say.** Which would you rather hear: "You don't spend enough time with me" or "I wish we could spend more time together, because I just love being with you"? Most of us would vastly prefer the second—and your man is probably no exception. Talk about what you'd like and how you feel, not about what he's doing wrong—even if you *know* he *is* wrong!

- **Offer solutions.** Open-ended requests often leave your partner feeling as if it's his responsibility to fix things, another recipe for defensiveness. So instead of simply saying, "I wish I could spend more time with you," perhaps go on to suggest, "Why don't I get us tickets for the game on Saturday, and then we can get some dinner afterward."

- **Tone it down.** Don't scream, yell, or snap. Honestly, this is very discouraging to your guy, and it can escalate until you are both yelling so loudly that neither of you can hear anything. You should not suppress your righteous anger, and sometimes a scream-fest (or a good cry) is necessary. Just don't make it a habit.

- **Touch ten times a day.** All sorts of flirty touching can communicate your feelings for your man—hugging, teasing, tickling, smooching. And since nonsexual touching conveys warmth and caring, why not talk with your heart and with your hands as well as your mouth?

Rest your hand on his arm, take hold of his hand, and always end every conversation with a kiss and a hug. You'll be surprised at how much closer it makes you feel.

- **Remember the power of "I love you."** You just can't say those three little words often enough. With the kiss and hug I just recommended, they're the perfect way to end every conversation.

QUESTION 2: SAYING WHAT YOU WANT IN BED

a. "Ouch! I'm not a doorknob, you know!"

Ouch, indeed! Of course, I deliberately exaggerated that response to make a point—but the point is an important one. Negative feedback in bed can be hard for any guy. Remember, lots of them think they're already supposed to know it all, and they feel royally embarrassed when they discover that they don't. That wish to "know it all" may come out of a deep desire to please you—and isn't that something you want to encourage?

So instead of saying "Not so hard," practice murmuring, "Oh, would you do that more softly?" Try replacing "That's way too fast" with "I like it so much better when you do it slower." And if you're thinking "Please don't touch me there," consider whispering, "I'd love it if you touched me *here*." Whenever possible, tell him what you want, not what you don't want. It sounds a lot better to his ears.

b. "Um . . . would you be willing to . . . go a little softer there? I'm kind of sensitive."

This response is pretty good, but you can see that the woman feels uncomfortable about saying it. That apologetic tone—while perfectly understandable—is going to make most guys feel anxious, uncertain, and once again, embarrassed. The more self-confident and relaxed you can manage to be, the more confident and relaxed he'll be, as well—and your chances of having a mutually satisfying time will improve accordingly. So put your guy at ease by putting yourself at ease. Feel your Passion Diva's confidence radiating through you, and know that your guy will be happy to accommodate you once you help him figure out how. Remember, people tend to live up—or down—to what we expect of them, so acting absolutely certain that *of course* your guy wants to please you is an excellent way to ensure that he does.

c. "I love it when you touch my breasts. . . . You know what would be great? . . . If you stroked them really gently, the way you'd pet a kitten."

Notice how this statement gives exactly the same information and accomplishes exactly the same goal as the previous two—but what a difference in tone and mood! If you were the guy, which of these three would you rather hear? Which would inspire you to perform greater feats in bed? Focusing on the positive and emphasizing how much he turns you on will carry you—and your guy—very far indeed.

d. (You take his hand and gently guide it the way you'd like it to go, while nibbling on his earlobe and sighing with pleasure.)

If you feel shy about stating your preferences out loud or worry that your words may not be exactly right, know that there are ways to get the idea across without saying anything at all! If you prefer to use actions instead of words, more power to you. Some men are also more comfortable with giving and receiving gestures. Whatever works for you and your guy is just fine—as long as it's positive and encouraging rather than critical and *dis*couraging.

THE *Passion Diva's Guide* TO SAYING
WHAT YOU WANT IN BED

- **Be playful.** The great thing about play is that nothing matters all that much. Don't make sex a competitive sport; you're not getting any gold medals here, not even if you break a world record! As long as you keep the mood light and playful, you've got lots of room to try stuff out, make mistakes, start over, and still rack up a pretty high score by the time the final buzzer rings.

• **Be truthful.** He's lying on top of you, your leg cramps up, and you cry out. Guess what? If your guy thought that was a cry of pleasure and you let him go on believing that's the case, he's going to lie on top of you that same way every night for the rest of your life. He's thinking, "Well, at least I know one thing that pleases her," while you're thinking, "*Please* get off my leg!"

There is *no* advantage in pretending when it comes to sex, and that goes triple when it comes to faking orgasms. I know you want him to feel good about what's he doing—or maybe you just want him to get it over with so you can go to sleep—but if you give him the impression that your sex was A-plus when it really was only B-minus, you'll be having B-minus sex for some time to come. And if he ever figures out you were faking it, he may take it as a breach of trust that shatters his confidence in himself and in your relationship. Put yourself in his place: How would you feel if he moaned with pleasure when you stroked his thigh or fondled his penis—and then later discovered that the move really left him cold, or at best, lukewarm?

What if he's doing his best to bring you to orgasm, and one night, it's just not happening? Consider a tactful response like the following:

~ Sometimes I just don't climax—but I love the cuddling.

~ I love being here with you—but it's just not happening tonight. Next time . . . !

And for those nights when you just don't have the energy right from the get-go:

~ You know what? Let's make this all about you tonight.

~ I'm really tired, sweetie—but how about if I give you a great oral treat?

Now what if you've been faking orgasms, and you've decided you'd like to stop? You don't necessarily have to tell the truth, the whole truth, and nothing but the truth. There is a more tactful way to turn the tide. Just stop giving any misleading signals. Then if he asks, "Are you there yet?" you say, "No, but go ahead and do what you want when you feel ready."

If he says, "I thought you'd climax while we were doing it," you can say, "I didn't, but I'd still like to! Let's try something different." Or, if he asks why you need something else now when you didn't before, you can simply say, "Oh, people change. What we're doing now is working great, and I have some ideas that might help things work even better." We'll get into these ideas in more detail later on, but now isn't a bad time to remind you: 75 percent of all women need to have their clitorises stimulated in order to reach orgasm, so for the vast majority of us, intercourse alone will never be enough. If you'd like to come clean, you might say casually, "Actually, before, I may have given you the wrong impression. But the last few times, I've really been climaxing—so let's keep on doing what works so well."

- **Be positive.** As we've already seen through the earlier examples, you should say what you want, not what you *don't* want. This goes hand in hand with my next point:

- **Be specific.** Remember, ladies, he *wants* to please you. But if you want your guy to be a star sexual athlete, you might need to give him some quality coaching. As we said in the previous chapter, every woman is different—it's your responsibility to make sure he knows what works for *you*. Here are some suggestions to get you started:
  ~ "That's where I like a firm touch. You can even press a little harder."
  ~ "Touch me very lightly there—just brush me. Yes, that's it—perfect."
  ~ "That's a place I like to be kissed."
  ~ "Oooh, I'm so sensitive there. Just a little touch really gets me going."

~ "Would you move your tongue in circles—like you're stirring something up?"

~ "You know what I like? First, you cover me with your whole palm, then sort of tickle me with one finger, then the palm, then the finger . . . a little of each one . . . Mmmm . . ."

If it's hard for you to say this all out loud—or if it's hard to talk while you're in the midst of making love—consider looking at this book with your guy and pointing to words, phrases, or even whole paragraphs. You can also stick a pretty Post-it beside your favorite suggestions and leave the book for him to find. Write a sexy little note on each Post-it, even something as simple as "Maybe tonight?" or "When you're in the mood . . ." so he hears it as a suggestion and not as a scold.

• **Use the language of love.** No, I don't mean French—I'm thinking of all the sounds and movements that lovers use to cue and guide each other, little sighs and moans along with body language to let him know what's working and what you'd like next. If you're stretched out on your back and you're ready to have him touch or kiss your clitoris, try pulling up one knee (keeping your foot on the bed) to make that part of your body more accessible. If he doesn't get the hint, then gently guide his hand or head where you want it.

Allow your satisfaction to translate into *mmm* and *ahhh* and *oooh*. Let your breathing be audible, so he can hear when your breath comes faster. Even if you're shy about talking, maybe try a whispered *yes* or an occasional "That feels so good." You'll be giving him worlds of information about what you like and loads of positive reinforcement that will keep him doing it longer. As an added bonus, you may discover that being more responsive involves you more, too. Instead of just lying back and letting him do his thing, you've suddenly become an active participant—and that may make the whole experience more intense, fun, and meaningful.

By the way, if you are usually vocal during sex and then one night you are quiet, he may ask you what's wrong. If something *is* wrong, you'll have a chance to tell him. If you'd rather not get into it, or if everything really is fine, just say, "I didn't realize I was being quiet—I'm certainly loving every minute . . ."

QUESTION 3: FINDING OUT WHAT *He* WANTS IN BED

a. "Hey, if you've got something more important to do, don't let me stop you!"

Again, ouch! I can well believe the woman who's saying this is frustrated, hurt, and anxious about what's going on, but she's making it really hard for her guy ever to have an off night. It's also quite possible that he really wants to be with you but just isn't in the mood to make a big production. Either way, you'll want to try a more positive approach.

b. "You're not having a very good time, are you?"

This remark opens the doors of communication, but it's certainly going to put him on the spot. No one likes to be called out or accused of feeling a certain way. After all, even if he seems a bit distant, he may be having a fine old time, or he may simply be worried about whether *you're* having a good time. Still, if you follow up this comment with some compassionate questions, you might actually find out what's on your guy's mind (and then you can stop worrying that the problem is you). Here's how such a conversation might go:

YOU: You're not having a very good time, are you?

HE: No, no, it's okay.

YOU: Honey, I can tell when you're into it—and you're terrific when you are—but tonight, I can see your mind is somewhere else. If something is bothering you, I'd really like to know what it is.

HE: It's kind of stupid. I called my brother today, and I guess I keep thinking about that.

YOU: Really? Why?

HE: Oh, he's such a jerk. I can never get along with that guy.

At this point, you've got a few choices. You might encourage your man to keep talking with the same kind of gentle questioning that has brought you this far. The important thing is to keep the lines of communication open, one way or another. If you don't feel like talking about his brother on your big date night, you can try to steer the conversation—and the action—back to a more sexual tone. If you are happy to listen to his problems, you can let him take the lead. You can also offer to talk about his brother another time, or encourage him to talk about his brother with the understanding that he'll save some time and energy for sex, or suggest that you make love first and talk afterward.

Of course, the problem might be closer to home and related to something concerning you or your relationship. Again, you can either let him choose what to do next or express your own preferences, but at least you've gotten him talking.

c. "Is there something special you'd like me to do tonight? You make me so happy . . . and I'd love to make you happy, too."

What if you don't *want* to get him talking? What if you really want to stay in the sexual moment? In that case, ask for some guidance on what he'd like in order to get himself more in the mood. Just remember that many guys are shy about telling you this. Sometimes they think they shouldn't "need" anything except what they can more or less get for themselves. Sometimes they're embarrassed about the particular thing that makes them feel good. Sometimes they don't really *know* what turns them on—especially if they're young or inexperienced—so the two of you may have to explore together. But asking your guy what he wants—in a positive, reassuring way—is a terrific start.

d. **(You think of something you know he likes—or some new move you read about in a magazine—and see how he responds.)**

As we've seen, actions can speak louder than words. Go ahead and try something you think he might like—and if that doesn't work, you can either keep trying or switch to verbal communication, using any of the positive suggestions outlined earlier.

QUESTION 4: PASSION CHAT

a. "What am I, a porn star? I don't think so!"

This can be a tricky area: What's the difference between just talking about sex and "talking dirty"—or, as we like to call it around here, passion chat?

Well, talking *about* sex is figuring out with your guy what either of you—or both of you—would like. It's having an adult discussion about your preferences and dislikes while guiding each other in a helpful way. But then there's also passion chat—what some people call "talking dirty" or "naughty talk"—the kind of language that in the bedroom or on the phone can help arouse either or both of you and make the whole act more exciting.

Lots of people of both sexes find passion chat intimidating, and if you really hate the whole idea of doing this, or if you can't stand the version of it that turns your partner on, of course you have the right to say *no.* But before you write off the idea entirely, maybe give it a try. As with so many sexual activities, learning that you can do it, you're good at it, and you can make your partner happy with it might easily turn an act that seemed daunting and distasteful into one that now seems delightful and delicious.

Think about it. You murmur a few words into his ear, and he begins to pant with desire. . . . You keep talking, and he gets more and more aroused. . . . Now he really wants you, but you say, "Not quite yet." You just keep whispering, as he wants you more, and more, and more. . . .

See what I mean? That could be something you just might learn to like!

And if you're the one who wants your guy to use some passion chat with you? Talk him through the basics if he's having trouble. Don't expect him to already know how to go about this and don't make him feel bad for doing it the wrong way. One little "Eew! Disgusting!"— however well deserved—will keep him quiet in the bedroom for a long, long time to come.

b. "I'll try, but I don't think I'm very good at it. Can you help me out? What would you like to hear?"

Here at Passion Parties, we generally stick with the clinical terms for sexual acts and body parts because we're adults and we want to talk about the topic in an adult way. That's the rule I'll follow in this book, too, but that's not necessarily how you and your man will want to talk in bed. You'll need to find out what works for both of you: "penis" and "vagina," or words that are a bit more down and dirty—which is exactly why they turn you on. If there are words that you just aren't comfortable hearing from your partner, share them with him, and invite him to do the same. If there are words that you find sexy, let him know that, too. Don't be afraid of admitting that you like saying or hearing certain things—passion chat can be a form of role play, and it can be good to experiment with different phrases or expressions to see if they heighten your sexual pleasure.

Some couples make up their own code words for sex, which has the added benefit of letting you talk about it in front of other people—especially your kids. I know one couple who referred to their sex play as "making cookies." "How'd you like to make some cookies later this weekend?" one or the other might ask when they were having dinner with their in-laws, and the sense of a shared secret makes the whole thing even sexier.

c. "Okay, let me tell you exactly what I'd like you to do to me. First, I want you to kiss me so passionately and deeply that I start getting wet. . . . Then I want you to trace your finger down my belly and slide your hand inside my panties."

Talking about what you'd like is always a good start, and it has the added advantage of helping him know what you want. If you go this route, be sure to tell him not only what you like but also how it makes you feel. An added bonus of this kind of passion chat is that it can help you feel more turned-on, as well. For example:

I want you to touch my breasts and play with the nipples . . . just a little . . . not too much . . . Oooh, I'm starting to get excited. . . . Now I want you to pinch them a little bit—not too hard. . . . Oh, that feels so good, I can hardly stand it. . . .

d. (**You ask him to get started, and then you start describing what he's doing.**)

One great technique for passion chat is to take your cue from what he's actually doing, and then you can describe—as explicitly as you can—what it feels like. Have you ever noticed that saying things like "I'm exhausted" or "Wow, this tastes good!" can actually make you feel more tired or more contented? Well, it works the same way with sex. Saying that you're excited can make you feel more excited. For example:

I love it when you get really hard. I can feel you deep inside me . . . deeper . . . deeper . . . Can you feel how I'm holding you in there . . . so tight . . . because I want you right *there. YES!*

You can also use this technique when your guy is out of town and you want to try some passion chat by phone. Talk yourselves through a whole sexual act, either a real encounter you might actually have in your own bedroom or a fantasy describing a setting and activities that turn you on. Some fantasies are never meant to be acted out, so the phone is a great tool for this kind of sexy communication; and, of course, you might end up describing some things you'd actually like to do! One more advantage of passion chat is that it can open up some creative ideas and options.

THE *Passion Diva's Guide* TO PASSION CHAT

• Remember, there's no wrong way to do this—and no one right way, either. Don't be limited by what you've seen in sexy movies—just be yourself. Of course, you can always take on a role if it helps you—maybe an attentive, sexy nurse, or perhaps a sultry temptress.

• Some women don't want to talk sexy for fear of sounding stupid, being put down, or rejected. If you're worried about this, let your guy know and ask for support: "I'd love to have some sexy talk in our bedroom, but I've got to be honest, I'm not used to it and I'm feeling a little bit shy. But if you give me lots of positive feedback, I promise I'll be talking sexy a lot more often!"

• If you'd like some extra security—or if your partner would—consider making rules for your passion chat: *No laughing; no judgments;* and *no put-downs* might be good places to start. You can also put a moratorium on any words that turn you off.

• Find your voice. Are you more comfortable with low, sexy grunts or high-pitched squeals? With loud demands or quiet whispers? Passion chat can reflect the way you normally talk or, if it helps you to feel freer, use different tones to surprise your lover. Experiment with speed, change the volume, sound commanding, sound uncertain, and everything in between. Once you see what turns him on—and what turns you on—you'll feel a lot bolder about trying out still more new things.

• If necessary, expand your vocabulary. If either of you wants actual "dirty" talk, don't use clinical terms like "testicles" or "vagina." If you need some ideas, read romance novels or watch sexy movies (but not porn: the talk is unimaginative and often degrading to women).

• Practice when you're alone, perhaps when you're self-pleasuring. Fantasize about sex with your partner and think of things to say. Start by hearing his voice and your voice in your mind, and work your way up to saying things out loud.

- Take your inspiration from what's going on. Think of yourself as doing a play-by-play narration of your sexual activity. "I love the way your hands feel on my . . ." You can move on to saying what you will do next, and then describe something you want him to do to you.

Question 5: Setting Limits

a. " *Stop that right now!*"

Now, here's a very important part of helping your Passion Diva find her voice: Setting limits. I'm all for it—every human has limits, and we all need to respect both our own and our partner's. I think this is so important. I'm going to say it again: *You have a right to your limits.* Never let anyone, no matter how much you love him, talk or pressure or bulldoze you into doing something that you really don't want to do, in or out of bed.

Having said that, I'm going to ask you to hold a second idea in your mind at the same time: Whenever possible, when it comes to the bedroom, see if you can be generous. What if you agreed to do something on the understanding that you'd do it just *once,* and you'd never have to do it again if you didn't like it? What if you agreed to do something, but only under the exact, specific conditions that worked for you, and you get to say what those are and stop immediately if your conditions aren't being met? What if you agreed to do something *he* really wants, on the condition that he'll turn around and do something that *you* really want? Do any of these ideas make you feel like maybe it would be worth it to push your own limits?

Again, your limits are *yours,* and nobody should ever make you feel bad for having them. A guy who won't take no for an answer—especially one who acts contemptuous or angry that you are saying *no*—is probably not a guy your Passion Diva wants to hang on to.

But if you're dealing with a good guy who generally makes you happy, think about going the extra mile, even if it's only that one time. Both of you may discover some wonderful, surprising things if you do. And if the whole experience turns you off? Get him to bring you some chocolate ice cream in bed afterward or have him give you a foot rub. If you please him, you can ask him to please you, too!

If you *do* want to set a limit, I think *"Stop that right now!"* is pretty good for times when you're feeling uncomfortable or unsafe—especially with someone you're not sure you can trust. I'm not only talking about the kind of sex I gave in the example, but about any kind of sexual activity that you'd rather not engage in, from an arm around the shoulders to a French kiss to any kind of touching or sex play. If a guy is doing something—anything—and you want him to stop, *"Stop that right now!"* will usually do the trick.

b. " *I really wish you wouldn't.*"

This might seem like the kinder, gentler option, but I don't think it gives the man nearly enough information. If you're sincere about saying *no,* especially in a casual or early-dating kind of situation, a guy may hear this as an invitation to keep trying to get you to change your mind.

Another confusing answer you should avoid if you're in a casual or early-dating relationship is *"Not now."* Does that mean you'll want it in five minutes, five weeks, five months, or five years? If your guy is into whatever he's trying to do, he may hear you saying, "Not now—but maybe in five minutes," and then be angry that you promised something you didn't intend to deliver. That's not what you meant at all, of course, but why set yourself up for a bad situation?

So if what you mean is "I don't want you to do that," "Please stop," or "No," then say so. If what you mean is "We'll have to know each other a *lot* better for that one," then state that specifically. So many times, we women try to do two things at once—please our guy *and* tell him to stop. I'm all for pleasing—but if you're serious about him stopping, he really needs to hear it. And if he doesn't respond with respect, then like I said, show him the door. Your Passion Diva can do a whole lot better.

c. "Honey, I'm not saying never, but let's not go there tonight."

This one's good for not breaking the mood. And then if you want, you can talk to him later about when, if, and how you do want to "go there." This response works pretty well in all situations, from the casual to the long-married, because it's so clear. It doesn't commit you to anything right then, but it doesn't close any doors, either.

d. (You take his hand, stroke it lovingly, and place it firmly somewhere you *do* want to be touched.)

I think this is a terrific way to keep things on track, but only with a guy you really trust to read your signals and take the hint. It won't work so well if you're making out with a new guy and he's trying to go all the way, since he doesn't know what your limits are. Many guys think—often with women's encouragement—that they're supposed to take the lead sexually and that even a good girl will expect them to press a little. She's expected to say no, and the guy is expected to change her mind. So while "showing" rather than "telling" might be nicer on the ego, don't leave any room for misunderstanding.

THE *Passion Diva's Guide* TO SAFE SEX

In addition to knowing how to set limits, Passion Divas also know the rules of safe sex, and they make sure that their partners get with the program. This can be one of the trickiest areas in communication between couples, particularly if the relationship is new. Here are some basic rules you can follow:

- **Always use a condom until the two of you are ready to commit to monogamy.** How do you know when it's okay *not* to use a condom? Here's the litmus test I'd advise you to use: When you're ready to give your guy $20,000 in cash and a deposit slip and send him to your bank, that's when you're ready to have non-condom sex with him. After all, aren't your health and your life worth at least $20,000?

- **Take responsibility for your pleasure and your protection—carry your own condoms!** A Passion Diva always takes responsibility for her pleasure, and carrying your own condoms, as well as any other birth control you use, is part of the deal. These days, you can buy some lovely designer cases to keep your condoms in. We sell some ourselves. And while you're at it, maybe you'd like to explore Elexa condoms specifically intended for a woman's pleasure. You and your partner can even make a game out of trying them all out: ribbed condoms, ticklers, pre-lubricated, colored condoms, neon condoms that light up in the dark, condoms made with thinner rubber for more intense sensations, and even flavored condoms. If you're keen to have oral sex, try applying some D'Lickious or Sweet Sensations on the condom to take away that latex taste.

- **If something hurts, stop right away.** Here is one time you don't have to be so tactful. You want him to stop *immediately*, because you don't want to risk tears, abrasions, or any other painful consequences. Sex shouldn't hurt, and if it does, you need to find out why. Often, it's a matter of not enough lubrication, in which case, some Revelation Lubricant, UltraGlide, or RomantaTherapy Warming Lubricant can do the trick. If he's too big for you or shaped in a way that doesn't suit your anatomy (rare, but it happens), you might use a "bumper guard" (more about this in Chapter 7). A bumper guard is also good for marathon sex, because it gives your pelvis and pubic area a little more protection.

- **Always wash your sex toys with a cleanser that's made specifically for them.** Purchase some Passion Parties Toy Cleanser Concentrate, Clean & Simple Toy Cleanser Spray, or individual toy cleanser wipes, and do the job right. Using anything other than a specially made cleanser can give you an infection or a rash—and believe me, the places adult toys go are not places you want itching, swelling, or inflammation. Some people believe that if you cover a toy with a condom, you don't need to wash it between uses. Not true. You have to cleanse a vibrator between each session of sexual activity: You can use it multiple times during one long day or night of continuous lovemaking, but if a few hours elapse between uses, you'll want to clean it before using it again.

- **Never use the same toy for anal and vaginal sex—in fact, don't put anything in the anus and then expect to put it anywhere else.** If you and your guy enjoy anal sex, more power to you—but please be safe about it. No matter how carefully you wash that area, it contains bacteria that you don't want to introduce into any other part of your body. Once fingers, genitals, or toys have gone there, they must be properly cleaned before they can go anywhere else. Again, putting a condom on a toy won't do it. You should cleanse the toy before using it elsewhere, or, even better, reserve certain toys for anal use only and never use them in any other parts of your body. We'll talk more about this in Chapter 9.

LET'S PLAY: THE *Passion Diva's Guide* TO BRINGING TOYS INTO THE BEDROOM

Some people think that sex toys and products make sex "unnatural," but that's not how we at Passion Parties feel. If you've ever painted your nails, highlighted your hair, or put a dab of makeup on your face, you know how much fun it can be to add a little something extra. And if you've ever pushed a button on an elevator rather than trudging up the stairs, or used a shopping cart to carry your purchases rather than staggering through the store with your arms full, you know there's no harm in using some equipment to make certain activities a little easier. We at

Passion Parties understand that toys are a positive, playful way of spicing up your sex life and making things more satisfying for both of you. Toys aren't a negative commentary on anybody—or on anybody's abilities in the bedroom—but it's true that people sometimes feel threatened. So if you want to introduce toys into your bedroom repertoire, communication and sensitivity are extremely important. Here are some suggestions:

- **Be tactful.** If your guy is excited about trying out a few toys, it's all systems go! But if the two of you have never used toys before, I wouldn't suggest dumping a shopping bag full of new purchases onto the coffee table. That can be a bit overwhelming. Consider instead one of the following approaches, either just before the sexual part of the evening or at a completely neutral time, so it doesn't seem like a backhanded criticism of your sex life:

  "Honey, I read about something in a book, and I thought maybe it might be fun. Are you willing to give it a try?"

  "I went to this party and ended up buying this product. . . . What do you think?"

  "My girlfriend bought this and gave it to me. Should we try it out?" (That way, he doesn't have to wonder if some lack in your sex life has sent you out shopping.)

- **Be creative.** Let's say you've just bought some Crèmesicle Edible Massage Cream, and you want to introduce it into your bedroom activities. You might start by giving your partner a little demonstration: "Here, honey, put some of this on your hands and imagine how good that will feel on other parts of you, as well—especially if *I'm* doing the caressing." Alternately, you could bring this right into your sex play. Or if he's the kind of guy who hates surprises, you could make it part of the pregame warm-up.

  Or let's say you've bought some RomantaTherapy White Chocolate Passion Powder, and you're thrilled with the idea of the extended foreplay it can provide. Brush some on four different places of your body—either your favorite erogenous zones or else some really creative places like the tip of your elbow or the back of your knee. Then, as the two of you are getting started, put some on your fingertip and put your finger in his mouth. Say, "I've put dabs of this flavor in five different places on my body . . . and you can't go on to the main event until you've found all five." Help him find the four, if you need to—perhaps by giving him hints or saying, "warmer/colder"—but encourage him to keep looking until you are totally ready. Then you can say, "Time's up!" and guide him inside you, or, once again, let your actions speak for you. Afterward, you can tell him the truth about your little trick—or if you've both enjoyed the game, you might consider repeating it, perhaps "playing fair" this time. (If you *really* like the game, try putting different flavors in different places, and let him have a scavenger hunt to find and identify the tastes!) Our Passion Parties Fireworks Lotion comes in ten yummy flavors for a fun variety. And since turnabout is fair play, you can invite him to create a treasure hunt for you, too.

- **Be positive.** Some men love the idea of toys, but they'll never make the suggestion, either because they think you'll be offended or because it simply never occurred to them. Once you open that door, though, they may have all sorts of ideas you haven't considered. I don't want you to go against your own feelings, but if your guy suggests something that makes you uncomfortable, consider moving out of your comfort zone, just for one night. Who knows, you may decide it's a night you want to repeat. That's what happened to Rita, a Passion Consultant and restaurant hostess in Pennsylvania.

One night, long before I ever heard of Passion Parties, I was talking to my husband (he was my boyfriend at the time) about toys. He asked if I had any, and I told him that I did have a couple of them, some vibrators I'd bought in college. He asked me if he could watch me use one, and I very quickly told him, "No way!" But he was very insistent and was so turned on by the thought that I eventually gave in. Though I was uncomfortable at the time, the experience opened lots of doors of communication in our relationship and really helped us express some things to each other that we had never expressed before.

- **Be patient.** Try taking it one step at a time, starting with the toy or product your guy will feel most comfortable with and building from there. If he's already good about using his mouth, suggest some edibles. If he likes a lot of attention to his penis, take out the Ring of Ecstasy, a gently vibrating ring of silicone that fits around the base of the shaft and greatly enhances male pleasure during intercourse, and say, "I was thinking it might be fun to buy ourselves some 'presents.' Here's one for you. . . . I'll show you the one I got for me later on! . . ."

- **Be playful.** If you look at vibrators, edibles, and other sexual products as adult toys—fun things you can share with your favorite playmate—you and your partner may both come to enjoy incorporating them into your sex life. Here's a story from Lucy, a full-time Passion Consultant from Kansas, that shows how useful it can be to keep a sense of play, not to mention a sense of the unexpected!

I had a client who really wanted to add a spark to her love life but she said her husband was very traditional and they didn't really ever talk about sex. She thought he might like the sensation of a vibrating toy but was afraid he would react negatively to the introduction of toys into their lovemaking and didn't know how to broach the subject. She bought a small vibrator, though—the Loving Spoon—for her personal use.

One day her husband came home early. When my client heard him come in downstairs, she hastily tucked the Loving Spoon into the pillowcase and smoothed out the bedspread. She ran downstairs and greeted him with a big kiss and forgot all about the toy.

Later that night when they were in bed, he became amorous. As the excitement built, he grabbed her pillow, tucked it under her hips, and dived in for the final round of pleasure. Somehow in the course of all that thrashing around, the toy's switch was activated, so that the pillow under her hips began to vibrate. And since his testicles were pressing against the pillow . . . Well, let's just say that he's now one of our biggest toy fans and is quite vocal about it, too!

Now that your Passion Diva has found her voice, let's move on to the next chapter and give her a Sexy Anatomy Lesson. I promise you, it will be lots more fun than anything you ever learned in school!

─୧ *In Your Passion Pantry* ୨─

- **52 Weeks of Romance.** Give your Passion Diva a little inspiration when each week you choose a separate "scratch and win" card. One for him and one for you—a great new way to open up communication with your partner.
- **52 Weeks of Naughty Nights.** A year's worth of delicious ideas with cards that can help you ask for naughty treats—and help your partner ask for them, too.
- **Spicy Dice, Dirty Dice, and Glo Dice.** One die names a body part (toes, nipples, lips); the other suggests an action (lick, kiss, tickle). The spicy ones can start some fun; the dirty dice take it up a notch; and the glow dice glow in the dark. Turn your bedroom communication into a delightful game.
- **Pretty Post-its.** Leave your guy some sexy little notes that can speak for you when you're too shy to speak for yourself—or when you just want to remind him that he's on your mind. . . .
- **Scented stationery.** Personalize your love notes by spraying the

perfume he loves most on your stationery and then connect with your guy in a surprise moment in his hectic day.

- **White Chocolate Passion Powder.** Sprinkle this delicious treat on four areas of your body and tell him you have put it on five. You decide when you will "come clean" and reveal your little secret!

- **Lover's Coupons.** The hottest way to say, "I love you" is these certificates that you can buy from us or make yourself to exchange for such activities as cuddling, pampering, a "quickie"—whatever the two of you enjoy. And if either of you has trouble finding the words, the coupon can speak for you.

3

Get to Know Your Body—and His

A Sexy Anatomy Lesson

Biology was never my favorite subject, so I'll admit I never thought a knowledge of anatomy was all that big a deal. I certainly never thought it could be an important part of sexual pleasure. The thing that set me straight was hearing a story from Rose, a full-time dental assistant and part-time Passion Consultant from Oklahoma. "Most of the women who come to my Passion Parties are shy at first," she told me, "but by the end of the evening, all they can think about is how our wonderful products will help them reach orgasm more easily." But a few years ago, a young, married mother of two at one of Rose's parties just kept shaking her head. She told Rose, "Oh, I can't have orgasms because I don't have the orgasm gene. My mama and my granny didn't have it, and they told me that I didn't get it either."

Well, Rose was completely staggered. Here were two whole generations of women who had never enjoyed this wonderful experience, and now there was a third generation being deprived in the same way. "I was heartbroken," she told me. "But at the same time I was thrilled that this woman had come to my Passion Party so I could teach her that her 'gene' was there. She just needed to know how to make it work!"

She sent the young woman home with a Bullet vibrator and some Revelation Lubricant and very detailed instructions on how to use them both. The young woman called Rose a few days later, bubbling over with excitement. After all those years of thinking that orgasms could never happen to her, she finally understood that it wasn't a matter of genetics. She just needed to know what to do. She felt as though a whole new world had opened up to her—and all because she had learned some basic facts about her own body. It's really true: Education *is* an aphrodisiac!

Most of us have probably never believed in "the orgasm gene." But when I heard that story, I realized that far too many of us women have spent too many years not knowing what's really going on down there. And many of us have just as little information about what's going on with our partners.

So this chapter is for all of you who'd like to get to know your bodies a little bit better, and who'd also like to know the biology behind your partner's sexual arousal. Think of it as a little tour of your pleasure factory, and his. In fact, if you'd like to get naked for part of the lesson, or maybe even study this chapter with your partner, you can have a direct, hands-on demonstration of where all the parts are and how they work!

To show you why this anatomy lesson is going to be a *lot* more fun than the ones you had in school, let's start with another little quiz—a true-false one this time. Unlike the other two, this one actually does have right and wrong answers, but even if you get some wrong, you may feel like the right answer is such good news that you are more than happy to learn the truth!

THE SEXY ANATOMY QUIZ

Decide whether each answer is True or False.

1. If your partner really turns you on, and you haven't yet reached menopause, you'll have no problem being well-lubricated by the time you're ready for intercourse.
2. If a man has difficulty becoming or remaining erect, the most common reason is his lack of sexual interest in his partner.

3. The most common reason for a man's premature ejaculation is his or his partner's lack of sexual experience.

4. If a man becomes sexually aroused and does not go on to have an orgasm, he might face serious medical consequences from the buildup of blood and semen in his genital area.

5. Only men ejaculate.

6. If your partner can't tell that you had an orgasm, you probably didn't have one or else the sex wasn't very good.

7. Most women can achieve orgasm from intercourse alone.

8. Vibrators can be used for solitary self-pleasuring, but they cannot be used while a man is penetrating a woman.

9. There is no way to prevent or reverse the loss in pelvic muscle tone that results from aging or childbirth.

10. The only organ in either the male or the female body whose sole function is to provide pleasure is the clitoris.

Okay, now let's take a look at the answers.

1. **If your partner really turns you on, and you haven't yet reached menopause, you'll have no problem being well-lubricated by the time you're ready for intercourse.—FALSE.** There are lots of reasons that women of all ages have difficulty remaining wet, including changes that occur over the course of the menstrual cycle; cigarette smoking; many over-the-counter antihistamines, cold remedies, birth-control pills, and other medications; travel and time-zone changes; stress; and many women's favorite— extended sessions of lovemaking. Fortunately, the solution is simple—incorporate Revelation, Embrace, or some other lubricant into your sexual encounters, and you'll be both more comfortable and more sensitive. In fact, some extra lubricant is a great idea, even if you're also naturally wet. Good lubrication is essential for good sex, so later in the chapter I'll tell you more about getting wet and staying wet as well as tell you how to use

lubrication to enhance your partner's pleasure. Needing a little extra lube isn't a sign of anyone's shortcomings. It's just that your body may have a little less fluid than you happen to need at the moment.

2. **If a man has difficulty becoming or remaining erect, the most common reason is his lack of sexual interest in his partner.—** FALSE. Most of men's erectile problems have biological causes. Smoking, drinking, stress, and environmental toxins can all make it harder for a man to achieve or maintain an erection, as can such conditions as diabetes, heart disease, high blood pressure, obesity, and depression. There are even some prescription medications that can contribute to the problem. His feelings about *you*, though, are rarely the issue. (We'll learn more about this in Chapter 7.)

3. **The most common reason for a man's premature ejaculation is his or his partner's lack of sexual experience.—FALSE.** Premature ejaculation *is* a very common problem: According to a recent survey by researchers at the University of Chicago, about one-third of men from age eighteen to fifty-nine are troubled by rapid, premature ejaculation. A wide variety of causes may be behind this condition, but sexual inexperience *per se* is rarely the issue. More likely culprits are the guy's masturbation habits—in effect, he may have "trained" himself to climax quickly; a pattern of rushing into sexual encounters that he would like to end quickly; excess stress (which orgasm can help relieve); anxiety; and some drugs, especially stimulants. (Again, we'll learn more about this in Chapter 7.)

4. **If a man becomes sexually aroused and does not go on to have an orgasm, he might face serious medical consequences from the buildup of blood and semen in his genital area.—FALSE.** But how many of us have heard this story from guys who were trying to get us to "go all the way"? Men call it "blue balls," and for years they've been using the phrase to convince women that

failure to ejaculate can be a genuine hazard to their health. There's no question that a certain degree of arousal without the sexual release of orgasm can be uncomfortable—for both sexes— so if your sexual limits don't allow for climaxing in each other's presence, you may want to gear your sexual activity toward less arousal, or else find ways for you to climax in private. But you can rest assured that there's no *medical* problem or any risk involved—just ordinary frustration.

5. **Only men ejaculate—FALSE.** This one might surprise you. But if your G-spot—that little cushion of nerve endings and tissue wrapped around the urethra—is properly stimulated, you, too, may have a response that involves the release of up to a quart of clear fluid. You'll hear plenty about that later in this chapter.

6. **If your partner can't tell that you had an orgasm, you probably didn't have one or else the sex wasn't very good.—FALSE.** Orgasms often come in waves, and they can be as subtle as the contracting of your vaginal PC muscles in a kind of ripply feeling, as dramatic as a headboard-banging series of full-body contractions, or anything in between. As we all know from watching *When Harry Met Sally,* women often use sounds to indicate that they have had an orgasm (whether or not they are being truthful), so if your guy would like more certainty about when you've climaxed, you may want to find some verbal or nonverbal way of letting him know. But let's not neglect the pleasures of the quiet orgasm. They can be just as satisfying as the other kind.

7. **Most women can achieve orgasm from intercourse alone.— FALSE.** This one is so important I'll say it again: false, false, *false.* Ladies, listen closely: Only about 25 percent of us can climax *just* from intercourse. The vast majority of us need some kind of direct clitoral stimulation in order to reach orgasm. The clitoris is that little button just above our vaginal opening, and you'll be hearing more about it in a minute. For right now, focus on this fact: Only about one-fourth of us get enough stimulation from

intercourse to reach orgasm—mainly from the incidental pressure of the man's penis against our clitoris while he is inside us. The other three-fourths of us need more than that—and even the lucky one-fourth might want more than that. Rest assured that we'll be offering many pleasing suggestions for clitoral stimulation throughout this book.

8. **Vibrators can be used for solitary self-pleasuring, but they cannot be used while a man is penetrating a woman.—FALSE.** As we just saw, clitoral stimulation is necessary for a woman's orgasm, and the vast majority of women can't get that stimulation from ordinary intercourse alone. Happily, there are plenty of vibrators that can help on this front, and we've developed a number that can be used during intercourse—while the man is either thrusting or resting inside you—to provide your clitoris with that necessary tingle. The Pleasure Curve, the Ring of Ecstasy, and the Lilac Elephant are all designed to be used this way. (You can read more about them in Chapter 7, too.)

9. **There is no way to prevent or reverse the loss in PC muscle tone that results from aging or childbirth.— FALSE,** thank heavens! Well, the part about losing muscle tone is true. But the wonderful Dr. Arnold Kegel has developed a series of exercises, known in his honor as the Kegel exercises, that can strengthen your pelvic floor muscles while offering a number of medical benefits, including an increased capacity for orgasm. These exercises are simple, no one can tell you're doing them, and they don't take very long. And to make them even easier, we sell Ben Wa Balls, Pleasure Pods, and Pleasure Pearls—small, weighted balls that fit inside your vagina to help you practice contracting your pelvic-floor muscles. If you want to know more, keep reading!

10. **The only organ in either the male or the female body whose sole function is to provide pleasure is the clitoris.—TRUE.** And aren't you glad to know it? Not only does the tiny clitoris have twice as many nerve endings as men have in their entire penis,

but also, unlike the penis, the *only* function of your clitoris is to help you achieve orgasm. Think about that for a minute. Your body possesses an entire organ whose *only* job is to give you sexual pleasure.

I hope this quiz has whetted your appetite for learning more about your body and all the wonderful things of which it's capable. So let the anatomy lesson begin! And while I won't give you another test at the end, I will encourage you to go out and put your knowledge into practice. It just might be the most fun you ever had, inside or outside of school.

The Anatomy of Pleasure: Your Version

Many women spend their lives trying not to look too closely at what's going on "down there." But ladies, the more we know, and the more comfortable we are with that part of ourselves, the more pleasure we'll be able to have. So I'm going to give you two choices, and I truly hope you'll take me up on both of them. There is a diagram on page 78 to help you get acquainted with your vagina and your genital area. And I'm also going to explain how you can get a good look—maybe your first look—at that part of your body, so you can see for yourself what's where.

Now I was raised in the South, and in my day, this was the kind of thing a lady just didn't do. Looking at your own vagina? Please! The very idea would have been enough to make me shut my eyes in total embarrassment.

But times have changed, and so have we, and I'd really like to encourage you to at least consider viewing this wonderful part of your anatomy that has the potential for making you so happy. I'll talk you through it here, and when you're ready, you can grab a mirror and look for yourself.

1. Find a time when you feel rested and relaxed and have plenty of time and privacy. Take a look at the illustration on the next page and read through the information first. Then, when you're ready,

wash your hands thoroughly and find yourself a small hand mirror, maybe five or six inches in diameter.

2. Take off your panties and prop your back up against a pillow either in bed or on a long, comfortable couch (in a room with the drapes closed, naturally!). If you're feeling tense, take a few deep breaths and "channel" your Passion Diva. She can help you move from anxiety to feeling natural and relaxed.

3. Keeping your feet flat on the bed or couch, draw up your knees to maybe a ninety-degree angle—nice and comfortable—and let them drop open. (Some women like to put some pillows under each knee for extra support.) Hold the mirror in one hand and position it between your legs, angled so you can see what's down there. With your other hand, spread apart your labia majora—the hair-bearing lips of the outer vagina—and take a look inside. Here's what you'll find.

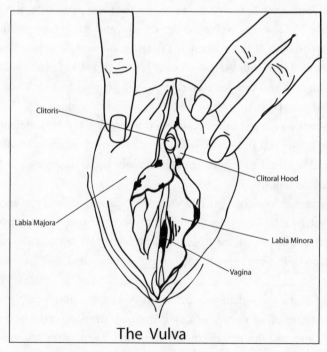

Clitoris

Clitoral Hood

Labia Majora

Labia Minora

Vagina

The Vulva

Okay, now you can see it all. But what are you looking at, and how does it relate to your sexual pleasure? Let's get to know this area of your body, because almost every one of these parts has the capacity to make you feel good.

VULVA

The external genital organs of a woman are collectively known as the vulva.

LABIA MAJORA

These are the outer lips of the vagina—in fact, the term is Latin for "big lips." The outside of the labia majora is often covered in pubic hair. The inside is pink and can be either smooth or a bit ridged. Here's where the pleasure begins, because the labia majora are packed with nerve endings, making them very responsive to stimulation. Having a man stroke or kiss this area can be a wonderful source of pleasure. As with all of your other pleasure areas, the labia are even more sensitive when they're wet, whether from your own lubrication, one of our products, or both. You can test this now, if you like, by gently touching yourself here and then moistening your finger with a little saliva or with some Revelation Lubricant and touching yourself again. Can you feel the difference? Don't neglect this area when it comes to making love—and for sure, don't neglect the lubrication. The difference in pleasure is like night and day.

LABIA MINORA

Now we come to the inner lips, tucked inside the labia majora. These inner lips also have a Latin name, which means "small lips." They're thinner, softer, and more flexible than the labia majora, and they have even more nerve endings and blood vessels, so stroking and kissing here can be even more pleasurable than farther out. Because of their greater sensitivity, lubrication is even more important for making any touch feel good. Again, the moisture can come from the man's saliva as he kisses you; from your own natural lubrication; from one of our products; or from some combination of the above. The more lubricated the area is, the more sensitive it becomes—and the more intense the pleasure.

By the way, labia minora come in a vast array of shapes and sizes, so if yours doesn't look exactly like the picture here, don't worry! They can be big, small, wide, or thin, and as with so many other aspects of sexuality, how you look has nothing to do with how much pleasure you're able to give and receive.

Urethra

If you gently pull back the labia minora, you'll find the urethral opening, which leads to the bladder. You'll also find the vaginal opening, but we'll get to that in a minute. The urethral opening is the much smaller top one, and it's where urine comes out when you urinate. While it's unlikely that you'll urinate during sex, some women do release a few drops now and then, or maybe even a small stream, so if this is a concern for you, you might make sure to urinate before you begin lovemaking, or even to limit your fluid intake for a few hours before sex. You can also do the Kegel exercises I describe at the end of this chapter, which will greatly increase muscular control in this area, or, as a last resort, see your doctor about prescription medications that can improve bladder control. By the way, sometimes you feel like urinating during sex—but actually, what you're responding to is not your bladder at all but your G-spot, which we'll get to in a moment. As we'll see, the G-spot can be the gateway to intense sexual pleasure, but stimulating it can also make you feel like you're about to urinate. Sometimes, too, G-spot stimulation causes you to release some clear fluids that are not urine but another type of urethral fluid. It's all part of the wonderful process of sexual arousal and nothing to cause you any concern.

VAGINA

Just below your urethral opening is your vagina, which leads into your uterus or womb. This is the place where babies come out and also the place from which your menstrual blood flows. During intercourse, this is the place into which the man inserts his penis, so let's get to know your vagina a little better.

The whole vagina is about three to five inches long—a little canal lined with soft, fleshy membranes. The outside open entrance to the vagina and the first inch or two are the most sensitive to touch, as this is where the majority of the nerve endings are located. What you can reach with your finger is the most excitable. Fingers and lips can make this area very happy, and so can the tip of a penis when it nuzzles and strokes. Again, lubrication can make a big difference in terms of the pleasure you derive, while lack of lubrication can make touching this area dull at best, unpleasant at worst.

What happens as you get farther inside? Well, ladies, the inner two-thirds of your vaginal canal has *no* nerve endings at all—none. So a penis, vibrator, or dildo thrust deep inside you may feel good for lots of other reasons (again, we'll get to the G-spot in a minute), but your vagina itself isn't really being stimulated, because it can't be.

If you're having a hard time believing me, check it out for yourself. With one finger, feel your way very gently into your vaginal opening and see how sensitive you are. Then push a little farther in—past the half-inch mark—and gently press your finger against the vaginal wall, kind of the way you might when you're inserting a tampon. You'll feel the sensation of your finger pushing inside you, but you won't feel anything like the same kind of stimulation you got in that first half-inch. That's truly nature's way of reminding us that penis length doesn't matter!

PERINEUM

Now here's a sensitive little area that lots of women—and men—don't know much about, and they should, because it can add a great deal of pleasure to your sexual encounters. The perineum is that flat space between your vaginal opening and your anus. (You may have heard it called the "t'aint," because "It t'aint the vagina and it t'aint the anus!") When you become aroused, this area may also become more sensitive, so that massaging it or applying gentle pressure can heighten your pleasure during either intercourse or clitoral stimulation. Maybe by now you can guess what I'm about to say next: Lubrication will also make this sensitive area easier to touch and more receptive to pleasure.

ANUS

Sometimes known as the "back door," the anus is the opening that leads to your rectum. Like your body's other openings, the anus is also full of nerve endings. Many women (and men) find that gentle stimulation either around the anal opening or just inside the anus offers another kind of pleasure, either as part of your journey toward intercourse and/or clitoral stimulation or as a separate kind of sexual pleasure (I'll tell you more about anal sex in Chapter 9). Once again, lubrication is key—especially in this area, which produces no natural lubrication of its own.

CLITORIS

I've saved the best for last. The crown jewel in your collection, the organ that's designed for the sole job of giving you sexual pleasure, is called the clitoris, and it's right there above your urethral opening—a little hooded organ that ranges in size from a half-inch to one inch outside the body, and another few inches that extend within you.

As we saw in our Sexy Anatomy Quiz, the clitoris—despite its small size—contains twice as many nerve endings as a man has in his entire penis. Twice as many, ladies. *Twice!* Think how sensitive you are right there, and imagine the enormous capacity for arousal and sensation that nature has given you. In fact, some women are so sensitive that they find direct clitoral stimulation to be almost too intense. Others like to be touched, kissed, or stroked there—but only very lightly. Still others prefer lots of pressure, the more, the better. There is absolutely *no* right answer when it comes to the clitoris, and only one wrong answer: ignoring it. This is the organ designed to bring you to orgasm. That is its only function, but I think that's enough, don't you?

As with all your other pleasure areas, the clitoris functions better in a nice, moist environment. While clitoral stimulation may help you produce more of your own lubrication, you can certainly start out with massaging Pure Satisfaction UniSEX Enhancement Gel to get things going, and you may want to keep adding lubrication as you go.

In Chapter 4, on self-pleasuring, I'm going to give you lots of suggestions for making your clitoris very happy indeed, and you may already be thinking of a few. Although, as we've seen, your body has lots of sexual pleasure zones—both in your genital area and elsewhere—for most of us it's the clitoris that makes the difference between having an orgasm and not having one.

True, some women can reach a climax when the clitoris isn't directly stimulated. A very few women were born with a biology that enables them to reach orgasm simply by thinking about it, or by having their

ONLY FOR THE BRAVE . . .

If you—and your partner—would like a better view of your genital area, there is one sexy, glamorous solution that's growing daily in popularity. It's called a Brazilian wax, and it's a five-minute procedure that, although somewhat uncomfortable at the time, leaves your pubic area smooth, hairless, and extra sensitive to sexual pleasure. Women who've tried the Brazilian recommend it for the way it leaves them feeling clean and super-fresh, for the way it turns on their partners, and for the new levels of excitement it makes possible.

Another fun version of pubic waxing is called the Runway. The hair is removed leaving a narrow strip down the center that looks like a runway (hence the name) that your guy can run his tongue along to reach your clitoris.

breasts massaged, or by being penetrated in a way that doesn't involve clitoral contact. Even for those lucky women, however, it's the clitoris that's regulating their orgasm. This powerful little organ is simply channeling the sexual arousal from elsewhere in the body to produce the group of biological responses that together make up a sexual climax. So the clitoris is where your orgasms come from, whether it's being directly stimulated or not. Once again, if you do need direct clitoral stimulation to reach a sexual climax, you can be sure you're not alone. In that respect, three-fourths of the earth's women are built exactly like you.

The G-Spot

Question: What's the difference between a TV remote and your G-spot?
Answer: A man will spend 30 minutes looking for the remote.

One day I was in San Diego driving along, when all of a sudden a young woman in a sporty and sexy convertible came racing by. The car sported a license plate with "G Spot" emblazoned on it. I could not believe my eyes. I thought, wow, she is either extremely proud that she has found hers or is just very in touch with herself. I tried to follow her to find out who this very special woman was, but she sped ahead and I couldn't catch up. Many years ago, that license plate would not have caught my attention, or if it did it wouldn't have meant a thing to me.

Even today, I am surprised at the number of women I meet who still don't know what the G-spot is or if it really exists (it does). If they do know about it, they may be still in search of the elusive and mysterious area. It's the tourist destination everyone wants to visit—but it's hard to find without a map. This is why men often miss it during sex. It's the gynecological UFO of body parts, and you have to take a magical mystery tour to find it.

It may take a while for either you or your partner to find your G-spot, but I encourage you both to keep looking, because once you succeed, the results may be thrilling! The "G-spot" gets its name from

German gynecologist Ernst Gräfenberg, and it's located about one to three inches inside your vagina, on the upper part of the vaginal canal. Because the G-spot is inside your vagina, you won't be able to see it with your mirror, but if you once again lie on your back and open your knees, you can gently reach inside your vaginal canal with one or two fingers and feel for it. It's there just about an inch and a half behind your pubic bone. Notice that your vaginal walls feel like the inside of your cheek. When you reach a fleshy section that feels like the roof of your mouth, with a bit of a rougher texture, you have found your G-spot. When you're sexually excited, your G-spot fills with blood and swells to two or three times its normal size, so you (or your partner) may actually have an easier time finding it when you're aroused.

So what exactly *is* the G-spot? Actually, there's some controversy about that. Many scientists believe it's a group of glands and ducts clustered around the urethra—the part of the body that releases urine.

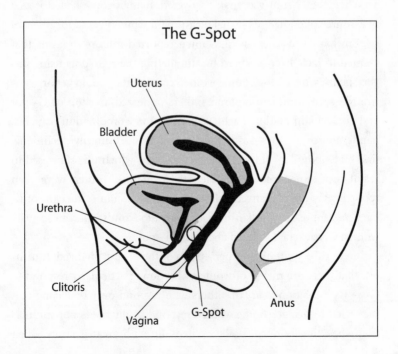

The G-Spot

Uterus

Bladder

Urethra

Clitoris

Vagina

G-Spot

Anus

Writer Nathalie Angier says that the G-spot is actually the place where the nerves of your clitoris intersect with your vaginal tissue on their way to your spinal column. And some experts believe that the G-spot is a kind of female prostate gland. In men, the prostate—located just behind the perineum—produces the clear fluid that carries semen out of the penis when a man ejaculates. In women, stimulating the G-spot can also provoke a kind of orgasmic ejaculation, sometimes causing the woman to release clear fluid through her urethra—possibly a few drops, or in some cases, as much as a quart. Not to worry; it will not stain the sheets.

Whatever its biology turns out to be, you should be aware that your G-spot may not be one single spot—and it may not stay in one place, either. Some experts believe that as your body changes and your hormones fluctuate, the G-spot shifts position slightly or even changes in size.

When the G-spot was first discovered, many people hailed it as a new source of enormous sexual pleasure for women—and for many of us, I'm happy to say, it was! Women reported intense orgasms that seemed to have been inspired by stimulating their G-spots using fingers, penises, or sex toys. Some women claimed they could get orgasms from G-spot stimulation alone. Others preferred a union of G-spot and clitoral stimulation—achieved with some combination of penis, hands, and/or sex toys—as in the famous "Venus Butterfly" technique, first made popular on the TV show *L.A. Law,* which was supposed to result in a super-intense double orgasm. Some women were even reporting G-spot orgasms that lasted up to half an hour. Since the ordinary orgasm usually lasts from four to eight seconds, you can see why women were excited to learn about the G-spot.

But as time went on, our perception of the G-spot changed. It turns out that there are plenty of women who don't particularly respond to G-spot stimulation, and still others who respond only by feeling that they need to urinate. Some women respond coolly to G-spot stimulation when they're not sexually excited and with great pleasure when they are. So you may want to explore this part of your anatomy—alone or with a partner—to figure out what works for you.

As with the clitoris, women who do like G-spot stimulation have a wide variety of preferences. Some want two fingers, a penis, or a sex toy to press deeply into their vaginal tissue at the correct spot. Others like the sensation of a finger or sex toy reaching into their G-spot and then curling back toward the vaginal opening in a kind of "come-hither" motion. Still others like to apply pressure from side to side. Some women find that they enjoy the added pleasure from adult toys that can press and/or vibrate against the G-spot, so perhaps consider an Aurora G-Spot Massager or Da'Bomb, or maybe a Nubby G, which also comes in a waterproof version called Nubby G Aqua. (You'll find more about G-spot vibrators in Chapter 4.)

Of course, G-spots can also be stimulated with a penis during inter-course, depending on the shape of your partner's penis. A penis that curves upward is more likely to reach your G-spot in the missionary position—the one where you're lying on your back and the guy lies on top of you. A penis that's uncurved or curves downward may be more likely to reach your G-spot if you have sex "doggie style" with you on all fours and the man entering you from behind. (For more on sexual positions, see Chapter 7, The Main Event.)

Again, you may want to explore different options, bearing in mind that your preferences may vary depending on your age, time of the month, and state of excitement, as well as on your partner, your use of sex toys, and your technique. In other words, there's no one right way to relate to your G-spot. But you and your partner can sure have a good time learning what ways might be right for *you*.

Having an Orgasm: Your Version

Now that we've figured out where everything is and how it works, let's look at where it's all leading: to the orgasm. In this section, we'll just focus on yours. A little later in this chapter, we'll get to his.

So what's an orgasm? Basically, it's the buildup and release of sexual pressure giving you intense, full-body waves of pleasure and relaxation. An orgasm is both an emotional and physical experience that can feel different depending on the circumstances, your partner, and your mood. You may feel tightness or a pleasurable tension in and around your clitoris and vagina. You may also feel your uterine walls contracting in a regular, rhythmic way. Most women's orgasms last from four to eight seconds.

An orgasm can seem like an event—the climax, or culmination, of a long process of sexual excitement. Let's take a closer look at the stages in this wonderful experience. The following steps happen more or less in the order given, though some may happen simultaneously or out of order.

PHASE ONE: EXCITEMENT/AROUSAL

As you start to become sexually excited . . .
- Your heart beats faster.
- Your breath comes more quickly.
- The muscles all over your body begin to tighten.

PHASE TWO: PLATEAU

As the excitement proceeds . . .
- Your breasts begin to swell and your nipples get harder, seeming to stand erect.
- Your clitoris swells slightly.
- You may begin to secrete vaginal fluids that either remain deep inside your vagina or that slowly make their way to your vaginal opening and then spread over your genital area.
- Your labia flatten out and open up a little, making it easier for a man to insert a penis (or fingers, or adult toys) inside you.
- Gradually, your vagina lengthens and widens, so you may feel it opening up inside you, making room for your partner's penis.
- Your face, neck, and chest may flush red—the so-called "orgasm

flush" caused by the opening up of blood vessels throughout your body.

- Your blood pressure, heart rate, and breathing rate continue to increase just the way they do when you're running hard or engaged in other vigorous aerobic exercise (although I personally think this kind of exercise is in a class by itself!).

PHASE THREE: ORGASM

- As blood vessels continue to open up throughout your body, blood rushes to your vagina, causing that whole area to feel pleasantly warm or even happily hot.
- Your clitoris also engorges, or fills with blood, right up until you climax. Then it begins to pull back and shrink a bit.
- You can feel the muscles inside your vagina and uterus throb and contract. If a man's penis is inside you, he can feel these contractions, which many men find quite exciting.
- The most intense part of the sensation—the throbbing sense of release as you reach your peak and then start to "come down"— lasts several seconds, though some women experience orgasm less as a single climax and more as a series of ups and downs of varying intensity. Again, styles, rhythms, and intensity of orgasms often vary for the same woman, depending on a host of physical and emotional factors.

PHASE FOUR: RESOLUTION

- Gradually, your genitals, breasts, heart rate, skin, and sensations return to normal.
- You may experience a dreamy, satisfied sensation known as "afterglow."

The important thing to remember about orgasms is that they vary enormously—from woman to woman, but also for the same woman.

Physiologically, all orgasms are the same in that they involve contractions of the pelvic floor muscles. I have heard women say, *"I can only have orgasms in one way,"* but it's not true. Sometimes your orgasm may feel like a tiny rippling sensation deep within your body, a little throbbing or trembling within your vagina as the muscles contract and release, contract and release. Sometimes your orgasm will feel like a slow, intense buildup of pressure that culminates in an even more pleasurable sense of release—a release that also feels like a huge relief. You may feel your orgasm in your clitoris, your vagina, and your labia; you may also feel it in your heart, your skin, and your spine, a kind of whole-body rush that feels like everything is opening up. (Biologically, what's going on is that your blood vessels are expanding very quickly and blood is rushing through your body.) Often, an orgasm is a very emotional experience that can make you feel happy, loving, peaceful, fulfilled, or "blissed out." At other times, it's more of a physical experience that doesn't carry such an emotional charge. As you explore your own responses, you'll come to know the different types of orgasms you have and maybe even learn what kinds of foreplay and sexual activity are likely to produce particular types of orgasms. (We'll learn more about this throughout the rest of this book!)

Many people think that if a man has to ask if you had an orgasm, you didn't have one. Actually, this isn't always true. Some men think the woman will thrash around like the actresses in a porn film, whereas many women don't behave at all like that. Some women have "little" orgasms, and the man doesn't know it. Sometimes her orgasms are pretty unmistakable, and everyone in the room knows for sure when they happen. But every now and then, she can have a subtle one. After the two of you have been partners for a while and paying close attention, he will know those orgasms also.

If you're looking for a foolproof way to know whether or not you've had an orgasm, there is one simple clue: You (or your partner) can insert a finger into your vagina. If you feel the vaginal walls contracting and releasing, you've had an orgasm. If you don't, you probably haven't (though you may have had a good time anyway). Those are the basics—but the fun, of course, is in all the variations!

So if you don't have orgasms when you have sex, you are missing out for a number of reasons. First of all, orgasms feel fantastic. They're a wonderful release. And they're good for us—orgasms are actually a health issue. Your mother probably told you to eat your vegetables daily, but I bet she never said, "Be sure to have an orgasm every day." Yet if you double the number of orgasms you have in one year, some people believe you add a year to your life. There's more good news: Our ability to have an orgasm stays with us our entire lives. It's never too late to discover how to have one.

Remember, though, that while orgasms are great, neither men nor women absolutely require them for enjoyable sex. Sometimes one lover is tired or just not interested and is happy to please the other and then stop. Sometimes an orgasm just isn't in the cards, and that can be okay. However, the great news is that the more orgasmic you become, the easier it is to have orgasms and the greater your chance to have multiple orgasms.

Multiple Orgasms: Even More of a Good Thing

Some women can reach orgasm more than once in a session of lovemaking, a response known as multiple orgasms. The fact that the clitoris, the G-spot, labia, vagina, and anal area can all be stimulated means that multiple orgasms during lovemaking or self-pleasuring are a very real possibility for any woman.

Like regular orgasms, multiple orgasms come in many different varieties. Sometimes you feel a series of orgasms that starts and won't stop. Sometimes you experience an orgasm, "rest" for several minutes—perhaps while other sexual activity is going on, perhaps while cuddling—and then feel ready to reach orgasm again, a process that can also repeat more than once. Sometimes the multiple orgasms build in intensity, sometimes they decrease, sometimes they stay the same.

LUBRICATION: WHEN YOU'RE
NOT GETTING WET

I have great respect for the work of pioneering sex researchers William Masters and Virginia Johnson, but they did lead us astray on one point. When they published their important works in the 1960s, they wrote that the vagina produces lubrication fairly quickly as the woman becomes aroused.

Sorry, Masters & Johnson, but for many women today, I'm afraid that just isn't so! Although some women gush with instant lubrication at the sight of their heartthrob, many of the rest of us simply don't, no matter how aroused we feel.

Why not? Here are some possible reasons:

- **Individual difference.** Some women naturally produce more vaginal lubrication than others. Just as height varies from person to person, so does lubrication. Unfortunately, some of us have been made to feel embarrassed about how "dry" we are, but that's just as foolish as guys agonizing over their penis size. We all know that size doesn't matter—and now it's time for us to realize that "wetness" doesn't either. You can buy so many different types of lubrication these days, it honestly doesn't matter how much you're producing on your own.

- **Age.** Levels of lubrication change throughout your life. In part, this is because of estrogen, the female sex hormone, which plays a key role in vaginal lubrication. Estrogen production declines as early as when you're in your thirties, and as it does, your lubrication may decline, too. After menopause, you're more likely to experience vaginal dryness, even if you take supplemental estrogen.

- **Your menstrual cycle.** You've got different levels of estrogen at different times of the month, so how much lubrication you produce—and how thick or runny it is—often varies.

- **Childbirth.** Nothing puts your hormones out of whack like giving birth, and as they fluctuate, so does your ability to produce lubrication.

- **Stress.** Everything from job hassles to relationship tensions can affect your ability to "get wet," which is a shame, because a good sexual experience is a terrific stress-reliever, while going without sex can make you feel tense. So turn that vicious cycle into a positive upward spiral: Get some Revelation or UltraGlide, enjoy a sexual encounter, and turn your mood around.

- **Illness.** Any illness may interfere with your lubrication, including such chronic illnesses as diabetes.
- **Medications.** Women have reported increased dryness from such medications as tricyclic antidepressants (Elavil, Anafranil, Trofranil, and Sinequan, among others), birth-control pills, antihistamines, cold formulas, and any type of medicine that dries out your mouth.
- **Cigarettes and alcohol.** A glass of wine may help you get into a sexy mood, but alcohol can also have a drying effect, as can cigarettes.
- **Travel.** When you cross time zones, you risk jet lag, and that may in turn temporarily decrease lubrication.
- **Extended loveplay.** Even women who produce a good deal of natural lubrication sometimes need to add some more during extended sex.

I'm a firm believer in the delights of a good lubricant—the slippery sensations can make you more sensitive as well as help both you and your partner move through your sexual experience more easily. So consider buying a Sensational Lube Sampler and discovering which lubricant you like most. For more on how to use lubricants to enhance your sexual experience, see Chapter 4 on Self-Pleasuring and Chapter 6 on Foreplay.

As you can see, there's no one "right" way to have either an orgasm or multiple orgasms. Not all women have multiple orgasms; and some women who do have them don't particularly enjoy them. They find the repeated sexual responses too intense. But if you're interested in seeing whether you can climax repeatedly, receiving clitoral stimulation even after you climax is definitely the best way. You can practice by yourself using your fingers or a vibrator to see what your body likes, or you can explore the possibilities with your partner. Just keep in mind that your clitoris is very sensitive right after orgasm, so be gentle with yourself—or have your partner be gentle with you—as you go for that second wave of pleasure.

You'll read more about orgasms and how to produce them in the next several chapters. But I'd also like to mention that doing regular Kegel workouts, as noted on page 76, may also help you achieve multiple orgasms, so if that interests you, look for the Kegel section at the end of this chapter. And once again, our top-selling product, Pure Satisfaction UniSEX Enhancement Gel, is too good to pass up for initial as well as multiple orgasms as it promotes and enhances sensitivity and arousal.

The Anatomy of Pleasure: His Version

Now that you've got a basic working idea of how *your* body is designed for sexual pleasure, let's look at your partner. Once you know how he is made, you'll find the whole process of lovemaking makes a lot more sense.

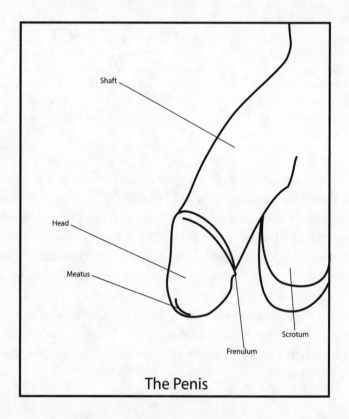

Shaft

Head

Meatus

Frenulum

Scrotum

The Penis

SHAFT

This is the main part of the penis. It's limp and flaccid before arousal, but becomes stiff and hard when the man is sexually excited. That's because blood flows into the shaft as the man becomes aroused. As the penis fills with blood, it extends and lifts away from the body.

You might be wondering if blood also flows out of the penis while a man is hard. Well, yes, it does, but the vessels the blood uses to travel out of the penis are smaller than the ones on which it travels in. Also, when the penis is erect, the engorged tissues (that is, the tissues full of blood) push the outgoing vessels up against the sheath that encircles the penis, compressing them and slowing the flow.

Touching a man's shaft can certainly give him pleasure, but it's not nearly as sensitive an area as your own genitals, so you can be a bit bolder with this part of his body than you want him to be with you. Think of grasping the shaft firmly without squeezing, the way you'd grasp the handle of a pot. Your guy will appreciate your confident touch.

URETHRA

The man's urethra is located inside his penis, and, just like your urethra, his is also connected to his bladder in order to carry urine out of his body. But his urethra has one more function that yours does not. It's also where his semen travels just before he ejaculates. A handy little valve inside his penis makes sure that when he's sexually excited, the canal that carries his urine is shut off, so that he can only release semen, never urine.

HEAD OR GLANS

This is a very sensitive part of the penis, and one that you'll want to get to know very well indeed! It resembles a hood that wraps around the top of the penis, joining on the penis's underside.

FORESKIN

Originally, every glans is covered by a foreskin, and if a man hasn't been circumcised, he'll still have one. The foreskin retracts naturally during erection, so if you're having sex with an uncircumcised guy, you may notice that a man's penis looks different at different points in the process. You should also know that the foreskin is a marvelously sensitive area—similar to the hood of your own clitoris—so handle it gently, but *do* feel free to kiss and touch. (We'll go into more detail in Chapters 6 and 8.)

MEATUS

Another wonderful sensitive spot on the penis is this opening at the top of the head. It looks like a slit, and its main function is to allow urine and semen to exit. Although you shouldn't insert anything into this opening, you can absolutely pleasure it with your tongue or stroke it very, very gently with your most delicate touch. (And don't worry about hygiene. If your guy is clean enough to have sex with, this part of his body is clean enough for you to kiss and touch.)

TESTICLES OR TESTES

The testicles, or testes, are two separate glands that are located below the penis in a loose sack of skin called the scrotum. (More about that in a moment.) The testicles resemble golf balls, but they're smaller, far softer, and very sensitive. They produce two crucial substances: sperm and testosterone. By the way, it's common for one testicle to hang lower than the other, so don't worry if you notice this.

SCROTUM

This is a sack of thin, loose skin that holds two glands known as the testes. Often it's sparsely covered with coarse hairs. Its main purpose is to regulate the temperature of the testicles so that they'll produce the right amount of sperm. When a guy's body is warmer, his scrotum relaxes so that testes can move away from his body, allowing them to get a little cooler. And when the temperature gets colder, the scrotum tightens to bring the man's testicles closer to the warmth of his body. By the way, stress can also cause a scrotum to retract, and it also retracts just before orgasm.

Most men enjoy having their testicles and scrotum fondled very gently, though here is one place where you don't want to apply too much pressure. Start out with a *very* loose grip and keep checking in with your guy to find out just how much pressure feels good. Even the slightest bit of "too much" can be *very* painful, and can also make a guy feel super-vulnerable. So please don't avoid this sensitive area. Why deprive your guy of another source of pleasure? Instead, get him to show you what he likes. A light fondle, squeeze, or playful kisses and licks are almost always welcome.

PROSTATE

The prostate is a gland that sits at the base of the bladder right next to the rectum. This is where sperm is stored before ejaculation and where semen and seminal fluid come together. The prostate also secretes a substance known as "pre-ejaculate," the clear fluid produced prior to ejaculation.

You can think of your guy's prostate as his version of your G-spot, which will help you remember that he often likes this area stimulated, too. Men who do enjoy this type of stimulation claim to have stronger, more intense orgasms.

PERINEUM

Here, the two of you are pretty much alike. He, too, has that same sensitive "t'aint" located between his genitals and his anus. You can stimulate your guy by applying pressure to the perineum with your hands or with a vibrator such as the Mini Bullet.

PLEASURING THE PROSTATE

Playful Plug

This flexible vinyl plug is designed to be inserted into the anus, so it's equipped with a secure finger ring for safe play. The shaft is widened for heightened sensations and its $3/4$" diameter is perfect for the first-time anal explorer. The Mini Bullet that you can also buy from Passion Parties can fit snugly into the finger ring of this toy for added stimulation. If the plug reaches over to the prostate, your guy gets a special treat known as a prostate orgasm.

Love Wand

This "tush toy" is a string of beads held together with plastic. When covered with a slippery lube such as Revelation and inserted into the anus, the Love Wand can stimulate your guy's prostate as well as his anal region.

ANUS

Once again, the two of you have the same equipment here. Remember that for both of you, this is a body part just full of sensitive nerve endings, so many people consider this an erogenous zone. For your guy, the anus can be an even more exciting area because it's the gateway to the prostate. Stimulating the prostate through the anus is a special pleasure for many men.

Having an Orgasm: His Version

PHASE ONE: EXCITEMENT/AROUSAL

As he starts to become sexually excited . . .
- His heart beats faster.
- His breath comes more quickly.
- The muscles all over his body begin to tighten.
- His lips, earlobes, nipples, and penis all become more sensitive.

PHASE TWO: PLATEAU

As the excitement proceeds . . .

- His nipples get harder, seeming to stand erect.
- His penis becomes firmer, and the color may deepen due to the rush of blood to his shaft.
- The skin of his scrotum starts to thicken and pull closer to his body.
- His testicles enlarge.
- Pre-ejaculate fluid may ooze from his penis.
- Ejaculate—semen mixed with other fluids—builds up in his prostate, so that he has the sense of building tension.
- His urinary tract shuts down, so there's no chance of him urinating during orgasm.
- His breathing, heart rate, and blood pressure continue to increase, and his muscles tighten.

PHASE THREE: ORGASM

- Three types of muscles contract for him: the ones in his anus; those in his sphincter, which control his urination; and his PC muscles, which propel the semen through the urethra.
- This intense contraction produces an equally intense release in a series of short spasms—up to ten contractions over a period of four to eight seconds in a spontaneous reflex that he can feel all the way down to the base of his spine.

PHASE FOUR: RESOLUTION

- Gradually, his bodily functions return to normal.
- His scrotum will return to its normal, loose state away from the body.
- His glans may be particularly sensitive.
- His penis will soften in two stages: The immediate hardness will

WHAT'S THE STORY WITH ERECTION DRUGS?

If you and your partner have been considering erection drugs such as Viagra, Cialis, Levitra, or the like, you'll need to know the ABC's of these sexual medications. They work by stopping an enzyme that inhibits erection. When a man is aroused, he produces a chemical called "cyclic GMP," which expands the penis's arteries and narrows its veins, creating a kind of "traffic jam," so that blood is entering the penis faster than it can leave. That's what causes the penis to get hard.

However, men with a physical difficulty in becoming erect—caused by such factors as diabetes, multiple sclerosis, vascular disease, or injuries—may suffer from a shortage of cyclic GMP. As a result, blood flows out of the penis about as fast as it flows into it, and the guy has trouble becoming hard. By stopping the enzyme that attacks cyclic GMP, erectile dysfunction medications allow more cyclic GMP to accumulate in the man's penis, so that an erection can be achieved.

Interestingly, some men with psychological problems, such as anxiety during sex, have experienced some positive effects from these drugs also. Some of these benefits are due to the placebo effect, by which the act of taking *any* pill causes a positive effect.

In fact, we don't yet know whether psychological problems can cause a shortage of cyclic GMP. So we're not sure just how helpful medications will be to men whose lack of erections is due to stress and anxiety. And, just so you know, a man who already gets relatively firm erections will not get an "erection of steel" if he takes one of the erection drugs. That's because there are a limited number of receptor sites for cyclic GMP to fill. Once they're filled up, that's it. So this is not a situation of "if some is good, then more is better."

The main thing to remember about Viagra, Cialis, Levitra, and the rest is that they are *not* aphrodisiacs. That is, they will not help a man achieve arousal if he's not already doing so on his own. All they do is help a man who's already capable of being aroused to have a somewhat firmer erection because of the additional blood flowing into the penis. In any case, erection drugs only work on about three-quarters of the men who take them. In some cases, there are important medical reasons *not* to take them. So if you or your partner are thinking about an erection drug, approach this possibility with caution and *only* under a physician's care.

soften immediately; then, as the blood begins to flow out of the penis, he will after several minutes return to a completely flaccid state.

- He may experience a dreamy, satisfied sensation known as "afterglow." Many men also experience a pleasant sense of tiredness, and some fall asleep, briefly or for several hours.

After sex is over, you may be wondering when your partner will be able to have sex again. Every man is different—and men also respond differently at different times. So your guy may need to wait as little as twenty minutes or as long as twenty-four hours.

Kegel Exercises: Sexercise Your Passion Diva!

Before the science lesson is over, I'd like to introduce you to a marvelous set of exercises that can keep your vaginal muscles toned and firm. Kegel exercises improve your capacity for sexual pleasure, including your ability to achieve multiple orgasms. If you do your Kegel exercises regularly, they can help you achieve orgasm more quickly and intensely, and they can make the whole experience more thrilling for your partner, as your vaginal muscles contract more tightly around his penis.

Kegel exercises also make it easier for you to give birth vaginally and to recover afterward. And they strengthen the muscles involved in bladder control. All it takes is two minutes a day, three times a day—and within only two weeks, you'll start noticing the results.

The first step toward doing your Kegel exercises is to identify your vaginal PC muscle. (PC is short for pubococcygeus, and don't ask me to pronounce that, either!) The PC muscle is a hammock-like muscle that stretches from your pubic bone to your tailbone, forming the pelvic floor. If you're not sure which muscles these are, try starting and stopping your stream of urine a few times as you're going to the bathroom. The muscles you use are your PC muscles, and those are the ones you

YOUR BASIC KEGEL WORKOUT

One set of three exercises should take you about two minutes. Try to do one set three times a day. You can do these in any position you like. Consider making them a part of your late-night routine as you watch your favorite TV program or the nightly news.

Contract and Hold

Squeeze your PC muscles and hold them for a count of ten. Then contract and hold for another count of ten. Continue doing this.

Flutter

Contract your PC muscles as quickly as you can. These won't be large squeezes but rapid light ones. Stop, take a rest, and then do it again.

The Elevator

Imagine there's a little elevator in your pelvic region that you want to raise up floor by floor to the top floor. Start at the ground floor and go up to the first floor, then up to the second floor, then to the third. Then gradually allow the "elevator" to go back down, stopping at each floor. Once you get to the ground floor, completely relax the muscles you've just exercised.

should try to isolate as you do your Kegels. At first you may find yourself contracting your chest, abdominal, back, and anal muscles, too, but with practice you'll be able to focus solely on the PCs.

If you like the idea of using Kegel balls to the max, start holding them in your vagina during everyday activities for up to thirty minutes. When you can manage one ball for this length of time, add a second. Be discreet until you're sure you can keep them in. Obviously, you don't want them rolling down the aisle of your local grocery store!

Some women like to start with larger balls, which are easier to contain. Joined balls also make the process easier for some women. If you've gotten good at holding on to connected balls, you can put one inside you while letting the second one remain outside your vagina.

Then, when you stand up, the outside ball pulls at the inner one, challenging your PC muscles even more. Eventually, you'll be able to spend an entire day holding on to your Kegel balls—and think how strong your PC muscles will be then! When you can urinate while still keeping Kegel balls inside you, you'll have reached your goal.

And don't worry about Kegel balls getting lost inside your vagina. There's no way they'll fit through your tiny cervical opening and work their way into your uterus. If you do have trouble getting the balls out of your vagina, you've only got to relax your muscles as far as possible while squatting or standing up, reach in with one finger, and scoop the balls out. Gravity will help you. You can also put the Kegel balls inside a condom and then simply pull the condom out with the balls inside.

So now that you're familiar with exactly how you and your partner's bodies work, let's move on to the next steps—using all of your bodies' lovely capabilities to reach new heights of sexual pleasure! Let's move on to Chapter 4 and some wonderful techniques for self-pleasuring.

⟶ *In Your Passion Pantry* ⟵

- **A mirror.** When it comes time to take a look at your intimate areas, choose a mirror with a long handle and maybe a magnifying feature.
- **Revelation Lubricant.** Use a dab or two of this silky-smooth lubricant when you're exploring your body—or your partner's body!
- **Condoms.** Because you know that every Passion Diva takes responsibility for her pleasure—in more ways than one! Try the new thinner, ultra-sensitive Elexa line that was designed just for women. Or choose some stimulating condoms with textured surfaces such as ribbing or studs (small bumps).
- **Condom case.** With their gold cases and designer tops, these lovely accessories let you be prepared and glamorous at the same time.

- **G-spot Stimulating Crème.** Looking for some G-spot pleasure? This cream will produce a stimulating, tingling effect to inspire excitement to your G-spot, making all types of G-spot stimulation easier and more intense.
- **Nubby G.** With its short, thick, curved shaft, and a nubby "hilt" about ⅔ of the way down the shaft, you can stimulate your G-spot, labia, and clitoris all at the same time.
- **Mini Bullet.** This small, easily handled vibrator offers you the clitoral stimulation that more than 75 percent of all women need in order to experience orgasm.
- **Pleasure Pods.** These weighted silicone pods are terrific for your Kegel exercises. Just insert them into your vagina and feel the thrill of vaginal stimulation while exercising your PC muscles. Recommended by gynecologists and obstetricians to increase vaginal elasticity and bladder control.
- **Pleasure Pearls.** These shiny, pearlescent-coated balls fit snugly into your vagina and can be worn comfortably and discreetly throughout the day, providing subtle yet wonderful vibrations as they make contact with each other. They also assist in strengthening your pelvic floor muscles for greater sexual satisfaction.

4

The Art of Self-Pleasuring

I'll never forget a movie I saw a few years ago, *Pleasantville,* a fantasy story in which two modern-day teenagers find themselves transported into a cheery TV sitcom of the kind that was popular in the 1950s and early 1960s. As did so many TV shows from that era, the fictional show in the movie presented an idealized view of life, and of course, everyone was literally black-and-white, the way they looked on early television. Most strikingly, passion of any kind was completely absent.

Then, the modern-day teenagers introduce passion into this bland world, and suddenly objects begin bursting into glorious, glowing color. As the people of Pleasantville start to feel passion, they, too, transform from black-and-white into color, reflecting the way that their lives have now become richer and more interesting.

The mother of the TV family—wonderfully played by Joan Allen—tries hard to fit the mold of the "good girl" that we all know so well: someone who keeps the house clean and serves her family nourishing meals, but who wouldn't think of giving her TV husband more than a peck on the cheek. Finally, as she watches so many of the other people in her world gaining color, she realizes that she, too, needs to discover the passion that she has never known. She marches up the stairs, draws herself a warm bath, and gets in the tub. While the movie stays away from explicit detail, you understand that she is pleasuring herself. And as she does, a marvelous thing happens. Not only does she turn from black-and-white into color, but the tree outside her bathroom window bursts into gorgeous red and gold flames. Think of it! A woman's passion and pleasure is so powerful—and so beautiful—that it can actually set her world on fire! The character goes on to discover passion in a sexual relationship in a way she'd never known, and we see that this private awakening is the beginning of a whole new life.

Part-time Passion Consultant and full-time counselor Sarah, from Arizona, shared with me a real-life story about her own awakening into a bright, new world.

For many years, I simply "checked out" of my body. Sex, for me, was okay. But I was always more concerned with whether my partner was happy with me than if I experienced any pleasure myself. By the time I was thirty, I had had my share of lovers, but I was never really satisfied. One day—and this was long before I ever became a Passion Consultant—my then-boyfriend gave me a gift, a Passion Parties Pink Passion vibrator. Who knows where he got it! But there it was—my very first sex toy. At first, I thought of it as a joke, but when I finally began experimenting with it, something unexpected began to happen. I actually started to feel things! You know the words of that old song, "How long has *this* been going on?" And where was I while it was happening??? I'm not sure I could ever have had these feelings for the first time while someone else was present, but I sure started having them by myself.

In a way, I had to make a decision. I had to give myself permission to welcome all these strange new feelings I was having, rather than avoid them. I had to give myself permission to lose control a little. Like I said, maybe I couldn't have done that for the first time—even for the first few times—with a boyfriend in the room, no matter how nice or thoughtful he was. Maybe I had to be by myself for a while to really feel safe.

Well, like I said, things started to happen, and I began to realize that there was so much more to a sexual experience than what *he* gets out of it. I started to see my body as something marvelous and unique. I started to communicate with my body again and began to ask myself questions. Did I like this touch? Did I like the feel of vibration in this area? What about over here? And there? And here again? Suddenly my clitoris had a voice, and she began to sing and shout so loudly that other areas of my body started to come alive as well. Suddenly, it was very important for me to know exactly what I liked in all aspects of my life.

Do you know, because of that one little change, I began to see my whole world differently! I began to feel that I was worthy of more than I had been allowing myself. I began to ask myself what I wanted in my life and I became unwilling to accept anything less. I began to build a relationship with the most wonderful, beautiful, funny, and sexy person that I know—*me!* And it has been the best relationship of my life. (P.S. My relationships with men got better, too!)

So now, every time I pause in front of the mirror, I give myself a special, secret smile, because I know within me lies a treasure box full of the most beautiful and special gifts I have ever known, and, amazingly, all I needed was the courage to use the key—in this case, a Pink Passion vibrator.

So, ladies, take it from me—and Sarah—and every Passion Diva who's ever allowed herself to get to know her own body. This is one area of your sexual life that you do not want to neglect. Although Good Girls like the Joan Allen character in *Pleasantville* may have been told that self-pleasuring is "dirty" or "immoral" or something that only men do, Passion Divas know that there are many reasons to include self-pleasuring in your sexual vocabulary. After all, men have been enjoying this sexy secret for years. It's our turn to get in on the fun! Here are my favorite "Sexy 7" reasons why a little private time is good for your Passion Diva:

1. It's a way to find out more about what you like.
2. It's a way to find out more about who you are.
3. The more comfortable you are pleasuring yourself, the more comfortable you may be experiencing pleasure with a partner.

4. Learning about the things that turn you on solo can give you valuable sexual information to share with your partner. After all, if *you* don't know what excites you, how is *he* supposed to know?

5. Self-pleasuring is a great way to get through those "dry spells" when you're between partners or when your partner is out of town, not feeling well, or otherwise unavailable.

6. Knowing you can pleasure yourself may make you feel more independent, self-sufficient, and empowered—all of which can help you attract a new partner or build a better relationship with your current partner.

7. Self-pleasuring can help you learn about sex toys and increase your comfort level with them—a knowledge and comfort that can spice up your sexual relationships, whether with a new relationship or a long-term soul mate.

As if that weren't enough, more women achieve orgasm through self-pleasuring than any other sexual activity. Since that's the case, it's good to know that some 97 percent of females have self-pleasured by the age of twenty-one.

So whether your previous experiences with self-pleasuring have been satisfying, unsatisfying, or nonexistent, keep reading. I'll share with you the secrets to making the most of this oh-so-delicious relationship with yourself—from "Self-Pleasure 101" to the Highly Advanced Course—and then, in Chapter 6, I'll also show you how to translate these solo melodies into the harmonies of a blissful duet! And if you've never had an orgasm, self-pleasuring is the key to learning what gets your body humming. You *can* have orgasms, and in this chapter I'll show you how. All it takes is a little time, privacy, and courage—and maybe a lubricant or a vibrator.

Lubrication: Wetter Is Better

If I had to pick only one product from the hundreds that we sell—just one product that would enhance virtually every woman's ability to

THE PASSION DIVA'S PRINCIPLES FOR SELF-PLEASURE

- **Be persistent.** As we say here at Passion Parties, "Practice makes pleasure." Some women figure out how to pleasure themselves in only a few minutes. For others, it takes up to an hour or may even require a few sessions. You were born with the capacity for feeling good—after all, the clitoris is the only organ designed exclusively for pleasure—so don't be afraid to give yourself the time you need to learn how your body likes to feel good.

- **Be prepared.** Arrange for a private, comfortable space where you feel safe and at ease. Some women—like the Joan Allen character—like to pleasure themselves in the shower or bathtub, where it's natural to be naked. Others prefer being naked in bed, or wearing their favorite sexy nightgown, or maybe some lingerie. Have some lubricant ready. Later on in this chapter, I'll help you figure out what kind you might like. If you want to try out a vibrator, have that ready, too (if you're going to use it in the tub, be sure it's waterproof). Read on for some suggestions about different types you might try.

- **Be creative.** There are so many ways your body can give you pleasure and so many wonderful kinds of pleasure it can give! If you come up with one or two basic self-pleasuring techniques that work for you, that's terrific, but you don't have to stop there. Try a different type of lubricant, another sort of vibrator, or a new "hands-on" technique. See whether there's a fantasy that turns you on, or maybe a special sensory treat—an evocative smell, a piece of music that makes you feel sexy, a way of combining sex and chocolate. Let your imagination run free, and if you like, fantasize about the ways your partner might pleasure you, too. You don't have to act on any of your fantasies—ever—but you never know; maybe you'll imagine one or two things that you'd actually like to try!

- **Be open to receiving help if you need it.** If you're simply not able to reach orgasm by yourself, or if you're feeling unsatisfied by your attempts to self-pleasure, don't despair—get help. A good sex therapist can identify any medical problems that might be getting in your way. Therapy can also help you understand your own anatomy and work through any barriers that might be interfering with your ability to enjoy your body and your sexuality.

achieve orgasm and enjoy lovemaking—I think that product would have to be some form of lubricant, or "lube," as some call it for short. That's because, as we saw in the last chapter, many of us don't always produce enough natural lubricant to make the path to arousal smooth sailing. And even those of us who are naturally wet may be surprised at how much better sex becomes—both solo and with a partner—just by adding a little more lube. For this reason, lubricants are ingredient number one when it comes to discovering your recipe for self-pleasure.

Still skeptical? Remember how in Chapter 3 you experienced the difference a little lubricant could make when you touched yourself? Try this ten-second lube test once again, and then tell me what you think:

- Close your mouth and dry your lips.
- Run the tip of one finger over your lips, very gently.
- Lick your lips, moistening them as much as you can.
- Touch your lips again.

Which caress felt more sensual? I'm willing to bet you said, "The one with the moistened lips." That's what lubricants are all about. A good lubricant can ease potential discomfort during intercourse, allow for extended lovemaking without soreness or abrasion, and even increase sensitivity during condom use. We'll get to all those aspects of lubricants in Chapters 6 (Foreplay) and 7 (The Main Event). First, though, let's take a look at how a lubricant can help you learn to reach orgasm like never before.

Now, for those of you who still feel a bit uncomfortable about the idea of using lubricant, I want to stress once again that there's nothing unnatural about this type of sex enhancer—no more than soft lighting, sexy music, lingerie, or a glass of wine. Anything that makes you feel sexy is good for your sex life. In fact, self-pleasuring is a perfect time to experiment with lube, if you don't want to incorporate it with your partner right away. As you learn solo about the ways lube enhances your sensitivity and eases your path to orgasm, you're preparing to take this knowledge to your partner, as well. As I see it, every square inch of the body is an erotic playground, and lubricants can help both of you feel fantastic all over.

Here are some tips for using lube in your self-pleasure sessions. Once you've gone "wetter," you'll *know* that it's better!

LUBRICANT: THE GREAT ESSENTIAL

Don't forget: Lubricant makes everything feel better against you or inside you. So any dildo or vibrator that you use should be coated with lubricant just before you begin to use it. You will want to moisten your hands with lubricant before self-pleasuring, too.

THE *Passion Diva's Guide* TO LUBRICANTS

- **Use your hands.** Some lubricants come in a tube, and some come in control-top bottles. Either way, you want to dispense the lubricant into the palm of your hand and then rub it gently between your fingers to warm it up. It can get pretty messy if you try to apply the lube directly from the container. Applying lubricant to your hand warms the liquid or gel, allowing it to go on more comfortably.

- **Don't forget the clitoris.** Your own natural lubrication starts deep in your vagina, and that moisture may or may not make it out to the clitoris by the time you're ready for it. If you're focusing on self-pleasure, the clitoris is probably where you want to start or at least where you want to get to pretty soon. Be sure this delicate, passionate part of your body is well-lubricated, so that when you're ready to touch, stroke, and fondle your clitoris, it is ready for you.

- **Be thorough.** If you're planning to use toys during any portion of your self-pleasuring, you'll want to lubricate both the toy and any body part it touches as you go. That way, you'll avoid any discomfort and feel only sexy stimulation.

- **Be safe.** Avoid all lubricants that contain the ingredient nonoxynol-9. Although for years, experts believed that this spermicide ingredient helped prevent the transmission of HIV, recent studies by the Centers for Disease Control tell us that nonoxynol-9 has no HIV-protection properties whatsoever. Moreover, it can be irritating to the vaginal tissue and can create open pathways in a woman's body that can actually contribute to the transfer of HIV. As a result, you're unlikely to find any lubricant with this ingredient still on the market in the USA or Canada, but take extra care when you're traveling or if you're using a product that was purchased some time ago.

- **Be aware.** There are four types of lubrication: water-based, oil-based, petroleum-based, and silicone-based. Each has its pros and cons, though at Passion Parties, we think that water-based products are superior for most sexual activity. In the past, some people have raised various concerns about side effects of silicone lubricants. Recent studies have shown silicone to be safe, but it can still cause possible irritation or allergic reactions in some women. Revelation, an exclusive Passion Parties lubricant, has the feel of silicone without the possible irritation or allergic reactions. To choose wisely, though, you need to know all the facts, so here's the lowdown on all four types of lube:

Water-Based Lubricants

Water-based lubes are the most common. Typically, they contain water; glycerine, an emulsifier; propylene alcohol, which helps the products retain moisture; and a preservative, typically methyl paraben, propyl paraben, or grapefruit seed extract. They're safe for use on your genitals and his, as well as in the anus. You can also use them with latex condoms and diaphragms; and during oral sex, you can safely ingest small amounts of them. Even when they claim to be taste-free, though, you may notice the slightly sweet taste of glycerine and/or somewhat bitter taste of grapefruit seed extract. Many water-based lubricants—including our own Revelation, UltraGlide, and Lickety

Lube—also use FDA-approved flavorings to encourage playful use during oral sex.

Water-based lubes won't stain your bed linens or your clothing, but some people do notice irritations or allergic reactions to some of the ingredients. If you think you're sensitive to a particular lubricant, stop using it. Keep trying other formulations. And don't use lubes as massage lotion or on large expanses of skin—they just won't work as well as products specifically designed for that purpose.

During extended lovemaking, your body heat may cause the purified water in water-based lubricants to dry out, though of course you can always apply more or revive them with a little water or saliva. After self-pleasuring or partner sex, just rinse these lubes off with a warm, moist washcloth.

Oil-Based Lubricants

Oil-based lubricants include vegetable oil (such as olive oil and corn oil), butter, and nut oils (avocado, peanut, and the like). These products double as genital lubricants and as massage lotions, and you can swallow them during oral sex. They are safe to use with condoms, diaphragms, and cervical caps, although the greasiness can cause condoms to slip off. Moreover, in some cases, they can provoke or encourage vaginal infections. Another "con": Oil-based lubricants might stain bed linens and clothing. As you might expect, it takes a good helping of soap and hot water to wash these oily products off your skin. For all these reasons, we don't sell any oil-based lubricants, but if you think you might enjoy them—especially for self-pleasuring, where condoms are not involved—go ahead.

Petroleum-Based Lubricants

This type of lubricant is made from petroleum jelly, mineral oil, or petrolatum—for example, Vaseline and baby oil. Because this type of lube destroys latex, it should never be used with condoms, diaphragms, or cervical caps. Even more important, petroleum-based lubes should never be used inside the vagina: The oil is hard to wash out, can irritate your vaginal lining, and can change your vaginal chemistry, increasing your risk of infection. They can also potentially irritate the outside of the vagina. You should never ingest a petroleum-based product, and you want to watch out for how it might stain linens and bedclothes. For all these reasons, you'll probably want to avoid petroleum-based products for self-pleasuring, though lots of couples like them for anal play.

Silicone-Based Lubricants

You can buy silicone lubricants that are specifically made for sexual purposes, but sometimes people also use silicone products that have been made for other purposes, such as industrial silicone products, including WD-40. I don't recommend using *any* lubricants if they haven't been explicitly made for sexual purposes. Fortunately, you can buy silicone lubricants that are made for sex, including our own Slip 'n Slide. Because there's no water in silicone lubricant, it never dries out. Since silicone lubes remain slick and slippery for a very long time, they're especially useful for anal sex play and for sexual activity in showers, bathtubs, and hot tubs. Silicone lubricants are condom-safe, but because they're *not* water-soluble, you'll have to use soap to wash them out of your linens and clothing, and they take a bit more work— and again, some soap—to get them off your skin. You can use silicone lubricant with plastic and jelly vinyl sex toys, but it will damage silicone toys and products made of cyber-skin or Futureflesh. Although silicone lubricants are more expensive than water-based ones, they also last longer, so it probably evens out in the end. If you're looking for the silky feeling of a silicone-based lubricant without the side effects, check out our exclusive Revelation Lubricant.

Lubricants: The Advanced Course

Now, ladies, I don't want any of you out there to be a one-lube woman. You need lots of different lubes for different occasions, so let me talk you through your options. All of these are water-based, condom-friendly, and available through Passion Parties.

- **Natural.** There are some lubricants on the market that mimic the consistency and feel of a woman's natural lubrication. They are perfect for self-pleasuring and intercourse. Since these are the closest to your natural lubrication, they're going to feel the most natural and should be a staple in everyone's lube collection. Some terrific "starter" lubes are Revelation and UltraGlide.

- **Gels.** Gel lubricants, like UltraGlide Gel, are very popular with women who like a thicker viscosity. The thicker consistency means they contain less water and therefore are long-lasting, making them a great choice for vaginal or anal play as well as for marathon lovemaking sessions. Gels are easier to handle than liquids, and they can be water-based or silicone.

- **Pump-dispensed lubricants.** It's great using lubricant that comes in a pump dispenser because of the convenience. You get the perfect amount each time, there's no unscrewing or pouring, and if the container gets knocked over, nothing spills, so no mess. Our best-selling pump-dispensed lube is Revelation, but I also recommend Embrace Sensual Lubricant, which comes in three popular flavors: strawberry, vanilla, and pear. (I especially recommend flavored lubricants for foreplay and oral sex; see Chapters 6 and 8 for more suggestions.)

- **Warming lubricants.** The perfect way to heat up your intimate moments may be a warming lubricant—I especially recommend RomantaTherapy Sensual Warming Lubricant. Many men will vouch that warmth greatly increases their pleasure because it makes them more sensitive, and you may notice the same effect. Warming lubricants create warmth upon contact and even more warmth in

EXCITING NEWS

In 1998, a group of scientists was awarded the Nobel Prize in medicine for their work on the nitric oxide pathways, the basis for penile and clitoral stimulation, erection, and sensitivity. Their breakthrough discovery has led to the introduction of some very exciting new formulas, including those made with L-arginine, an amino acid that promotes clitoral and penile sensitivity and arousal. L-arginine is a key ingredient in Pure Satisfaction UniSEX Enhancement Gel, which rapidly became our number-one product and remains so year after year. Tens of thousands of women say that Pure Satisfaction Gel allows them to enjoy faster, stronger, and more pleasurable orgasms. And, from what we hear at parties, their partners like it, too! When Dr. Jennifer Berman, formerly of the Female Sexual Medicine Center at UCLA, was asked about Pure Satisfaction UniSEX Enhancement Gel and why it was so successful, her answer was simple: "Because it works."

response to friction, which encourages play and exploration, alone or with a partner.

• **Topical stimulants.** Using a stimulating lube can add some extra sensation to your self-pleasure. Spend a few minutes massaging some topical stimulant on the top, around the sides, and underneath the hood of your clitoris to promote blood flow to your genital region, making your climaxes both easier to achieve and more intense. I recommend our number-one seller, Pure Satisfaction UniSEX Enhancement Gel, with its companion Personal Finger Smitten—a little massage mitt with subtle jelly nubs that fits over your index finger. Pure Satisfaction contains aloe vera for smoothness; peppermint for a warming sensation; and L-arginine, an amino acid, to promote circulation.

Self-Pleasuring with Dildos

The word itself comes from the Italian *diletto,* which translates to "delight" in English. A dildo is a shaft shaped like a penis, made of soft

TWO STIMULANTS THAT
ARE NOT LUBRICANTS

If you're looking for a milder sensation, consider Fresh & Frisky, a stimulant that excites genital skin and provides additional sensitivity. One spritz from the handy 360-degree sprayer on your labia and around your vaginal opening, and you'll feel fresh and confident without any harsh chemicals or artificial scents.

For an even less-intense sensation that nonetheless leaves you feeling stimulated, try Ready To Go, a cooling, sensitizing cream containing menthol that you apply directly to the clitoris. The cooling sensation encourages arousal. While not all women respond to Ready To Go, about 80 percent do.

And for your G-spot, try our specially formulated, exclusive G-Spot Crème, which temporarily increases the size and sensitivity of your G-spot once you massage a small amount into that very special area.

or hard plastic, jelly, or lifelike "future flesh." While vibrators are motorized, dildos are not, which means they can be used quietly anywhere, without batteries, for self-pleasuring or couples play. You can stroke and rub a dildo over any part of your body, but they're especially exciting against your labia and clitoris or within the first inch or so of your vaginal canal.

One of our favorite dildos at Passion Parties is Glow Boy: It has a concave bottom that can create suction so it can be planted firmly to a chair, floor, bathtub, or wall, enabling you to have some leverage in your self-pleasuring activities. The Glow Boy also glows in the dark for added fun.

Another favorite is glass dildos, which are especially good for women who have allergies to jelly vinyl. They can be warmed in warm water or cooled in the refrigerator for temperature variety. They're nonporous, which makes them easy to clean. They can even be put in the dishwasher. Our number-one seller is the Mystical Moments Glass Wand.

Dildos also come in strap-on versions. The inside of the dildo itself is hollow, allowing a man's penis to fit inside. Strap-ons can be a great way for men who have difficulty achieving or maintaining erections to have intercourse with their partners.

Your Ticket to Orgasm: The Vibrator

In your exploration of self-pleasure, you're selling yourself short if you don't consider using a vibrator, at least occasionally. These buzzy little objects, which are designed to vibrate gently against your clitoris or within your vagina, can help you achieve orgasm in a variety of ways—some of them even reach your G-spot! And if you've never had an orgasm before, I have terrific news for you: The vibrator is your ticket to this experience of ecstasy. It's just a matter of learning how to use it. In the past few years, lots of new types of vibrators have come onto the market, too, so if you haven't thought about using a vibrator in a while, you may be surprised.

If you're shaking your head as you read this, you're not alone. Our guests at Passion Parties just love the edibles and the lotions, but some do get a bit antsy when the consultant starts opening up the toy box and pulling out the mechanical objects. They're full of questions like the following:

"Isn't it unnatural to use something with batteries for sex?"

"What if it's too much stimulation for me?"

"Shouldn't I be able to do this on my own?"

"Will a vibrator ruin me for regular sex?"

And my all-time favorite: "Will I end up liking the vibrator more than I like my husband?"

All these questions are completely natural. Even Marilyn, a part-time Passion Consultant and full-time bank teller in San Francisco, had to overcome her own initial reluctance about vibrators. "I know just how these ladies feel," she told me, "because before I ever became a Passion Consultant, I also worried about using a vibrator. I had all those questions, but I now see that they all boiled down to the same question: Was it *really* okay for me, a proper wife and the mother of four, to buy myself something whose only purpose was to make me feel good 'down there'? Wasn't it just a tiny bit selfish?"

Here's what Marilyn found out: "The better time I had by myself," she explained, "the more energy I had for my husband, my family, and everything else I was involved in. I know it sounds strange, but because using a vibrator gave me so much pleasure, I felt I could be more generous with everybody else. I no longer resented those little things that used to irritate me—the way my mother would always call just around dinnertime or the way my oldest son drank milk right out of the carton no matter how many times I told him not to. Because I had this nice thing I could do for myself, I ended up being a lot more relaxed and easygoing with everybody around me.

"And no, I did *not* like my vibrator better than my husband! But I *did* like the feeling that sometimes the only person's pleasure I had to worry about was my own."

I loved Marilyn's philosophy, because it echoed two of our Passion Diva principles: *Sex is good for you* and *Even if you're a good girl, you get to have great sex.* And she was very clear that using a vibrator didn't "ruin her for regular sex," any more than driving a car "ruined her for walking." Both the vibrator and the car simply get you to your destination a little bit sooner. Your body craves stimulation, whether from fingers, tongue, penis, or vibrator. And if you've never used a vibrator, you may be surprised at how useful it is in helping you to respond to other types of sexual stimulation. Vibrators can increase your sexual self-knowledge, which can make it that much easier to enjoy a relationship with a partner.

So let me tell you the basics about the four different types of vibrators. Then I'll help you pick one out. And a bit later on, I'll tell you how to use one.

THE *Passion Diva's Guide* TO VIBRATORS

- **The Bullet.** This is a good first-time vibrator, versatile and powerful, providing stimulation to your clitoris as well as to many other sensitive areas of your body. You can use the Bullet to buzz gently against your breasts, stomach, thighs—any place you like attention—and then move on to the direct clitoral stimulation that at least 75 percent of us need to reach orgasm. The Bullet is a small, egg-shaped vibrator, $1\frac{1}{2}$ to 2 inches long and about 1 inch in diameter. It fits easily into the palm of your hand. The basic version is smooth, but you can also buy a variety of sleeves and covers made of a soft jellylike material if you prefer that texture or if you simply like variety. You can also find Bullet sleeves in a number of cute animal shapes with sensuous little nubs for enhanced clitoral stimulation. Little elephants, dolphins, and bunnies bring some humor to the bedroom, and if you later want to introduce your vibrator into sex play with your partner, you may find that he's more receptive to a sex toy in the nonthreatening shape of, say, a little purple elephant with a tiny vibrating trunk!

The Bullet is a frequent companion to the Super Deluxe Smitten, a nubby massage mitt that fits over the Bullet for an excellent full-body massage. Sleeves like the Beaming Bullet Buddy have soft nubs to enhance sensations and are also glow-in-the-dark. Pleasure Safari sleeves are animal-shaped and are made of silicone for a velvety touch. The rabbit ears tickle the clitoris; the elephant trunk has a steadier vibration; and the turtle is great if you want direct pressure along with the vibrations.

The Magic Mushroom mini-vibrator is essentially a vibrating egg encased in a soft flexible material. It has an attached controller that easily adjusts intensity with the slightest movement of your thumb. Velvet Pleasure is an elongated four-inch bullet, soft and smooth, covered in material known as "the Velvet Touch." It's equipped with multi-speeds and it's also waterproof. A Double Bullet offers twice the fun—one bullet to stimulate your clitoris while the other goes against your breasts or other sensitive areas. And the Pulsing Orbiter offers another variation—pulsing rather than buzzing—as well as five tempos that range from a slow pulsing to a rolling pleasure of vibrations.

- **Hard cylinders.** Some women like more firmness and pressure, and they also like an extended vibrator that offers them an easier grip. For these women, a hard plastic vibrator may be the perfect choice. You can get a hard-cylinder vibrator in many different lengths, from pocket-size to full length. The Pocket Rocket, Handy Massager, and Nubby Satisfier all double as excellent clitoral massagers and all-over body massagers. You can even find a Waterproof Dancing Dolphin for shower and bathtime fun.

- **G-spot stimulators.** The Aurora G-spot Massager is designed with a curved end to stimulate your G-spot—and it, too, is waterproof. I also recommend the Nubby G for the first-time G-spot explorer, with its amazing jelly vinyl tip curved upward for G-spot stimulation and stimulating nubs for labial and subtle clitoral stimulation. If you like bath and shower self-pleasuring, get the waterproof Nubby G Aqua.

- **Multitaskers.** You can get both vaginal penetration and clitoral stimulation with a multitasking vibrator. The Jelly Osaki and Thumb Pleaser are both basic vibrating shafts with an attached vibrating stimulator. The Jack Rabbit (you might have seen it on *Sex and the City*) has rotating beads in the shaft to pleasure your vaginal opening. The Pearl Dolphin offers dual reversible bead rotation. For life-like action, choose the Ultimate Stroker, with its seven functions and six speeds: Its shaft thrusts, pulses, and throbs, and also has a butterfly clitoral stimulator for additional pleasure. You can see the glow-in-the-dark controls if you want to change settings. For an adult toy with a high-powered motor, try the Decadent Indulgence, which features eight levels of vibration, three patterns of motion, and a set of rotating beads. Finally, the Escalating Elephant has twenty-one different ways to thrill, with three rotation speeds on the shaft and seven different vibrating patterns on the clitoral stimulator, plus those fabulous rotating beads.

SOLIDARITY FOREVER . . .

One of the most heartwarming vibrator stories I ever heard came from Alicia, a Passion Consultant in Vancouver. One of her guests came to Alicia's party saying that she'd heard about a new type of vibrator that she just had to have. She'd heard that a woman could walk around, fully clothed, while wearing the Adventure Arouser—a sleek, slender, glittered device that rests on the vaginal lips, resonating waves of pleasure and providing intense, focused clitoral stimulation. Operated by a power pack, the Adventure Arouser is held in place by adjustable thigh straps and can't be seen under street clothes. Fortunately, Alicia had an Adventure Arouser available to sell her guest, but she was curious what was so urgent about the matter.

"I'm going on strike tomorrow," the guest explained, "and I'll be walking the picket line all week long. I have to have something to keep my spirits up."

The strike, Alicia told me, lasted for a week. But the guest, Alicia learned, continued to wear the Adventure Arouser all month long!

Choosing a Vibrator

Now that you know the four basic types of vibrators, let me talk you through the process of choosing one—or perhaps, more than one! Here are a few of the questions you'll want to ask when making your choice:

- **Where do you want to be stimulated?** Some vibrators, like the Bullet, focus on the clitoris while others offer more attention to the labia (Adventure Arouser), vagina (Magic Monarch), or G-spot (Nubby G). If you've already pleasured yourself by hand, you'll probably have a good idea about what kind of stimulation is most important to you. If you're interested in giving your G-spot more attention, look for a vibrator with a forward-tilting tip and reversible rotating action. The Nubby G is a special favorite at our parties. Its sister product, the Nubby G Aqua, is designed for use in the bath, which means that if you're one of those ladies who ejaculate after G-spot orgasms, your fluid will flow right into the water.

- **What size do you want?** If you're looking for a vibrator to insert into your vagina, look for one that's about as long and thick as the penis of your "ideal lover." A good basic beginning size is the Pearl Shine. If you often feel that your partners are too thick, you might like the Pink Passion. If you often feel that your partners are too long, try the Perfect Jewel. And for women who'd like to try something with a little extra girth, I recommend the Jelly Cliterrific.

- **What's your idea of "fun vibrations"?** There are so many different ways a vibrator can move, but the most popular motions are twirling, rotating, vibrating, pulsating, and escalating to multi-speeds. Some vibrators light up, which adds to the fun. You can certainly get a combination vibrator that does all of the above.

- **Do you want dual action?** Vibrators that offer both clitoral and vaginal stimulation have dual motors, which can be used either individually or in unison. Once you've moved beyond the simple Bullet, you might enjoy a dual model such as the Loving Spoon or the Jelly Osaki, which have two stimulation actions—one that stimulates your clitoris, the other that excites your vagina and perhaps also your G-spot. You can turn on both motors, reach a clitoral orgasm, and then turn off the clitoral motor and enjoy the continuing sensations of the vibrating shaft against your vaginal walls, labia, or G-spot.

- **What kind of material do you prefer?** One choice is hard plastic or glass, which will be firm and easy to clean, but which may feel a bit unnatural. The Aurora G-spot Massager, Pocket Rocket, and Nubby Satisfier are some good examples of this "hard, clean" approach. For a more natural, flexible, porous feel, try a vibrator made of jelly

BATTERIES SHOULD BE INCLUDED

If you buy a vibrator from one of our Passion Consultants, the batteries are often included. If you purchase one from a store, ask to have some batteries placed in it—even if you have to pay for them—so you can make sure that all the different types of movement it offers are working properly. Since sex toys are almost always a nonrefundable item, you want to be sure the one you've gotten is in proper working order.

vinyl, FutureFlesh, or silicone, such as the Jelly Tropicana, Pink Passion, or Thumb Pleaser.

- **What about texture?** Glass and plastic vibrators are generally hard and sleek, but they may also come with a few smooth ridges for some extra sensation, such as the Mystical Moments Glass Wand or Nubby Satisfier. Some silicone and jelly vinyl vibrators simulate the look and feel of a real penis, including ridges, a head, and other textural features. The Pearl Shine is especially lifelike. For extra vibrating pleasure, products like the Decadent Indulgence or Perfect Jewel include moving beads and pearls set into the shaft about a third of the way down from the tip. One of our latest offerings is the Mini Tongue, a soft silicone vibrating tongue. Add a bit of lube and you won't be able to tell the difference between it and a real tongue— except, of course, the toy tongue never gives up!

- **How much control does your vibrator offer you?** Before you buy a vibrator, check out the on-off switch: Some allow you to smoothly and infinitely control the speed and move the vibration level up and down; others require you to switch from high to low without offering many power nuances in between. Japanese-made vibrators are generally stronger, quieter, and longer-lasting than other products, and in my opinion, they're worth the extra cost. Think about it. A

Japanese car can run for 300,000 miles, while a Japanese vibrator might last for 300,000 orgasms!

- **What color do you prefer?** Of course, your vibrator's color won't affect how it feels against you or inside you—but it will affect how you (and maybe your partner) feel about it. Some women like a vibrator that simulates the "real thing" all the way down to skin tone, and for sure, you can find some pretty good replicas. Most women enjoy the opportunity to make a fashion statement by choosing bright pinks and purples, fluorescent aquamarines, vibrant greens, pastel tones, and glow-in-the-dark specials.

- **Do you want a lighted vibrator?** Some vibrators literally light up in the dark—which some women consider a turn-on for them, too. If you're using the vibrator with your partner, he may have his own preferences, but it's true that lots of guys like to see what's going on, and what better way than by the light of your vibrator? If one of you likes the lights on and the other prefers the dark, a vibrator light may be an even better compromise than a bedside lamp.

- **What kind of noise do you prefer?** Some vibrators hum softly; others make more noise. And while some women like the gentle humming, which they find relaxing, others prefer the more discreet softer sounds.

TRY BEFORE YOU BUY

If you can, try the vibrator you want to purchase by pressing it very gently to the end of your nose. That will give you the best approximation of what the toy will feel like as it moves against your clitoris. Placing the vibrator under your arm will help you get a sense of how it will feel in your vagina. Since you can't return a vibrator after you've bought it, you want to be sure you've chosen a toy that's right for you.

In general, hard plastic battery-operated vibrators and some large wand vibrators are louder, as are many vibrators with a variety of moving parts; simpler models may be quieter. Remember, though—the place where your vibrator is going will naturally muffle the sound!

YOUR *Passion Diva's Guide* TO VIBRATOR CARE

- Proper care, cleaning, and storage of your passion toys will not only keep them safe and sanitary for use, it will also extend their life. Vibrators should be cleaned after every use and before storage. Of course, if you're engaged in a marathon lovemaking session, you can wait till the next morning to clean your toys, but don't use them in another session before cleansing them.

- Batteries should always be removed from vibrators when not in use. Batteries contain corrosive materials that may leak and ruin the internal mechanisms that make your vibrator work. Removing your batteries will also preserve their life.

- The best cleansers are those specifically designed for adult toys. Regular soap or alcohol can dry out and damage your toys and might even leave a residue that will irritate your vaginal tissues. The Passion Parties Toy Cleanser is specially formulated to meet your needs. It comes in three choices:

  1. A concentrated liquid to which you add water. One bottle yields more than sixty quarts of cleanser—an economical solution to the care and cleaning of your favorite waterproof toys as you can create a little bath in your sink and submerge them.
  2. A spray toy cleanser like Clean & Simple Adult Toy Cleanser Spray. This is ready to use and can easily be sprayed on your toy, wiped, and rinsed off.
  3. Clean & Simple Toy Cleanser Wipes. These are convenient and easy to use, at home or away.

- Unless your toy is waterproof, don't put it under running water to rinse it. You might flood the motor and render it useless. Instead, use a damp washcloth, and always completely dry it before storing.

- When cleaning your toys, make sure you get in between any ridges, nubs, or crevices in order to prevent bacterial growth. And remember, not cleaning your vibrator is simply not an option. An unclean vibrator is a breeding ground for bacteria, which could lead to urinary tract or bladder infections, if not worse.

- Store your toys in a cool, dry place: Moisture and heat are the most damaging elements to any vibrator's life. One great storage option is Passion Parties' discreet Hideaway Heart Pillow. It can be placed on your bed for decoration, and you're the only one who needs to know the sexy secrets hiding within. Also available from Passion Parties are individual silky toy bags.

- Store adult toys separately and not touching one another, since some materials will cling to and melt each other.

Self-Pleasuring: Some Basic "Hands-on" Techniques

Now that you've read about lubricants and vibrators, two delightful accessories that can greatly enhance your experience of self-pleasure, let's move on to how exactly to get started. Using your fingers to stimulate your clitoris is the most basic technique for bringing yourself to orgasm, but there are plenty of variations and none of them are "right" or "wrong." Some women prefer to self-pleasure with only their own hands; others like to use a vibrator; still others prefer a combination of the two. So in this section, I'll talk you through first one way, and then the other. Either way, be creative. Mixing it up is part of the fun! See what happens when you vary pressure, speed, and strokes, and come up with your own variations and combinations, including your position on the bed or couch. Some women like to lie on their backs; others prefer to lie on their stomachs for more clitoral pressure; still others vary their positions, depending on what they want at the moment. Whatever you try, though, don't forget to apply lubricant to any dildo or vibrator that you might use. While some women are happy using only their own natural moisture, you might want to have some Embrace or UltraGlide handy—remember that ten-second lube test and the increased pleasure you were able to get just from licking your lips! So put a bit of lube into your palm—a dollop the size of a quarter will do—and, after warming it between your fingers, gently massage it all over your clitoris, labia, and vaginal opening so that everything is nice and slippery. You may discover that you get some new ideas for self-pleasuring just from applying the lubricant!

SETTING THE SCENE

Many women begin their self-pleasuring with some sort of fantasy to help them create the mood. A fantasy may be as simple as picturing yourself in a sensuous setting or with a real-life partner; or it may be a complex scenario involving stories, situations, and people you invent. Some women find it helpful to think of a scene from a movie or book, to read a passage from a sexy book or romance novel, or to listen to some music that makes them feel sexy. Perhaps a particular smell evokes your sensuous side, or maybe you get turned on by the texture of a particular fabric or the feel of a sexy piece of lingerie. Take some time to learn what turns you on, letting your Passion Diva guide the way.

Some women feel anxious or self-critical if they can't immediately figure out what turns them on. But to me, that's like blaming yourself for not knowing right away what kind of clothing looks good on you and what colors flatter your complexion. Think how long it took you to develop your own personal fashion sense—what styles, shades, and accessories go best with your own body, personality, and lifestyle. Why shouldn't it take you a while to find out your own personal passion style, as well? And since your fashion sense changes as you get older, why shouldn't your passion style change, too?

Many people enjoy fantasizing about actions or situations that they'd never choose in real life but which, in the privacy of their own minds, turn them on. This is perfectly natural and normal, and I encourage you to give yourself total permission in this ever-so-private realm. *Nothing* you think or imagine here is wrong. The whole point of fantasy is that it's just that—fantasy.

Still, some women are a bit taken aback to find themselves fantasizing about scenarios that don't necessarily interest them in real life, including multiple partners, situations involving a celebrity, and same-sex partners. Sometimes these are fantasies they enjoy acting out in some other way, such as role-playing with a partner. Or they might like describing these fantasies to a partner. (For more on either type of shared fantasy, see Chapter 9, Great Adventures). Sometimes, though, a woman will choose to keep these fantasies in "the vault" as private images that she shares with no one but her Passion Diva.

Whatever you choose—and whatever you fantasize about—remember that it's your body and your very private pleasure. Allow your mind to roam free and let your body enjoy every moment of your favorite fantasies. It may take a while to learn what turns you on—or what turns you on *now*—but give yourself permission to enjoy the learning process. This is one situation in which *getting there* can be just as much fun as *being there*.

CLITORAL STROKING

Here is a list of moves you can try when figuring out what works for you. These are not successive steps, so feel free to mix them up or combine them in any way that feels good. The clitoris is one of your most sensitive places, so go easy at first, but be prepared for some intense and thrilling sensations.

SOME LIKE IT WET . . .

Lots of women enjoy self-pleasuring in the shower or bathtub. Some also enjoy having sex there. After all, you're already naked, it's a sensuous environment, and it's also a very private place. An inflatable bath pillow is good for supporting your neck and head in the tub, while a shower hose attachment offers yet another chance for stimulation as you direct a stream of warm water on your clitoris. Since many women can't reach orgasm solely by water stimulation alone, you might want to start by stimulating yourself with a shower massage attachment. You can have fun massaging yourself with a Smitten plus waterproof Mini Bullet. Then, after you've become aroused, "graduate" to a water-safe toy, such as the Nubby G Aqua vibrator. This waterproof vibrator can either be inserted or used for clitoral stimulation: It has little nubs that you can press up against your clitoris or that stimulate your vagina. The Nubby G Aqua also curves up slightly, making it good for G-spot stimulation as well.

- Gently "sandwich" your clitoris between your index and middle finger. Start with a soft up/down motion to stimulate both the clitoris and your inner labia. Increase the pressure to your liking.

- The basic movement of clitoral stimulation is up and down. But you can also try mixing this technique with side-to-side or circular movements that help you explore your body's unique sensitivities.

- Using two fingers side-by-side, rub your clitoris in a circular motion. This method is great when your fingers get tired from other techniques but you don't want to stop the feeling.

- For full-coverage pleasure, use three to four fingers side-by-side, fully covering the entire clitoris and inner labia by placing your hand flatly between the outer labial lips. Apply pressure and stimulate your clitoris with your palm using your favorite technique: One that often works well is an up-and-down motion from your clitoris to your vaginal opening. Some women like to alternate between "full-palm action" (and pressure) and a lighter, more tickling motion of fingering their clitoris and/or playing with their labia.

• For even more focused and direct stimulation, gently squeeze your clitoris with your index finger and thumb, lift upward, and roll your clitoris back and forth, as if you were passing it from thumb to index finger and vice versa.

• A popular technique for fuller stimulation is to rub your clitoris in a circular motion and alternate with the same motion on your labia.

• Some women like to place a pillow, something silky, or something furry—or even just have their panties or a towel—between their hand and their genital area. You can try all of these techniques through the "barrier," which both eases the intensity of direct clitoral stimulation and offers some exciting new sensations. If your "barrier" is big enough, you can get some added stimulation from where it presses against your inner thighs—an area that many women (and men!) find highly erotic. Squeezing your thighs tightly around something soft, with a pleasurable texture, while reaching for your clitoris "through the barrier" can be a very exciting experience. (Lots of men like silk, fur, and other exciting textures against their penises, too, and against their inner thighs; so as you discover your own pleasure, remember that he may like many of the same things you do.)

Finger Fun

After stroking and playing with your clitoris for a while, you may be feeling quite aroused and ready for further stimulation. At this point, you can insert a lubricated finger into your vagina while using your other hand to continue the clitoral stimulation above. Once you're comfortable, try using two (or more) fingers to heighten the sensation. You can move your fingers around, teasing yourself, moving in and out, or using them in whatever way feels good. This alone may be enough to bring you to orgasm. But if you're eager for more intense sensations, or your clitoris needs a bit more stimulation to reach climax, you can go on to incorporate a vibrator.

USING YOUR VIBRATOR

Vibrators can be the first, last, or middle stop on your road to orgasm, depending on what you like. Some women like to start with their hands and move on to a vibrator; others like to start with the vibrator and ride its delicious tingling sensations all the way through. If you've tried self-pleasuring with your own two hands as just described, and are still having trouble achieving orgasm, the addition of a vibrator can make all the difference. Give it a try, and you'll soon be singing with pleasure! Read on, and I'll walk you through the process.

The Bullet

Since this is my favorite "beginner" vibrator, designed to focus on clitoral stimulation—the key to orgasm for 75 percent of us women— let's begin here.

Gently caress your clitoris, labia, and vagina with a generous helping of your favorite lube. Then stroke your clitoris to build sexual excitement. Your body will become warm and relaxed, and your clitoris will become slightly swollen and extra sensitive. Of course, all this time you may have a sexy scenario running in your mind as well.

Then lightly lubricate your Bullet. (Too much lubrication and it may slip from your fingers!) Finally, press the Bullet gently against your clitoris. Experiment with the type of pressure and the level of lubricant you like. Roll the Bullet back and forth, up and down, or in a circular motion. Some women like to tease themselves, working around their labia and ending up at the clitoris. Other women just like to sink into the sensation of sustained vibrator action. You may find that you enjoy a wide variety of approaches, or you may figure out a surefire favorite that always works for you. That's the beauty of a vibrator—it's there at your beck and call, ready to experiment as long as you are!

The Hard-Cylinder Vibrator

As we've seen, the Nubby Satisfier, Pleasure Curve, and many other hard-cylinder vibrators are designed to fit inside your vagina, where many women enjoy being stimulated as well. You'll probably want to begin with some manual stimulation to ensure that you're feeling sexy and turned on and ready to go. When you are ready, lubricate your vibrator, turn it on, and ease it carefully into your vagina. Now you can experiment a bit: Glide your vibrator in and out or move it around in a circular motion. Most vibrators have controls to vary the speed. Experiment to find which intensity is most pleasurable for you. You might also try elevating your hips at different angles to see what types of sensations this produces when the vibrator is inside you.

Remember that you'll probably still need clitoral stimulation to reach orgasm, even with a vibrator inside your vagina. To achieve this, you can continue to use your fingers, press the vibrator against your clitoris, or use one of the multitaskers I describe on page 134. Either way, you'll have a chance to explore and determine the combination of clitoral and vaginal stimulation that works best for you.

The G-Spot Vibrator

If you'd like to use a G-spot vibrator, such as the Nubby G or Aurora G-spot Massager, you can experiment with a variety of sensations. Some women like the pressing of a hard vibrator against their G-spot, while others prefer vibrations. Adding some G-Spot Crème can increase your G-spot sensitivity. You can apply it internally with your fingers or put it on the tip of a G-spot toy, using the toy like a little paintbrush to put it on the right spot.

The Multitasker

Finally, if you're interested in a multitasker, the possibilities are—well, multiple! But here are a couple of suggestions to get you started. Consider playing with the sensation of the twirling, free-moving beads in the Jack Rabbit and Pearl Dolphin, which you can work forward or in reverse (so if you find a spot you like, hit the reverse function and find it again!). If you prefer firmer, more consistent stimulation, experiment with the Perfect Jewel, which also contains beads, but they are evenly aligned and in a fixed position. You can also experiment with the relationship between clitoral and vaginal stimulation by turning the dual motors off and on—perhaps beginning with some clitoral stimulation, moving to a double sensation, turning off the clitoral function, and then alternating between clitoral and vaginal or clitoral and G-spot stimulation.

You should also be aware of the variety of clitoral stimulation these multitaskers offer. The elephant on the Escalating Elephant has a firm little trunk that can target one particular area. The Decadent Indulgence's hummingbird offers a beak to target one spot and two wings to flutter against you. The butterfly on the Magic Monarch flutters against you with two little wings that nudge the labia while its antennae tickle your clitoris. And our popular model, the Turtle Frenzy, features a turtle stimulator with a round, solid head that offers a different kind of pressure.

KEGEL PLEASURE

As we saw in Chapter 3, Kegel balls are terrific for your sexual health because they strengthen PC muscle tone. That's good for childbirth and recovery from childbirth; for bladder control; for your ability to contract your vaginal walls around your partner's penis; and for your orgasmic potential. But there's another advantage to Kegel balls—they're wonderful for self-pleasuring as well. Just put the balls inside you and then lie on your back, rocking gently back and forth. For extra pleasure, slip two fingers inside yourself and press one or both balls against your G-spot, rubbing gently. (You can also ask your partner to do this for you.)

Whatever you do, though, don't insert Kegel balls into your anus. They really could disappear in there. If you'd like a little pleasure in that area, check out Chapter 9—we offer other products for that!

THE JOYS OF PLEASING OURSELVES

Many of us women want a fabulous guy to know us better than we know ourselves. And sometimes, it's true, a loving man can give us pleasure that we never expected. That's part of the joy of a sexual relationship. Still, it's always a good idea to know yourself what you like, what works for you, and what turns you on. After all, just because your guy can give you a fabulous piece of jewelry or a gorgeous sweater doesn't mean that you'll never go shopping for yourself, does it? So everything you've learned about happy self-loving will stand you in good stead when it comes time to make love with your partner.

I think it's just about that time—so let's move on to the next section, where you can begin preparing for passion. You may find out that the preparation holds a pleasure all its own.

⚬ *In Your Passion Pantry* ⚬

- **A variety of lubricants.** No need to rely on just one! Passion Divas know that choice is half the fun. Start your collection with a natural, water-based lube like Revelation, and go on to add some gels, stimulants or warming lubes, and edibles, like our Embrace Sensual Lubricant.
- **Bullet.** This egg-shaped vibrator is a terrific way to pleasure yourself. Try it with the Super Deluxe Smitten for an excellent full-body massage or check out the variety of sleeves or accessory

rings. For twice the pleasure, try the Double Bullet—one for your clitoris and the other for your breasts, stomach, or any other part of you that wants a little extra buzz.

- **Jelly Osaki.** This multitask vibrator with vibrating shaft rotates deep inside your vagina while its attached tongue teases your clitoris. The separate sliding controls on the base allow you to easily select the right intensity for both types of stimulation.
- **Dildo.** One of our most popular, realistically shaped, and versatile dildos, the Glo Boy even glows in the dark when the lights go out. Waterproof for use in the bath or shower, its concave bottom can fasten to any hard, smooth surface, including a bathtub, hot tub, shower wall, or chair.

Part

II

Preparing for Passion

On February 8, 2003, Pfizer—one of the world's leading pharmaceutical companies and makers of the wonder drug Viagra—announced that after many years of research and millions of dollars spent, they had given up the search for the female "sex pill." Why? Because although they had been able to find a relatively simple way to help men achieve erections, a woman's arousal and desire were a lot more complex than they had originally anticipated.

It all comes back to Passion Diva Principle #8: *Your most important sex organ is your brain.* How you feel about yourself, your body, your partner, and your life in general will all affect the kind of sex you have. And as the Pfizer Corporation found out, women's thoughts and feelings are too complex and interrelated to be easily affected by a simple pill.

But here's some really terrific news: Even if the Pfizer Corporation couldn't help you ramp up your sex life, there's a lot *you* can do to make things more exciting in bed. It's all in the preparation.

Ginnie, for example, was a bookkeeper in suburban Long Island who came to one of our Passion Parties. She listened eagerly to her Passion Consultant's presentation about the wonderful toys and lotions she could buy, and when it came time to make her purchases, she bought several things. But Linda, her Passion Consultant, had the sense that Ginnie was holding something back.

"I've been married for about ten years, and our sex life has always been fine, I guess. But I always thought I'd have more romance in my life," Ginnie admitted when Linda tried to draw her out. "I mean, the sex is okay. But it's just not what I thought it would be."

Linda realized that Ginnie might not be giving her Passion Diva enough support in preparing for passion. She suggested some of the romantic bathing rituals I'll describe for you in Chapter 5 (our Luxurious Bath & Shower Gel, Vibrating Bath Ball, and Salt Glow Body Scrub—all from our exclusive RomantaTherapy collection—are terrific bath aids). She also told Ginnie that one of the most common complaints women express about their sex lives is that they are not getting enough foreplay. It seems that most of us women are getting about twenty minutes less than we would ideally like! She shared some special foreplay secrets with Ginnie—delicious, exciting ways of extending that portion of her lovemaking, assisted by such products as Passion Pudding and Powder, and the Super Deluxe Smitten combined with Passion Massage Lotion. (Don't worry, I'll tell you all about these ideas in Chapter 6 and show you how you, too, can ensure yourself the kind of long-lasting, slow-building, super-delicious foreplay that will both fulfill your need for romance and pave the way for great sex.) And she told Ginnie about the ten Passion Diva Principles that could help Ginnie connect to her own personal Passion Diva.

Ginnie ordered some of the products that Linda suggested, and when they arrived, she began to try out some of the passion preparation activities that Linda had described. She decided to begin with the RomantaTherapy products she'd bought from Passion Parties' exclusive line, products we developed to help busy women make the transition from "stressed out" to "make out" by waking up all five senses. After all, as Passion Diva's principle #6 reminds us: *You need all five senses to make sex great.* So Ginnie luxuriated in a bath infused with Plumeria using RomantaTherapy Sensuous Bath Salts, which left her feeling sensuous, relaxed, and ready for love. She also made a point of clearing all distractions out of the bedroom—no laundry baskets, stacks of bills, or bedside laptops to remind her and her husband of all the household and work-related chores of the day—and sprayed her sheets with Silky Sheets scented with Plumeria, our own special fragrance that freshens linens and creates a sensuous aura in your bed. Ginnie discovered that making just these few specific preparations for a night of love helped her and her husband focus on each other, so that their lovemaking became more attentive and satisfying.

Encouraged by her success, Ginnie decided to put into practice Passion Diva principle #7—*For sex at night, foreplay starts in the morning.* She made sure to connect to her husband in both affectionate and intimate ways on the days she knew they'd probably have sex. She found new ways to let her husband know she appreciated him and enjoyed his company, and she also focused on waking up her own sexuality. She began wearing silky, glamorous lingerie under her daily work clothes, and at Linda's suggestion, she dabbed some Pure Instinct Attraction Cologne behind her ears each morning. To Ginnie's amazement, the pheromones in Pure Instinct worked like a magic love potion, evoking subtle responses from the men she met each day—responses that reminded her that she was a sexy, desirable woman. She also made a point of putting a few drops of Pure Satisfaction UniSEX Enhancement Gel on her clitoris right after her morning shower. The tingly, exciting sensation of the gel made Ginnie feel as though she was carrying her own special secret throughout the day, an affirmation of her body, her sensuality, and her sexual desire.

Ginnie felt as though her sex life had improved immeasurably, and she hadn't even approached her husband about making any changes! But she was putting into practice Passion Diva Principle #4: *If you take responsibility for your pleasure, your pleasure will pay you back.*

It turned out that the more pleasure Ginnie got from her sex life, the more she wanted, a perfect example of what I call the pleasure-positive upward spiral. Tentatively at first and then with more confidence, she began to find ways of encouraging her husband to make their foreplay more satisfying and exciting. She showed her husband the Crèmesicle

Edible Massage Cream she'd bought at Linda's party and suggested that they learn how to give each other sensual all-body massages. She introduced the strawberry Crèmesicle edible product into their foreplay, applying the delicious cream to the places on her body where she wanted more of her husband's attention. The delicious, sensuous taste was a pleasurable reminder to him of where she wanted to be kissed, nuzzled, and nibbled, and soon he was using Crèmesicle to cue Ginnie about where *he* wanted more attention, too. The two of them began to communicate more passionately—and eventually, much to Ginnie's surprise, her ten-year marriage of "just-okay" sex had been transformed into a far more romantic and loving connection.

"I consider Ginnie one of our greatest successes," Linda told me. "We not only sold her products that made a difference in her life, we shared a philosophy that transformed her whole relationship." I was happy to agree. Ginnie, it seemed to me, had truly mastered the Passion Diva principles, especially Passion Diva #10: *If you want great sex, bring the right woman to the bedroom.* She had learned how to focus on herself, her sexuality, and her partner in a way that was practically guaranteed to ensure great sex and to improve her relationship. Ginnie had learned how to prepare for passion, and her life would never be the same.

As you can see, I'm a big believer in preparing for passion—and that's what these next two chapters are all about. In Chapter 5, I'll help you bring the right woman to the bedroom by sharing with you a whole range of RomantaTherapy secrets that will help you feel more sensual, sexual, and loving, every minute of the day. Then, in Chapter 6, I'll show you how to make your foreplay more satisfying, exciting, and romantic, with enormous benefits to your entire sexual life. After all, you wouldn't drive a car without making sure you had plenty of gas in the tank or prepare a new recipe without making sure you had all the necessary ingredients on hand. Doesn't your passion deserve the same degree of preparation and care? So come on, Passion Divas! You may discover that preparation is half the fun!

⌒ 5 ⌒

RomantaTherapy

Bringing the Right Woman to the Bedroom

This chapter is all about the steps you can take to prepare yourself for passion long before you ever slip between the sheets. It's about how you can live your daily life in such a way that your Passion Diva comes to the surface, enhancing any relationship you're already in or drawing a wonderful new relationship to you. Chapters 6 through 9 will give you lots of delicious suggestions about what you can do *in* the bedroom, bringing you and your partner closer together, deepening and enriching your sexual connection. But none of those suggestions will mean very much if you're not bringing the right woman to the bedroom in the first place—and all of them will mean so much more if you are.

Before you can bring the right woman to the bedroom, you need to know who she is. I'll tell you a secret: The right woman isn't Britney Spears or Catherine Zeta-Jones or any other movie star, pop star, diva, or model. The right woman—the woman you need to be bringing to the bedroom—is *you*.

That's right. You. Because here's another little secret you may be glad to know: A lot of research has shown that most men in relationships don't want *another* woman. They want a more spontaneous and playful version of the woman they've already chosen. As we've seen time and time again, becoming a Passion Diva isn't about imitating some other woman, but rather about freeing your own inner capacity for passion, pleasure, and romance.

So who is the *you* that you need to bring to the bedroom? Well, you need to be *aware, good to yourself, in the mood,* and *committed.*

Let's take a closer look.

Be Aware: Remaining Physically Aware and Alive

How can you expect to have a good sex life if, when the moment comes, you're too pooped to participate? How can you expect to enjoy your partner's caresses or to get pleasure from caressing him if your senses aren't fully alive? You can't drag yourself through twenty-three miserable hours of half-numb overcommitment and frustration and then expect that one hour in the bedroom to be magical and fulfilling. So your first step in bringing the right woman to the bedroom is to be sure that you are fully aware, alive, and awake to all the pleasure and excitement that your senses have to offer you, twenty-four hours a day. (And no, that's not a misprint! Later in this chapter, I'll show you how to set up your bed so that even your sleeping hours are sensually pleasing, restorative, and nourishing to your senses.)

THE *Passion Diva's Guide* TO BEING AWARE

BECOME AWARE IN ALL FIVE SENSES

So many of us shut down our senses and physical awareness for huge portions of our waking lives. We gulp down a hurried breakfast, rush off to work in a fog, and sit at a desk in a drab office. No sweet-smelling flowers in a graceful bud vase or heartwarming photos of our loved ones to brighten our daily experience. Or we're surrounded by sensory possibilities, but they've become so familiar, we barely notice them anymore, ignoring the flowers and the photos while doing business on the phone or scanning a memo.

If your primary work is at home, you may feel even more overwhelmed by the demands of childcare, household maintenance, food shopping, and bill-paying. We rush from chore to chore, thinking only about how soon we can be done with it all, so that we might be able to grab five minutes with our feet up or ten minutes in front of the tube. Our idea of relaxation is not tuning in to our bodies and our senses, but rather, tuning them out—numbing ourselves with television or a hurried trip to the gym or maybe a sugary snack that we gobble down so quickly and guiltily that we don't even give ourselves time to savor its taste in our mouth.

And then, after a day like that, we expect to come to the bedroom and make magic? We expect our partner to touch our cheek and *then* suddenly we'll come alive? I don't think so! After a day spent making ourselves *less* aware of our bodies, our senses, and the world around us, we're not exactly primed for a passionate sexual experience.

So if you'd like to bring the right woman to the bedroom, start thinking of ways that you can remain sensually and physically alive and aware throughout every minute of your day. Even if you've got to focus on other things—kids, bills, memos, bosses—you can at least see that your sensory burner stays on "low" and is never totally "off." I'll be the first to admit it's challenging, but I can tell you from personal experience that it's worth it. Here are some ideas for how to maintain that glorious state of physical awareness every single minute of your day:

- **Savor every beverage you drink.** Whether it's coffee, tea, juice, or water, make each moment of drinking a moment of concentration, invoking taste, smell, sight, and physical sensation. If you've lost consciousness of your physical self for a moment, let the physical experience of sipping, swallowing, and tasting bring you back home to your body.

- **Take two five-minute walks or one ten-minute walk each day.** Not only is this good for your heart, lungs, stress level, and waistline, it's good for your sense of "alive and aware," because you can make every minute of these brief walks a full-body sensory experience. Don't let your mind wander to your grocery list or to your upcoming deadlines. Invite your awareness to remain with all five senses. If you're walking in a lovely environment, you can turn your senses outward, noticing what you see, smell, hear, and feel. If you're walking in a less-inspiring place, turn your attention inward: Become aware of the beating of your heart, the intake and exhale of your lungs, the play of your muscles. Feel the blood coursing through your veins, and check in with your sexual center as well. Give thanks for your body, celebrate your ability to feel and move. Treat your walk as a moving meditation and then know that you can enter this state of appreciative physical awareness every time you're in your partner's arms.

- **Surround yourself with sensory treats.** Can you delight your eyes with lovely ornaments; treat your ears to soothing background music; awaken your sense of smell with incense or flowers? Can you take a moment out of your busy day to rub your hands with sweet-smelling, silky lotion (try some RomantaTherapy Alluring Body Lotion or RomantaTherapy Solid Parfum!)—not absentmindedly, but with awareness? Can you add some tart lemon or pungent lime to your glass of water, or choose a different natural juice each day and let its distinct taste linger on your tongue? Even the busiest, most hectic life can accommodate these kinds of sensory treats if you put your mind to it. And awareness, after all, is what we're going for.

- **Wear lingerie or other undergarments that feel marvelous against your skin.** And then check in with yourself. Be aware of your skin and notice what rests against it; experience the sensation of silk or satin or lace as it brushes and caresses you. In fact, I suggest that you do a little "lingerie check" each time you leave the bathroom—not with your eyes, but with your inner awareness. Make sure that at least once or twice a day, you're allowing yourself to experience the sensual comforts of your own skin.

- **Try some Pure Satisfaction.** This extraordinary gel, especially designed to stimulate a woman's clitoris, is our top-selling product. And once you try some, I'm sure you'll see why. If you want your sexual center to be tingling and purring all day, a dab of Pure Satisfaction UniSEX Enhancement Gel applied to your clitoris in the morning will get you on track right from the beginning of the day, helping you recall at every moment that you're a sexual woman who's fully alive to her own body.

BECOME AWARE OF YOUR PHYSICAL SELF

The daily sensory activities I've just suggested are the equivalent of stopping by the market periodically to pick up the things you need for supper. But what about stocking your shelves with long-term supplies? You also need to engage in some long-term physical activities to keep yourself physically alive and happy with your body. Here are some ideas:

- **Move.** I much prefer this term to "exercise," because "exercise" conjures images of "should" and "ought," and we're going for "alive" and "aware." But here's the important point: If you can find a way of using your body physically a few times a week, I promise you that your sex life will be better for it! Regular, pleasurable movement will help you relax, give you more energy, and boost your self-esteem. Besides, you can't let your body remain idle all through the week and then expect it to perform for you Saturday night. I'm not talking about being "in shape" or even about losing weight. I'm talking about feeling in touch with your body, excited about being inside it, alive to its many possibilities. A physical activity as simple as a thirty-minute walk three times a week can do the trick, and, when the time comes, it will make you feel enormously sexy! Consider walking, rebounding (bouncing on a small trampoline), swimming, biking, or some other way of using your muscles and remembering that you have a physical self. Yoga, t'ai chi, stretching, and martial arts all require a combination mind-and-body awareness that I think is terrifically conducive to good sex. If you find even one way to pleasure yourself physically, your sexual pleasure will grow by leaps and bounds.

- **Baths, showers, and lotions.** Sink into a warm tub, perfumed with sandalwood or lavender . . . or stand under a soothing shower, rubbing yourself with rose, plumeria, or bergamot. Feel the bubbles pop against your skin and soak up the healing oils, and then step out of the warm water and wrap yourself in a plush towel. If you're a woman who enjoys body powder, a delightful alternative is a lotion that glides on creamy and then dries like a powder: RomantaTherapy Plumeria Liquid Body Silk gives you cool instant freshness without the mess that powders can leave behind on the bathroom floor. Or slowly, gently, rub your skin with Strawberry Champagne Passion Body Dew or RomantaTherapy Alluring Body Lotion . . . mmmmm. Now *there's* a woman who's in touch with her body. And *there's* a body that will come alive to her partner's touch—and then some! Bathing and beauty rituals of all kinds are one of the best ways to arouse your senses. We cover all sorts of ideas on this front later in the chapter.

- **Try some sensuous dancing.** One fun way to remain present to yourself and your body is to do a private sensual dance. We'll get to stripteases and partner-pleasers in Chapter 6. For now, let's focus on the kind of dance you do by yourself, just to wake up your body to the sensual moment. This might sound a little hokey, but moving your body to a thrilling, sexy, or soothing rhythm naturally activates your sex energy, especially if you surrender to the music. So sometime when you're alone, I encourage you to let go of your inhibitions and give it a try. It's not about choreography or looking good for anyone else, it's about opening yourself to the rhythm while staying present in the movements.

You can do a sensuous dance in any number of ways, but here's one of my favorites: Start by undressing—remember, you're alone—and tie a big silky scarf around your hips, sarong style. If you like, you can dance in front of a mirror, or you may prefer to experience your body from the inside out. Put on some music that appeals to you and begin to move in any way that feels natural. Let your sexual side come to the fore: Roll and thrust your hips, let your arms sway, pulse with the beat or flow with the melody. Allow yourself to dance the rhythms, gestures, and feelings of making love. Feel the heat of your own sexual energy and stay present in your limbs, your muscles, and your skin. If you can, keep going for about fifteen to twenty minutes. You'll feel super-present in your body by the time you stop!

If you're looking for some musical choices to get you going, here are some CDs that Passion Consultants have listed as their favorites:

Coltrane for Lovers, John Coltrane

Come Away with Me, Norah Jones

The French Album, Celine Dion

The Icon Is Love and *The Ultimate Collection,* Barry White

Love Deluxe, Sade

Love Songs, Grover Washington, Jr.

Love Songs, Etta James

Midnight Love, Marvin Gaye

Nada Como El Sol, Sting

Canon in D Minor, Pachelbel

Rhapsody, Anita Baker

Romanza, Andrea Bocelli

The Unforgettable Nat King Cole, Nat King Cole

BECOME AWARE OF YOUR PARTNER

So often, in our rush to finish the chores of the day, we shove aside not only our own physical awareness but our awareness of our partner, as well. We forget how we feel about him and how he can make us feel. We don't stop loving him, exactly, but we put the love to one side like a piece of clothing from the wrong season. Sure, we'll get to that wool sweater *after* the summer is over, but given that temperatures are currently hitting ninety degrees, we can afford to forget all about it. Time enough to get it out of storage when winter comes.

But our relationship is *not* some piece of clothing that will be there, exactly as we left it, after a long period of neglect. A relationship is a dynamic, living entity, more like a plant that needs to be watered every day and occasionally treated to some extra-nourishing plant food. I'm not suggesting that you wander around in a dreamy romantic state, though at the beginning of a relationship or during a second honeymoon, that can sure be fun! But I am suggesting that you remain alive to the sensations that your relationship awakens in you.

Here's one of my own favorite ways to stay alive to *my* dear husband and long-cherished marriage. I like to keep a picture of my sweetheart right there on my desk, where I can see it every moment of the day—and not just any picture, but a photo that evokes one of our best moments, reminding me of exactly what I love about him and our relationship. I also like to change this photo periodically, so it doesn't "wear out" by becoming too familiar. Then, every so often—but at least once a day—I take a "five-second escape," imagining myself with Ollie and allowing all my tender feelings for him to come fully alive.

If you like this idea and you're not currently involved with anyone, try the same technique using a picture of yourself at your most "Passion Diva"—in a great outfit, or with a friend you really love, or in a physical place whose very memories make you feel more alive. And take a five-second escape to come alive to *yourself* and your warmest, most loving and appreciative feelings for your own special being.

Be Good to Yourself: Happy Women Have Great Sex

One of my favorite characters in *Sex and the City* was the irrepressible Samantha, the sexy "older" woman played so well by Kim Cattrall. Samantha was always telling her friends, "You're fabulous—we all are!"

That's what I loved about Samantha. She didn't just think she was fabulous—she *knew*. And she knew her friends were fabulous, too. As a result, she allowed herself to indulge in all sorts of fabulous pleasures: designer clothes, plenty of cosmopolitans, decadent meals at all of New York's hottest restaurants, and of course, lots and lots of sex. Samantha Jones was the very essence of a woman who was good to herself, because she knew that's what she deserved.

Alas, few of us are able to feel as entitled as she did to treating ourselves well. After all, we face some pretty formidable barriers, including our feminine tendency to put others' needs before our own. Most of the time, we're the nurturers—in the family, in the office, for our friends—and sometimes it seems that we nurture everyone but ourselves. Sometimes, though, it's okay to put *yourself* first. It might even be an unselfish act to do so, because once you connect to your Passion Diva—that sexy, entitled woman of passion—you'll bring a new sparkle and vitality into every situation, and your family, friends, colleagues, and loved ones will benefit accordingly.

How I wish I could personally speak to every woman who's reading this book and say, just as Samantha did, *You're fabulous—we all are!* If only I could wave a magic wand and grant every woman on earth that wonderful sense that she *deserves* pleasure in all areas of her life!

Since my magic wand is in the shop at the moment, I'll have to be satisfied with some basic suggestions, but hopefully they'll work just as well.

THE *Passion Diva's Guide* TO BEING
GOOD TO YOURSELF

Pamper Yourself

If you don't treat yourself as a precious, wonderful, physical being, how can you expect your man to treat you that way? We've already talked about sensual baths and showers, but now I'd like to suggest that you expand your self-pampering into an extended cleansing ritual that leaves every inch of you feeling cared for, silky-smooth, and oh-so-ready to touch. A vibrating bath sponge is a pleasant way to stimulate your body and get your circulation going. A salt scrub, like RomantaTherapy Salt Glow Body Scrub, can be invigorating as well as sensual. When you're removing unwanted hair, try some special RomantaTherapy Soft & Silky UniSEX Shaving Creme followed by After Shave Protection Mist, so that your guy sees that your skin is just asking to be stroked and caressed. Rub your body with Alluring Body Lotion or Honeysuckle Passion Body Dew so that you remember how much you enjoy it when your man touches you. Pamper your hands and feet with manicures and pedicures, both so that they'll look lovely and cared-for, and to give yourself that forty-five minutes of luxury in the nail shop when someone else is attending to *your* needs. And every so often, treat yourself to a full-body massage that will help you remember how many pleasure centers you have in your skin and your muscles and even your bones. Just the relaxation alone can help you feel centered, calm, and powerful—and how sexy is that?

For some even-more-decadent pampering, decorate yourself with Passion Parties Jewels, glittering body lotion, and Passion Parties Gold Dust, and maybe spray your genital area with Passion Parties Fresh & Frisky "so your guy can go downtown for dinner," as Michigan Passion Consultant Velma likes to say. Now you're bringing the right woman to the bedroom in two senses: You're modeling for your guy how you'd like to be treated, and at the same time, you're reminding yourself that you are a special, lovable person who's entitled to great sex.

BUY YOURSELF SOME LINGERIE

Now, you *know* that Samantha wasn't wearing just any old undies underneath those stylish clothes! Of course, not everyone finds lingerie as sexy as I do. But I've been struck, over my years with Passion Parties, at how many women would wear lingerie if only they felt that they deserved it. If buying a silky little camisole or a sexy little G-string makes you feel sensual, special, and desirable, then I think the price for the extra-nice underwear is definitely worth it, because it's a way of reminding yourself that *you're* worth it. And of course, wearing lingerie under your daytime clothes feels like a naughty little secret that can make you feel sensual all day long. If you like, buy your guy some matching male silk boxers and set the mood for both of you. As each of you dresses for the day, you'll not only get the hint of things to come but will think of sex throughout the day as the silk rubs softly against your skin. There's no way you *won't* be bringing the right woman to the bedroom after that!

GIVE YOURSELF AT LEAST ONE TREAT A WEEK—AND WORK YOUR WAY UP TO ONE TREAT A DAY!

I can already hear what some of you are thinking—"No way do I have time for that!" Now, before you turn the page, take a moment to realize

SENSUOUS BATHS

When it comes to pampering, there's nothing quite like the luxury of a delightfully scented, sensuous bath. Here are some of my favorite recipes. You can buy the glycerin in any drugstore, and you can find the essential oils in a health-food store or even in some pharmacies. Stir the glycerin and water together, then add the essential oils. Use immediately or store in a pretty jar with a tight-fitting lid.

Lavender-Patchouli Sensory Wake-up Call
You'll emerge from this tingly bath both relaxed and awakened to all your sensory possibilities.
5 drops of lavender oil
4 drops of patchouli oil
1 quart of distilled water
4 ounces liquid glycerin

Mind-Clearing Eucalyptus-Rosemary-Mint Soak
This combination of pungent eucalyptus and stimulating rosemary-mint will revive your spirits and energize you for an evening of great sex.

6 drops of eucalyptus oil
3 drops of peppermint oil
3 drops of rosemary oil
1 quart of distilled water
4 ounces liquid glycerin

Life Is Just a Bowl of Cherries Bath Scrub

For those nights when you want to feel fresh, new, and innocent, you can scrub away your cares with a washcloth or loofah, or you can just add this mix to your bathwater and let it soak into your skin.

$1/2$ cup unscented shampoo, such as baby shampoo
$3/4$ cup water
$1/2$ cup of coarse sea salt, kosher salt, or Epsom salts
15 drops cherry fragrance oil

Arabian Nights Bath Salts

Add a few tablespoons to your bathwater and then dream of fairy-tale lovers and steamy romance.

4 drops of musk fragrance or essential oil
3 drops of jasmine fragrance or essential oil
3 cups of coarse sea salts
1 cup of baking soda
2 teaspoons liquid glycerin

Cleopatra's Milk Bath

I don't advise you to imitate Cleopatra's history with men, but she did have an over-the-top sex life! Her daily bath rituals were legendary—now *there* was a woman who knew how to prepare herself for passion! You can pour these ingredients right into your bathwater to treat yourself like the Queen of Egypt.

2 cups powdered milk
2–3 drops of rose or lavender oil

You can also use $1/4$ cup Sensuous Bath Salts and some Luxurious Bath & Shower Gel from our RomantaTherapy collection for a sensuous, stimulating bath. Take a Vibrating Bath Ball into your tub with you and massage yourself from head to toe, stopping anyplace in between that feels good!

that I'm defining a "treat" in a *very* doable way: Five minutes that are devoted entirely to you and that make you feel happy *right then.* I know that for some of us, even five minutes is too much time to take out of a long and busy day, but with all my heart, I urge you to try. We all need some way to make ourselves feel special and entitled as our day wears on. If your entire day is devoted to others, you run the risk of forgetting that you, too, deserve lovely experiences—including fabulous, romantic sex. I've graduated to monthly leg waxes and facials, and twice-monthly massages, manicures, and pedicures—my salon loves to see me coming!—but I asked the women around my office what they'd do with their five minutes. Here are some of their ideas:

- sipping a glass of wine while walking outside in my garden and enjoying the weather
- slipping into an outfit—maybe even a fancy outfit—that feels good to wear
- having some chocolate
- just being—enjoying a quiet time
- indulging in a fantasy
- drinking a cup of coffee, tea, hot chocolate, or hot milk—perhaps flavored with some Bailey's Irish Cream . . .
- reading
- taking a hot shower
- sensuously removing my makeup and applying tingly toner and silky moisturizer for a five-minute "mini-facial" as a nightly time to unwind
- meditating
- listening to music and/or dancing to music
- having someone else give me a five-minute massage or a five-minute foot rub (By the way, my six-year-old granddaughter loves to do this—she pretends she's a masseuse!)

Almost as important as what you do with your five minutes is the spirit in which you approach it. Declare this your treat time. Make it a big deal, at least to yourself. Be in the moment and enjoy your time to the fullest. Tell yourself, "I'm doing this because it's my treat, and it's fabulous—and I'm fabulous, and I deserve it!" And when your partner realizes what a difference there is in the bedroom after you have treated yourself so well, he may even volunteer to do the dishes—just to make sure you get all the treat time you need!

Be in the Mood: Setting the Stage for Romance

If you want romance to happen, you need to be ready for it—in your mind, body, and spirit—and you need to be in the setting you create for you and your partner. You can't simply show up for a night of sex, tired and cranky, and expect to have a wonderful time. Nor can you walk into a neglected bedroom whose every detail screams, "I'm too busy to enjoy my life!" and expect to find a romantic haven. If you want to enjoy romance to the fullest, you have to spend some time getting in the mood. Here are some ideas for making sure that you're ready for whatever passionate possibilities come your way.

THE *Passion Diva's Guide* TO BEING *IN THE* MOOD

PREPARE THE PLAYGROUND

Your bedroom isn't just a place to sleep. It's also the setting for your nights (and maybe your days!) of pleasure. So make your bedroom an oasis, a place of refuge, and a site for your most intimate and romantic communication.

In my opinion, it all starts with the bed. Invest in a good mattress— firm, but soft. (A firm mattress with a pillow top on either side can give you the best of both worlds.) I know mattresses can be expensive, but consider that you spend at least one-third of your life sleeping on that mattress—and ideally, a great deal more time there having excellent sex! Find some comfortable blankets and pillows, perhaps a nice feather duvet. Play with colors and textures so that your bed feels like a cloud and looks like a haven.

Then consider the sheets. Perhaps invest in Egyptian cotton or silk, and on the nights you're planning to have sex, spray some perfume on the sheets for a lovely scent, or perhaps our own special pear-fragranced Silky Sheets spray to make your cotton *feel* like silk. (Allow for about fifteen minutes after spraying to let the fragrance settle.) Create an unencumbered area that's not cluttered with household obligations or work-related chores. And if you possibly can, get the TV out of the way. Or at least turn it off and cover it with a scarf. Both of you should be focusing on other kinds of entertainment, not to mention that watching TV or using computers within an hour of bedtime can disrupt your sleep cycles.

Remember the role of all five senses, and put on a CD that plays soothing, sexy, or romantic music. Or go for one of those "nature sounds" CDs: re-create the aura of rain falling or evoke a nighttime forest. Throw another pretty scarf over your lamp or change to a colored bulb. Through your attention to detail, show your partner that you've taken the time to honor the relationship. Sometimes bringing the right woman to the bedroom is also bringing the right bedroom to your man!

READ SEXY BOOKS

Reading can be a terrific way to put you in the mood. A good sexy book can bring your sexual feelings to life, so that by the time you come to the bedroom, you're turned on and rarin' to go.

In fact, scientific evidence shows that reading sexy scenes fills your body with the same arousal hormones as does actual foreplay. What a terrific illustration of Passion Diva principle #8: *Your most important sex organ is your brain!* One of these hormones is called phenylethylamine (PEA for short). Similar to amphetamine, PEA boosts sexual arousal and helps fight depression. It's the same ingredient that makes chocolate so satisfying—with the added bonus that reading is calorie-free! Sexy reading material can also boost your levels of such sex-stimulating hormones as estrogen and testosterone.

You may like to keep your favorite stash of sexy books tucked away in a bedroom drawer, or perhaps even read one in the tub. Besides using books for your own private RomantaTherapy, you can also make them part of foreplay or Passion Chat. Share your favorite sexy passages with your partner as a prelude to lovemaking or read them over the phone for long-distance sex. I believe so strongly in the power of reading that I asked my Passion Consultants to share their favorite romantic books with me. Here are some of their top choices: *All Night Long,* by Jayne Ann Krentz; *Angel's Fall,* by Nora Roberts; *Beauty's Punishment,* by A. N. Roquelaure (also found under Anne Rice); *Beauty's Release,* by A. N. Roquelaure (also found under Anne Rice); *Belinda,* by Anne Rice; *Born in Fire* trilogy, by Nora Roberts; *The Butcher and Other Erotica,* by Alina Reyes; *Chances,* by Jackie Collins; *The Claiming of Sleeping Beauty,* by Anne Rice; *Coming Out,* by Danielle Steele; *La Cucina,* by Lily Prior; *Delta of Venus,* by Anais Nin; *Exit to Eden,* by Anne Rampling (also found under Anne Rice); *Grand Passions,* by Jayne Anne Krentz; *Henry and June,* by Anais Nin; *Journey,* by Danielle Steele; *Like Water for Chocolate,* by Laura Esquivel; *Little Birds,* by Anais Nin; *Lovers,* by Judith Krantz; *Lovers & Players,* by Jackie Collins; *Nectar,* by Lily Prior; *The Other Side of Me,* by Sidney Sheldon; *Possessions,* by Judith Michael; *The Real Mother,* by Judith Michael; *Sleeping Beauty,* by A. N. Roquelaure (also found under Anne Rice); *Spring Collection,* by Judith Krantz; *Tell Me Your Dreams,* by Sidney Sheldon; and *Temptation,* by Jude Deveraux.

ENGAGE THE POWER OF FANTASY

One of the reasons men tend to have a higher sex drive than many women is that they are more comfortable with fantasizing than we are. Some men think about sex as often as every seven minutes, and most of the time, those thoughts are fantasy—what he'd like to do, what he might do, what he'd never do in real life but nevertheless enjoys imagining. Have you ever met a man who seemed continually "in the mood," as though sex might happen at any minute, even if you were in a meeting or at the post office? Sexy men have that indefinable aura because they actively fantasize about sex even when they're *not* on their way to the bedroom, and with a little practice, you can do the same. You can fantasize about your partner, about strangers, even about situations that, in real life, you'd never actually choose. On some level, your brain—that super-powerful sex organ!—can't tell the difference between what you're actually doing and what you're only thinking about: It starts the sex hormones flowing just as it does when you're reading. So let your imagination roam free!

Opening the door to your fantasies allows you to be in the mood more fully and quickly when it comes time to actually having sex. So don't limit your fantasies to bedtime. Allow yourself to fantasize in the shower, at the store, at work, while making dinner. Become aware of specific details that turn you on—textures, colors, clothes, settings. Then you'll have lots of images to bring to mind—or even into your actual practice—during sex; either way, they'll wake you up, making you more tingly, alive, eager, passionate—and that's definitely the right woman to bring into the bedroom!

I wanted to find out what the guests at our Passion Parties were fantasizing about, so I asked our Passion Consultants to do a little research. Here are the scenarios they reported as most common:

On the beach
In flight (first class, of course!)
With a sexy stranger
In a public place
With a movie or music star
While other people are watching, either out in the open or from the
   shadows

LET PHEROMONES WORK FOR YOU

Pheromones are the chemical scents that every animal on earth produces, with the goal of attracting sexual mates. We aren't consciously aware of smelling pheromones, but believe me, we *do* pick them up unconsciously and respond accordingly. We at Passion Parties are so convinced of their ability to spark sexual attraction that we've created our own pheromone fragrance called Rendezvous. We also sell Pure Instinct Attraction Cologne, a unisex product made from artificial pheromones that mimic the action of real ones. I won't guarantee that these artificial pheromones or natural fragrances work in every single situation, but I've seen too many reports on their effectiveness to take any chances: I never go out without dabbing some on my pulse points and behind my ears, as well as in some more mysterious places— behind my knees, in the bend of my arm, in my navel. Pheromones have been known to turn an admirer into a lover, and an acquaintance into your biggest fan. If you work on commission or for tips, expect to see an increase when you wear pheromones. If you need to talk to your boss about something important—a raise, a new assignment, or a Monday off—be sure to wear your pheromones. Male or female, your boss may find it that much harder to refuse your request. Our Passion Consultant Laura, from South Carolina, reported that one of her guests, a single woman, never had to pay for a single drink when she went clubbing wearing her pheromones. The men were literally lining up to pay. I know what she's talking about, because I always wear pheromones when I travel, and I've sure gotten a lot of mysterious first-class upgrades! Zoya, a consultant from New Jersey, told me that she could go to bed wearing pink rollers and flannel gown, and if she was also wearing her pheromones, her man always found her hot and sexy.

We also include another type of natural attractant, the flowery scent of plumeria, in the rest of our RomantaTherapy lotions and potions, so that whenever you use them, you'll carry this attractive fragrance. You can even wash your lingerie in fragrance-infused bath gel such as RomantaTherapy Luxurious Bath & Shower Gel, and let the romance take over.

Now, why am I talking about pheromones and plumeria under the

SEXY BETS

Margie, a Passion Consultant from southern California, shared this wonderful idea with me, and I can't wait to share it with you: Make sexy bets with your partner. If you are arguing over who starred in a particular movie, say, "I bet you ten minutes of oral sex that I'm right." If you're not thrilled about oral sex (or if he's not), choose an activity that you both like. Make this a very special kind of bet where everyone wins.

You can use the same approach for housework, too: "You'll do the dishes and I'll sweep the floor and whoever finishes first gets ten minutes of his or her favorite sexual act." Of course, you've got to make these wagers about activities you really enjoy, because you never want to make sex a bargaining chip or use it to manipulate your partner. But integrating sexual pleasure into your conversations and household chores—now, *that's* what I call being a Passion Diva!

heading of "being in the mood"? Well, getting that kind of admiring attention—from both men and women!—reminds you at every turn that you're a sexual, alluring, and physical creature. When your daily life is full of sexual attention—or even just friendly glances—that can only help when it comes time to bring the right woman into the bedroom.

Be Committed: Making Sure That Romance Can Thrive

There's one final component involved in bringing the right woman to the bedroom—and that's your commitment to good times for both you and your partner while you're in there. Just a little effort can allow you to expand outward the attention you've been paying to your own body, mind, spirit, and sexuality, so that you are also attending to the physical and emotional environment in which the two of you will make love. This expanded effort may require only a slight shift in focus from thinking primarily about yourself to thinking about the relationship.

For example, Cindy, a Nevada housewife and Passion Consultant, told me that the single biggest change in her own sexual pleasure came when she began wearing more lingerie, not so much because of how she felt about it as for the effect it had on her husband.

"I have never been a lingerie kind of girl, because I thought it was too expensive and I'd rather spend the money on something else," Alicia explained. "But once I started wearing it, and saw the response that it got out of my husband—especially Passion Parties' Fishnet Fantasy body stocking—I began trying to buy something new every few months!" Alicia was bringing the right woman to the bedroom in both senses—doing something that she knew would give her partner pleasure, and then deriving her own pleasurable anticipation from the romantic treatment she knew she'd get as a result.

Or consider Martha, the fifty-year-old woman who attended a Passion Party in Appleton, Wisconsin. As the party wound to a close, Martha met with the Passion Consultant in the private ordering room and asked for a wedding gift suggestion. She'd only come to the party, she explained, to get something for her favorite niece. Lois, the consultant, recommended some bath products and then asked Martha if she wanted to buy anything for herself and her husband.

"Oh, no," Martha said promptly. "We don't do that anymore."

"Why don't you just buy one of these couple's games," Lois suggested. "Just to try."

Martha thought about it for a minute. She was one of those real Midwestern ladies who never likes to say no if she can help it, so after a while she said, "I'll buy it if you put it in a double bag."

Lois was pretty sure that was the end of it. But a few weeks later, as often happens, she got a call. Martha had tossed the game on a top shelf in a closet and forgotten all about it. But her husband found it, opened it, and asked her what it was. When Martha explained, her husband said, "Okay, let's play." One thing led to another: The game opened the door to a new kind of intimate communication, and that in turn paved the way for a long, lovely session of making love. "And do you know,"

Martha told the consultant, "the next day, that was the first time my husband *ever* sent me a dozen roses!"

Clearly, Martha had brought the right woman to the bedroom—and then some! As her story shows, being committed to a good time for both of you doesn't have to involve enormous effort. In fact, sometimes I think of this part as the "microwave of love," because you can do it in less than five minutes to help prepare the evening for romance.

THE *Passion Diva's Guide* TO BEING COMMITTED

SET A REGULAR DATE NIGHT

For those of you in a regular relationship—especially one that involves children—I can't stress the importance of this one too strongly. For your relationship to remain vital and nourishing to you both, you have to give it some attention, and what better way to do that than to have a regular date? Even if you're both swamped with work, commit to having one two-hour date every two weeks, when it's just the two of you enjoying each other's company. And if you're too exhausted and stressed out to manage both a two-hour date and a chance to make love, honestly, I'd recommend the date. The sex you eventually have will be much better and more satisfying if you feel like you're not having it with a stranger.

I know it can be difficult to make this kind of time when children are involved, especially if you don't have a lot of money for a sitter. But what if you put your kids to bed and then just sat together in the back yard or on your front steps, having a glass of wine and enjoying each other's company? Or perhaps you and another couple can trade off: You leave your kids at their house one night, and they leave theirs with you another. Maybe you can set up a babysitting co-op. One night, you take the neighbor's kids to sleep at your house; another night, your neighbor returns the favor. Maybe, too, you and your partner can have a day date—two hours on the weekend while your kids are playing at a friend's house. You may have to trade off for that, too, but I'm willing to bet it will be worth it. If you allow your whole life to rotate around your kids and don't make time for you as a couple, what's going to happen when the kids are gone? And meanwhile, what kind of loving adult relationship are you modeling for your children? Two hours every other week. It may not be easy, but you can do it if you're committed.

PRESENT YOURSELF AS A SEXUAL PERSON

Let's be very clear. I am *not* saying you should imitate anyone's idea of a "sexy woman." I *am* saying you should come up with a look and style that makes *you* feel sexy, and then present yourself accordingly. If wearing comfortable old sweats gives you a sensuous, tingly feeling, you're going to communicate that to your partner just as much as if you were wearing a red teddy and black garters. But if *you* feel like a more sexual, alluring creature in the teddy and garters, then give yourself and your partner the chance to see you that way.

Of course, there are lots of sexual styles—as many, probably, as there are women. Perhaps you like clingy cotton T-shirts of deep purple or bright rose. Maybe you enjoy satin pajamas or a silk robe. You might feel at your sexiest in workout clothes that show off your plus-size curves or in a cozy sweater that only hints at the delights beneath. Whatever your style—even if you have to experiment a bit to find it—I strongly encourage you to find a "casual, at-home" look that brings out your sensual side as well as your need for comfort. It's hard enough feeling like a Passion Diva when you're working a fourteen-hour day or running around after your toddler, but if you're wearing clothes that scream, "Don't look at me, I'm just trying to get through the evening," you'll have an even harder time bringing the right woman to the bedroom. So I'm going to give you two choices: Either wear those sloppy clothes to get you through the evening and then, an hour before bed, change into something sexier; or else spend the whole evening in casual but sexy outfits that make you feel like the Passion Diva that you are.

RELATE TO YOUR PARTNER AS A SEXUAL PERSON

Again, I know this can be hard, especially after a difficult day or when children are around. But the effort will be worth it, because both of you will remain aware and alive to the passionate connection that can exist between you. Particularly on the evenings when you expect to have sex, look into your partner's eyes a few times during dinner and make that silent connection that can be so powerful. Create your own set of little buzzwords, as described in Chapter 2, to let each of you know that sex is forthcoming—making cookies, feeding the cat, or whatever code the two of you invent. Help your partner get his mind off the events of his day and onto the here and now with you. Offer him a massage or a foot rub; suggest taking a shower together and then scrub his back. Or, if you prefer, ask him for that kind of attention. Lots of guys are happy to oblige when they know what their woman wants of them, particularly if they see it as part of a whole evening of preparation for sex. (What they don't like is either being "demanded of" or having to guess.)

If you're in doubt about how to help your man "step up," ask him: "What should I do to help you unwind, so that when it's just us later tonight, you'll be fully present?" Whether subtly or directly, try to engage your guy and give him what *he* needs to make the transition from "stressed out" to "make out."

Lots of women tell me that the household chores become so overwhelming, they're just too tired to have sex, and then they come to resent the husbands who expect them to make love after an evening of housework. If your thinking falls along those lines, I have two questions for you:

1. Do those dishes really *have* to get done, especially if a night of romantic sex is the alternative?
2. If the dishes really *do* need to get done, what about asking for help? You might say, "Honey, if you help me do the dishes, we might be able to get to bed earlier," with a suggestive wink. Or

swat him with the dishtowel and murmur seductively, "If you'll dry, we could be done a whole lot faster." Turn your requests for help into a flirty offer rather than nagging, and see if your sex life—and your relationship—improve.

From Romance to Foreplay

So far, we've been focusing on RomantaTherapy—what to do for yourself so that you can bring the right woman to the bedroom. But I can't resist sharing with you the story of Wendy, a part-time Passion Consultant and full-time librarian in New Hampshire, who turned her private RomantaTherapy bathing rituals into a loving, sensuous connection with her husband.

My husband isn't always the most romantic lover but when he is, he goes all out for me. One night, he knew that I needed a bit of pampering and called me into the bathroom. He had the lights down, some candles glowing, and a nice hot bubble bath waiting for me. As I sank into the warm water, he returned with a glass of wine. He left me to soak and relax, returning later for a relaxing, sensual back wash. He then led me from the tub to our bedroom, where he had been preparing for my massage.

While I was in the tub, he put a cotton blanket in the dryer to warm up. He turned down the sheets and invited me to climb in. With warm blankets wrapped all around me, he gently pulled the covers off and proceeded to give me a hot-oil massage. His tender touches melted away all of my tension and stress. Then his caresses turned sensual. Removing his clothes, he joined me in the warm nest of blankets. Words were not needed to express our love for each other that night. The look of love in our eyes and the feeling of our bodies touching expressed the deep connection we have for one another. I fell into a deep and peaceful sleep that night in the loving arms of my husband. He gave me a night I will never forget.

Wendy was able to enjoy this unforgettable evening of romance and love because she had done a wonderful job of preparing for passion. And clearly, she had taught her husband how to prepare for passion, as well! You'll read more about love baths and massage in Chapter 6 as we move on from preparation to the first steps of the big event itself: Foreplay. But first, let's stock up your Passion Pantry with plenty of RomantaTherapy treats.

In Your Passion Pantry

- **Pure Satisfaction UniSEX Enhancement Gel.** Apply a small amount of this stimulating gel on and around your clitoris, massaging it for several minutes into the soft tissue on the underside of your clitoral hood. You can also enhance feeling in your vaginal area with a bit of gel there. If you put some on in the morning, it will keep you feeling tingly and sexy all day long.

- **Some sexy books.** Don't forget to stimulate your most important sex organ—your brain! Try some Judith Krantz, Danielle Steel, Anne Rice, or Sidney Sheldon to turn you on before your partner ever even enters the bedroom.

- **Mood music.** Whether you go for the classical romance of Pachelbel's *Canon* or the smooth stylings of Luther Vandross, you can use music to get you and your partner in the mood, helping you make that transition from stressed out to make out.

- **RomantaTherapy Sensuous Bath Salts.** These soothing Dead Sea salts relieve the tension of the day, helping to prepare your mind and body for passion.

- **RomantaTherapy Luxurious Bath & Shower Gel.** The naturally attractive scent of plumeria helps you feel passionate and sensual, while the aloe vera in this gel pampers and softens your skin.

- **RomantaTherapy Alluring Body Lotion.** Our nongreasy, aloe vera–based lotion leaves your skin feeling irresistibly touchable during your sensuous massage, while the naturally attractive plumeria fragrance will draw your guy closer, and closer, and closer . . .

- **RomantaTherapy Soft & Silky UniSEX Shaving Crème and RomantaTherapy Soft & Silky After Shave Protection Mist.** You'll be amazed at how silky and smooth your skin will get with this special shaving cream, and how beautifully the after-shave mist protects and moisturizes your skin, discouraging possible irritation to sensitive areas.
- **Scented candles.** Soft lighting and fragrance will help set the mood in your bedroom. Consider using votive candle holders for extra protection against fire.
- **Vibrating Bath Ball.** Here's a great Diva secret: Recline in the bathtub or Jacuzzi, place the Vibrating Bath Ball gently at the back of your neck, and feel your stress dissolve. Or move the Vibrating Bath Ball from your neck to your toes, stopping anyplace in between that feels good.

➸ 6 ᐣ

Foreplay

Recently I saw a rerun of an old *Friends* episode that I thought perfectly exemplified the problems that so many couples face when it comes to foreplay. The perpetually single guy, Chandler, had just started dating a new girlfriend with whom he was madly, passionately in love, but unfortunately, the sex was not so exciting for her. Chandler confides in Rachel and Monica, and Monica, ever ready to take charge, sets out to explain the secret to great sex. The female body is divided into seven erogenous zones, she explains, places where the woman is most likely to feel sensual and sexual pleasure. On a piece of paper we never see, she diagrams the various zones, giving each a separate number, and then becoming a bit excited herself as she talks Chandler through the process. "Okay," she says, "start with 1. Then a little 2. Then go on to 3. Then maybe 4. Then mix it up a little, 4, 5, 4, 5, 6, 6, 6—7 . . . 7 . . . 7!!!!!" Later in the show, Chandler's ecstatic new girlfriend bursts into Monica's living room. "Thank you!" she cries. "Thank you, thank you, *thank you!*"

I really enjoyed this episode, because it was so clear that Chandler was eager to find out what made his girlfriend's motor hum. He just needed a little help. And, as the episode also made clear, foreplay is the key. You don't want to skip all the way to zone number 7 without paying attention to the other zones first. So we might say that foreplay is what you do together to become aroused before the activities that lead directly to climax—from your first gentle kiss to mutual self-pleasuring and anything in between. (Foreplay often includes oral sex, as well, but that area of sexual pleasure is so important and unique that we've devoted all of Chapter 8 to it.) Or we might broaden our definition and say that foreplay is anything that makes you and your partner feel good on your way to sex: a sensual massage, a delicious bath or shower ritual, a striptease. And of course, there's Passion Diva principle #7—*For sex at night, foreplay starts in the morning,* which means that you might consider foreplay to include the sexy little note you left in his briefcase or the seductive smile you gave him as he left for work.

The important thing to remember is that foreplay isn't separate from sex—for women, in particular, foreplay *is* sex, or, as we say here at Passion Parties, foreplay is *the* play. Beginning with how you feel about your guy and continuing on to the moment when you reach orgasm, you might see everything that the two of you do together as a kind of foreplay—a sexual, sensual, and emotional expression of your feelings for one another.

In this chapter, we're not going to go that broad—we'll focus much more specifically on the actual things you might do to make the sparks fly, and how the two of you can continue to please and arouse each other up to the moment when intercourse begins (at which point we'll go on to Part III). I want you to hold this very broad definition of fore-play in your mind, however, because for a lot of couples, this is where the problems arise. Many of us have been conditioned to think of sex as the moment when the guy penetrates the woman, and then, if that moment isn't satisfying, we're at a loss. But in almost all such cases, it's not the intercourse that lacks excitement, passion, or romance. The problem lies in what came before, or rather, in what *didn't* come before.

If you're lucky, your partner already understands the importance of foreplay. Often, though, men have been socialized to believe that their job is to "get to the finish line" as quickly as possible. They may be shy about knowing how to please a woman, or unconfident, or worried that their lack of experience will show. A man—especially a younger man—may be anxious about the prospect of climaxing too soon. Men don't always realize, either, how different every woman can be; perhaps your guy is doing moves on you that his former girlfriend thought were terrific, never suspecting that he's leaving you cold. Or if your man's previous experience was with a woman who hadn't yet found her own Passion Diva, he may have learned that his partner actually preferred him to get it all over with as soon as possible, because she didn't seem particularly interested in sexual pleasure.

Of course, some guys are just plain selfish, but I honestly believe those cases are rare. The vast majority of men are thrilled to please their sexual partners, even if they need a little guidance when it comes to slowing down the process and enjoying every moment of the journey. Sex is a journey, not a destination, though I'll be the first to admit that the destination can be fun! It's a lot more fun, though—for both you *and* him—if you take your time, build excitement up to its most intense, and save the actual intercourse for when you're both overcome with desire. In this chapter, you'll find suggestions for how to do just that.

From His Point of View . . .

Let's start by assuming that your guy is happy to do anything that makes *you* happy, especially in bed. He loves knowing that he gives you pleasure and takes direction like a champ. But he ought to enjoy foreplay for his own sake as well as yours. What might make him feel good before intercourse begins? What might arouse his five senses and intensify his anticipation? What parts of his body hold secret treasure-troves of pleasure? The more excited your guy is before intercourse begins, the more intense and pleasurable his orgasms will be, too.

Both you *and* your partner will benefit from extending foreplay to make it a more thoroughly fulfilling all-body experience for the two of you. Part of foreplay is learning what your partner likes and making sure that he gets it. Each of you needs to take to heart Passion Diva principle #4—*If you take responsibility for your pleasure, your pleasure will pay you back*—while at the same time paying attention to each other's pleasure, too.

What's hard for guys, I think, is to feel as though they have total responsibility for both your pleasure and their own. That can make even the most experienced guy sometimes feel as though he just wants to get the whole thing over with, rather than risk failure and humiliation. Much of this problem stems from old-fashioned notions of the guy being the leader in all things, especially in the bedroom. And sometimes our men are more experienced than we are, and sometimes we do want them to take the lead. But men are well aware that women see them this way, and they in turn feel anxious or embarrassed when they don't intuitively know exactly how to please every woman they're intimate with. It may even be that you are actually more relaxed than he is about trying something new or making an unexpected suggestion.

RELAX YOUR WAY INTO ECSTASY

You and your guy will enjoy foreplay a whole lot more if you're both relaxed, and one of the best ways to relax is simply to breathe. If you need to make the transition away from the day's worries and clear your mind before you can get in the mood, you might simply take ten long, slow, deep breaths, breathing in and out on a count of first two, then four, then six, then eight, and finally, ten—a very loooooooong, deep breath that will slow down your heartbeat and open you to pleasure. To breathe in a deeper and more relaxed way, put one hand gently on your tummy and feel that area puff out as you inhale; then feel it sink back down as you exhale. Your goal is to breathe from your diaphragm, way down in your abdomen, rather than from your chest. You'll be amazed at how quickly you relax once you do.

If you like this approach to relaxing and opening, listen to one of the sensual-relaxation CDs in the Mental Foreplay collection by www.MoreInLove.com and allow fresh, life-giving oxygen to fill every fiber of your being, bringing a kind of euphoria that is a terrific preparation for sex. After all, the more relaxed you are, the more pleasure your body can receive.

If you do happen to be blessed with that one special guy who can perform bedroom magic based on intuition, good for you, but even he may not always feel so confident that he's chosen right, without feedback from you. So this chapter is all about helping you to imagine some things that might please you, please him, and please the two of you together. Be patient, be creative, and above all, have fun! Remember, no one gets it all right the first time, and anyway, perfection isn't the goal—pleasure is, and that goes for both of you!

Foreplay: The Basics

Let's go back to that episode of *Friends*. I'm curious about what was on Monica's numbered list, aren't you? Since I'll never really know, I made my own list of sensual places on a woman's body—and guess what? All of them are pretty sexy places for guys, too. I even came up with more than seven! So if you'd like a very basic road map for some satisfying foreplay, think of kissing, stroking, or otherwise stimulating the following body parts. Either of you can take this list in any order you like, and of course, it's fine to skip a place or two. And as Monica pointed out, you are invited to mix it up a little—vary the order or go back and forth between two or more areas. But if you're looking for a great place to start your foreplay, you can't go wrong with some version of the following:

1. mouth
2. throat
3. ears
4. breasts or chest (Men's nipples are often very sensitive and men, too, like to be kissed, caressed, and teased there.)
5. back
6. feet
7. buttocks
8. stomach
9. tops of thighs

10. inside of thighs
11. genitals (Don't worry—we're going to give a *lot* more detail about this one, for both of you, toward the end of the chapter!)

As I said, those are the basics, but, of course, every person has his or her own special places. Here are some others you might want to add—can you think of still more?

inside your elbow
the back of your neck
under your shoulder blade
the back of your knee
your belly button

The Sensuous Art of Kissing

Ah, kissing! For most of us, romantic kissing is our first type of sexual contact, and most women never get tired of it, even after moving on to more advanced activities. If you were dating in junior high or high school, maybe you had long make-out sessions with your guy, where kissing was pretty much the main event. Then, eventually, you went on to other things. But now, perhaps, it's time to go back to kissing, not instead of the other pleasures but as a wonderful prelude to them.

According to the *Kama Sutra,* the Indian manual of sexual pleasure, there are over seventeen types of kisses and over four hundred different places lovers can enjoy kissing. So if you *really* like kissing, pick up a copy of the *Kama Sutra* and start exploring it with your mate!

Meanwhile, here are some fabulous kisses that you and your partner might try. And remember, practice makes pleasure! Remember, too, that it's okay to be creative—even a little sneaky—about getting what you want. If you feel comfortable asking straight out for a longer kissing session or a chance to try some of the techniques listed below, that's terrific. If not, leave this book lying around with these pages marked.

SEXY SIGNALS: WAYS TO GET HIM
IN THE MOOD

Since foreplay starts in the morning, what can you do to get your guy in the mood before he even gets to the bedroom? Here are some favorite suggestions from our Passion Consultants—and if you can come up with any more, drop us a line! We're always looking for new ideas.

- That morning, lay out your silky underthings—and his silky underthings—in a place where he can see them.
- Leave a piece of lingerie on his pillow.
- Send him a sexy text message or e-mail (though not on the company account!) or leave him a voice mail message. "Can't wait for tonight," or "See you at 10," or "You know what I'm waiting for" are all guaranteed to have him meeting you that night halfway in the mood already.
- Put a sexy note in his briefcase, lunch box, or gym clothes.
- When he gets home (or meets you at your home), suggest that you take a shower together. Or draw a bubble bath and invite him in.
- Flirt with him outrageously over dinner.
- Meet him at the door in a raincoat—with lingerie or nothing at all on underneath.
- Set out some sensuous foods. Passion Consultants recommend the following, either because they are traditionally considered aphrodisiacs or simply because they are very sensual to eat: asparagus, caramel, chocolate, chocolate pudding, fresh figs, grapes, ice cream cones, jumbo shrimp, orange segments, oysters, raspberries, ripe peaches, strawberries, whipped cream. Eat them slowly, sensuously, licking your fingers, letting the juices flow . . . maybe even feed them to each other, licking each other's fingers . . . mmmmmm. Now who's ready for a little foreplay?

Or suggest a contest: "What if I set the timer for five minutes and we just kissed for that whole time? Come on! Let's see if we can do it!" As we saw in Chapter 2, positive communication is always welcome. What guy wouldn't want to hear, "I love kissing you, and I'd like to do more of it"? If you're married, you might say, "Don't kiss me as though I'm

your wife, kiss me like I'm the lover you just can't wait to seduce!"
Model for your guy how to approach kissing in a passionate but lighthearted spirit, pop some breath mints, and then, let the kissing begin!

THE *Passion Diva's Guide* TO FABULOUS KISSES

CLASSIC FRENCH

Start kissing gently with your lips just slightly parted. You can either
close your eyes or keep them open and continue looking into your
partner's eyes. Now lightly draw your tongue across his lips and gently
prod his lips apart. As your mate opens his mouth, you can begin to
slowly explore his tongue with yours, using a light licking and flicking
motion. Or you might try sucking very gently on his tongue, or using
your tongue to explore other areas of his mouth. The roof of the mouth
is very sensitive, so try tickling it with your tongue. Or caress the sides
of his mouth with the sides of your tongue.

LOWER LIP TUG

Begin with a gentle kiss, your lips just slightly parted. Then use your
lips to softly tug and suck his lower lip, moving back to gentle kissing
every few seconds.

TASTY KISSES

Here are several tasty variations on how foods and flavors can make
your kissing even more delicious:

- **Chocolate kiss.** Take a bite of chocolate and then French kiss,
  spreading the flavor throughout both your mouths. Try it with any
  chocolate you enjoy, but consider the advantages of the Milky Way,
  which has creamy caramel inside!

- **Menthol kiss.** Apply a tingly edible menthol balm to your lips for an extra-heightened sensation. You can use any menthol product such as our Nipple Nibblers, and as the name suggests, you can put that other places as well! More about that later.

- **Pop Rock kiss.** Put a few Pop Rocks in your mouth for an explosion of kissing fun and flavor.

- **Trade-off kiss.** One of you sucks on cinnamon candy, and the other pops in a mint. While French kissing, switch them from time to time.

BREATH EXCHANGE

To create a major anticipation during a hot moment, just barely touch your partner's lips with your lips slightly parted. Then inhale your partner's breath as he exhales. When you exhale, he inhales your breath, and the two of you continue to exchange breath. After you've got the hang of it, you can move your head slowly to experience different sensations, all while touching your lips on and off of his very slightly. It's a very teasing sort of kiss and builds tremendous passion.

TOUCH KISS

After you and your partner have been making out for a while, vary the pace by touching just the tips of your tongues, no lips involved. Try it both ways: with your tongues still and with them moving.

LAP KISS

While your partner is lying with his head in your lap, lean over and kiss him. Your bottom lip will be on your partner's top lip, and vice versa. You can even French kiss while in this position.

THE BUTTERFLY

Put your eye quite close to your partner's cheek and flutter your lashes upon his skin. You can also flutter your lashes on his lips.

THE NUZZLE

Gently using your nose, nuzzle your partner in all the places on his face and throat where he might enjoy being kissed. This can be a very tender, playful way to begin, continue, or transition out of a kissing session.

When You Don't Like the Way He Kisses You . . .

I was surprised to see this topic, too, taken up in prime-time TV, this time on the popular program *Boston Legal.* One of the lawyers—a hunky blond ex-Marine who could clearly get any woman he wanted—confesses to his pretty colleague that his girlfriends keep leaving him because he's such a lousy kisser. The colleague, of course, has to demonstrate, and—well, you can imagine what happens next. But I loved the fact that the show was so clear about the problem: Even a handsome, virile, big-money guy might *not* know how to kiss, and it was up to some woman to teach him better.

So if your guy needs a little help on this front, no harm, no foul. Maybe he's imitating something he saw in a movie or read about in a book, or maybe he's kissing you exactly the way his former girlfriend liked to be kissed and he hasn't yet figured out that your tastes are different. Just pull back gently, regroup, and start again, using a combination of words and actions to show him what you'd prefer. Here are some of the typical ways that kissing can go wrong, and how you can take the lead.

THE ST. BERNARD

Some guys just seem to do it with a lot of, well, slobbering. The direct approach is best in this case, but always, always be kind. Pull back and say sweetly, "Oh that's just too wet for me. Can we try it just a little dryer?" If he still doesn't get the idea, ask him to swallow, invite him to do nothing, and then insert your own appropriately moistened tongue inside his mouth. Demonstrate your best romantic French kiss, and then say, "Did that feel good? Now, *you* try it!"

THE SNAKE

What if he flicks his tongue quickly in and out of your mouth, really fast? Try teaching by example, holding on to his tongue with your lips and your own tongue, and gently, sweetly, sucking for a moment or two. If that doesn't work, you might say, "Honey, you're going a bit fast for me. I feel like I'm not getting enough of you. Here, I'll show you what I'd like," and then again, demonstrate with your tongue inside his mouth.

THE RACER

If your guy just likes to get in, get out, and call it a night, consider slowing him down with a chocolate kiss or one of our other tasty treats. Murmur, "I really want this to taste delicious . . . so let's take our time . . ."

THE DEEP THROAT

Some men like to go very deep into a woman's throat, and, in fact, some women like that. If you don't, then try taking hold of his tongue with your mouth and sucking on it or caressing it with your tongue, so that you're getting the depth you prefer. If you can't quite control the action this way, you might say, "Darling, the roof and sides of my mouth are *so* sensitive, and you feel *so* good there. Do you think you can stay in that part of my mouth? I'm just not getting enough of you there!"

THE GRAND CANYON KISS

If his kiss is so big your nose is in his mouth, you know he's gone too far. Try a few minutes of closed-mouth kissing to reestablish lip-to-lip contact. Then say, "I love your lips on mine. Do you think you can keep them there while we kiss? I'll feel so deprived if you don't."

THE TORNADO

Some men spin their tongues around in your mouth, and again, some women like this. But if you don't, once again, you might try taking hold of his tongue and caressing it with your own tongue and mouth, showing him how you'd like his tongue to lie. If this doesn't work, say, "I like to really savor you, and when you go so quickly, I just feel like I'm missing out. Can we slow things down so that I can really taste you?"

THE FLOP

What if his tongue just flops around inside your mouth—no direction, no control? Yet again, take hold of his tongue with your own mouth to model what you'd like. If necessary, say, "You know what I'd really love?

THE ELVIS KISS

Our Passion Consultant Nina, from Memphis, Tennessee, was actually lucky enough to be kissed by the King, Elvis Presley himself, when she was about seventeen. When she described this kiss to me, we both knew we had to share it with you. If you like, read Nina's story to your favorite guy and spend some time together practicing the Elvis Kiss.

I was standing at the gate of Graceland one day, when Elvis rode up on his golf cart, zipping by to give his fans a big hello. As he left, I asked if he would kiss me goodbye. To my amazement, he grabbed me playfully, took me in his arms, and slightly tilted his head toward mine. He planted those famous perfect lips, partially parted, on my mouth and tenderly sucked on my upper and lower lips. It was very soft and gentle. The kiss melted me all the way down into my soul and is one that I have never forgotten to this day.

Try kissing me like *this,*" and then show him, with your own tongue in his mouth.

Frequently Asked Kissing Questions

How Do I Handle My First Kiss with a New Partner?

If you're at the point of a kiss, you've already got some electricity happening, so relax. Take it slow and soft, starting with a closed mouth. See if the kiss takes a "French" direction, or else save the open mouth for the second kiss.

What Do I Do If Our Teeth Bang Together?

Again, no harm. Such things happen. Just back away and laugh it off. The more relaxed and lighthearted you are, the more he'll follow your lead. Then gently re-approach the kiss again.

How Do I Become a Great Kisser?

The secret to kissing is variety. Sometimes you're gentle, sometimes you're more enthusiastic. Don't be afraid to vary the pace and intensity. But above all, pay attention to how your partner is responding. Doing so will ensure that you're kissing in harmony and finding it an equally pleasurable experience. Tenderness, passion, sensitivity, and being relaxed about the whole situation are also terrific kissing aids.

How Do I Banish Bad Breath?

Bad breath often comes from poor dental care, so in addition to getting boosters from breath mints, brush your teeth twice a day, using a tongue brush, if necessary, and floss daily as well. Have regular dental cleanings and checkups.

PRIVATE PLACES

The skin is the largest sensory organ for both men and women, so don't overlook its out-of-the-way nooks and crannies. You may be surprised to find your lover thrills to you tickling his inner wrist, lightly brushing his eyelid with your lips, or caressing some other special, private place that only *you* have taken the time to discover. Here is where tenderness, sexual arousal, love, and romance meet and meld into a single exciting experience that neither of you will ever forget. And if your lover enjoys your special attentions, what better way to encourage him to attend to you in exactly the same careful and tender fashion?

Marvelous Massages

What's the largest erogenous organ on your body? What about on your lover's body?

If you answered "skin" both times, you were correct! Our skin covers every inch of us, and sometimes it's simply longing to be touched. Touch and massage can be a terrific intimate prelude to other kinds of sexual pleasure.

If you've never had a good massage, you might want to get one before trying to give one. Treat yourself to a professional massage—it's the ultimate in luxury pampering—and take mental notes about the kinds of strokes and pressure points that feel the best to you. Professional massage therapists know the importance of all five senses, so they often burn incense, use scented massage oils, warm their massage oils, play calming music in the background, and use soothing light to help you relax—all great mood-enhancing techniques that you can re-create at home.

For you and your partner, massages are a great way to begin an enchanted evening. You can massage each other either in a nonsexual way, with no intention of having sex, or as foreplay, with sex very much in mind. Both types of massages begin the same way. The difference

SET THE SCENE FOR YOUR MASSAGE:
THE BASICS

- Massage oils and creams—such as RomantaTherapy Sensual Massage Oil or Crèmesicle Edible Massage Cream—Orange
- A comfortable surface, covered with a sheet or blanket—your bed, the floor, even a professional massage table
- Mood candles
- Heated towels and robes—warm them up in the dryer
- Sensuous or soothing music
- Incense
- Essential oils
- Time—from thirty to sixty minutes for a relaxed, thorough massage

comes in the way they end. Either way, I encourage you to pay close attention to your partner's responses. This is one great way to learn a lot about where and how he likes to be touched. The same goes for him, when it's his turn to massage you. The massage doubles as your treat and his "learning experience."

THE *Passion Diva's Guide* TO MARVELOUS MASSAGES

- **Keep it warm.** Your partner will be naked when you give him a massage, so make sure to warm up everything that comes in contact with his skin. Use your dryer to preheat towels and linens. Warm up your hands by rubbing them briskly together before you touch him. Submerge your tube or jar of massage oil in a pot of hot water or let it stand for a few minutes under a running tap.

- **Keep it peaceful.** Shut off all phones, turn off the TV, and make your space as private as you can. This is your time to luxuriate in each other. Place candles—perhaps scented candles—around the massage area, and turn off any too-bright lights. Put on your favorite soothing music.

- **Keep it relaxing.** Have your partner begin facedown, with his hands stretched out by his sides. You might want to put a pillow under his stomach to ease any strain on his back. Some people like a pillow under their knees also. Start at the top by massaging his head with the tips of your fingers—with or without massage oils. Then apply a small amount of oil to your palms, rubbing your hands together to create some more warmth. Or for a terrific massage alternative, put some oil on a Super Deluxe Smitten Massage Mitt and insert a Mini Bullet inside the Mitt's little pocket. Either with your hands or with your Mini Bullet vibrator and Mitt, gently massage your partner's shoulders and biceps, then work your way down his back. Next, massage his buttocks, thighs, and calves, using your entire body to create more pressure on these larger muscles. Finally, attend to his feet, which are a very sexy part of the body and which connect to all of your body's organs and sexual-response zones. When you're ready, whisper gently in his ear, "Now turn over." Place a pillow under his knees—and if he's got a bad back, encourage him to leave his knees gently bent, feet flat on the floor or bed. Now begin once again from the top—scalp, face, shoulders, chest, hips, thighs, calves,

MASSAGE MITTENS

Love Smitten (for a firmer massage) and Super Deluxe Smitten (for a gentler massage) are massage mitts made from a very soft jellylike vinyl covered with hundreds of little nubs that feel like one hundred butterfly wings gently tickling your skin. The Super Deluxe version also has a little pocket designed to hold a vibrating Bullet for extra massage pleasure. And if you'd like to give each other a foot massage? Try some Tingling Tootsies Herbal Foot Cream, delicately scented with spearmint to tempt the nose and and soothing herb to reward the feet. This shea butter formula—which allows for the ultimate in moisturizing and softening—can be applied to the feet before massaging them with a Super Deluxe Smitten and perhaps also a Bullet.

and yet again, the feet. Imagine a twelve-inch circle around his penis—what I like to call the "invisible circle"—and avoid that magic area where he is most likely to become sexually stimulated. Save it for the very end, though you can feel free to brush his testicles or penis with your hand if you're in the neighborhood.

- **Keep it creative.** If you like, use a Handy Massager or Nubby Satisfier to soothe the tension out of his neck. If you're planning on a sexual massage, you can tease him a bit with the Bullet around the invisible circle, approaching it and then backing away. Watch for his responses. You may find that he's begging you to enter the circle.

- **Make it sexual.** This is the point at which a sensuous massage can become a sexual one. If you're going "all the way," you can stimulate him just under his testicles with the Bullet. Or use your own magic fingers to play with his testicles and massage his penis. (We'll talk more about "The Hand Job of Happiness" later in the chapter.) Alternately, too, you might repeat your massage journey with your lips, kissing him all over—now you know a lot more about the places he likes!—and eventually culminating in oral sex. Or you might invite him to begin kissing and/or massaging you.

Games for Adults

Here at Passion Parties, we believe sex should be playful whenever possible, and what better way to remain playful than to use a toy—or, in some cases, a game? Games can be a great way for you and your partner to vary your foreplay. Consider playing "strip" versions of checkers, Uno, or Twister. Or for more explicit sexual suggestions, take a look at our two premier games: *52 Weeks of Naughty Nights* and *52 Weeks of Romance,* in which you and your partner draw cards with sexy or romantic suggestions. Or check out our *Lover's Coupons:* twenty-five perforated certificates redeemable for cuddling, pampering, a "quickie," and other such

THE MOST FUN YOU CAN HAVE
WITH YOUR CLOTHES ON . . .

If you want to get the evening started before you're actually in the bedroom, consider the sexy possibilities in stimulating each other's genitals while your clothes are still on. Say you are both dressed up and ready to leave the house but with a few extra minutes to spare. Or perhaps you find yourselves alone for a moment at a party or in a restaurant. Back into him and rub up against his genitals with your buttocks. Or have him approach you from behind and gently rub himself against your backside. For fantasy play, begin an encounter this way as you imagine all the daring public places you might be.

treats. Sexy dice and other spicy card games offer similar variations on the theme: instructions for trying various sexual positions, settings, implements, and activities can help you and your partner explore new things while having fun together. *Spicy Dice,* for example, is a set of two dice that gives you a body part and an activity, so that you might be told to kiss his lips, while his roll instructs him to nibble your toes. For a bit of extra nighttime fun, try *Glo Dice,* which glow in the dark.

If you do decide to play, keep it playful. We're not talking Olympic medals here, so figure out together what boundaries you'd prefer. You might agree that neither of you has to do anything you find uncomfortable or that either of you should offer a creative substitution for any of the activities the game suggests. The goal isn't to put each other on the spot, but to enable you to loosen up and have fun.

For the do-it-yourselfers among you, consider making your own card game with some card stock and a pretty gold or silver pen. Keep the cards in a private place, and then, when he wants a special treat, he can select a card, or you can choose one and give it to him to fulfill. Your cards might include such items as:

- a twenty-minute foot massage
- twenty minutes of kissing on the couch

- one night of unabashed lovemaking
- a pre-breakfast shower together
- sex with ten minutes of cuddling afterward
- one evening of skinny dipping
- oral sex
- blindfolded sex
- "Your choice."
- "Surprise me!"

You can even make your own sexy dice with some wooden cubes from the crafts store. Write activities on one die and locations on the other—then take turns rolling. Here are a few flirty suggestions:

Activities	Location
Lick	Breast
Kiss	Above waist
Blow	Surprise me
Squeeze	Lips
Nibble	Below waist
Suck	Toes

However you decide to play, use your games as a way to open up your sense of fun and communication. Passion Consultant Rita from Colorado told me how her experience with a game led to a whole new vitality in her sex life with her husband.

My best sexual experience happened one night when my husband and I were playing a game for my birthday. He drew a card in the game that told him to "be a photographer" and he was really shy about it at first. But then he picked up our digital camera and took some incredible photos of me. True, the first few were corny, but then they evolved: from beautifully artistic, to suggestive, to sexy, to downright racy. He was really turned on, which I guess didn't surprise me, but I was amazed at how much *I* was turned on by the whole experience. Now we make pictures and picture-taking a part of our sex life fairly often, and it's remarkable how much we both enjoy it.

Romantic Bathing

Water is one of the most relaxing, sensuous, and stimulating elements I know. In Chapter 5, we talked about bringing the right woman to the bedroom by preparing yourself with a luxurious soak in the tub or a sensuous scrub in your shower. These bathing rituals take things a step further, however. Designed for you and your partner to share, they are a wonderful type of foreplay.

THE SENSUAL ROSE BATH

What You Need:
   ½ dozen red rose petals
   ½ dozen white rose petals
   ½ cup almond oil
   1 CD of romantic music
   30 or 40 tea candles or votive candles

Run a hot bath and throw in some almond oil. Then sprinkle some of your red and white rose petals on top of the water. With the rest of the petals, make a path to the bed and then adorn your bed. Surround the tub and your bed with lit candles. Turn on the music, turn off the lights—and invite your lover to join you in a bath of roses, maybe sipping a glass of red wine to heighten the mood.

For sensuous variations, you can also . . .
   • use peach and pink rose petals
   • use red and orange rose petals

- use lavender and white rose petals
- pour five drops of rose-scented essential oil into the bathwater
- put a dish of fresh strawberries (plain or chocolate covered) by the tub for the two of you to nibble on
- bring along a bottle of champagne and two champagne flutes
- lay out his & her white satin or silk robes
- lay out some heated towels

LAVENDER LOVERS SHOWER

What You Need:

5 to 7 drops of lavender-scented essential oils
your favorite lavender foaming bath gel or soap
lavender linen water
lavender-colored rose petals
2 robes
2 heated towels

Heat your robes and towels in the dryer and then spray them with linen water for a delicious lavender scent. Run the shower until it is hot and steamy, then moisten your fingers with the lavender oil and wave them in the air to diffuse that scent into your shower. Now invite your lover to join you under the water. Begin by lathering yourself slowly and sensuously with the foaming bath gel. Then lather his body starting feet first and again, slowly and sensuously, working your way up.

When you're all nice and soapy, rub your bodies together. Try to create friction and lather without using your hands. Let yourself feel the soft sensuality of the soap against your skin. Take your time and enjoy the experience using all five senses.

HINT: If your guy is one of the many whose erections are stronger in the morning, take this shower while he's still standing at attention. . . .

WATER WARNING

Baths and hot tubs are terrific for foreplay—but not for actual inter-course. The water washes away your natural lubrication along with water-based lubricants and spermicidal creams or jellies. The com-bination of vigorous play, chemicals added to the tub, and hot water can irritate your genitals and your urethra, possibly increasing your risk of a vaginal or urinary tract infection. So enjoy your time in the bath or shower, and feel free to enjoy oral sex and hand play there. But save the intercourse and anal sex for somewhere drier.

CHAMPAGNE SHOWER

What You Need

2 dozen strawberries

2 plastic champagne flutes

1 bottle of quality champagne (for drinking)

1 bottle of less expensive champagne (for your shower)

Let your shower run until it's nice and steamy. Then invite your lover to join you. Spray your partner with the less-expensive bottle of cham-pagne and invite him to shower you with champagne, as well. Then find as many ways as you can to feed each other the good champagne and the strawberries. For example, you might lick champagne off each other or feed each other the strawberries.

Fabulous Foreplay with Feet: The Tantra Tootsie Massage

Most of us are unaware of the incredible sensual energy locked away in one of our body's most unexpected places—our feet. Did you know that through the feet you can indirectly stimulate several other erogenous zones, including the nipples, breasts, penis, and vagina? Try rubbing some cinnamon-flavored Fireworks—a clear warming lotion—between his toes and watch the sexual heat rise. (If his feet are squeaky clean, go ahead—blow and lick his toes, because the cinnamon taste will delight your tongue even as your tongue delights his toes!) Or try the following extraordinary foot-play for some unexpected foreplay:

What You Need:
portable foot spa or bathtub
Passion Parties Tingling Tootsies herbal foot cream
Passion Parties Fireworks cinnamon-flavored lotion
one clean, moist, warm towel
one clean dry towel
1 cup Epsom salts or RomantaTherapy Sensuous Bath Salts

Start this particular activity with clean, relaxed feet—soak your partner's tootsies for five to fifteen minutes in some warm water and Epsom or bath salts. Then dry his feet thoroughly and don't forget the area between his toes.

Massage the foot cream gently and completely into one foot: top and bottom, toes to ankle. Then do the other foot. You want both feet to be relaxed and soft.

Proceed with each of the following steps, attending to first one foot, then the other, before moving on to the next step:

• Move your thumbs in between the bones you feel on top of the foot.

• Press smoothly and firmly from his ankle toward his toes, in long, smooth strokes. Use enough pressure so it's not ticklish, but don't go so deep that it hurts.

• Move on to the soles. Using your thumbs, make circular motions that cover the entire bottom surface of his foot, moving from the base of his toes toward his heel. Keep the pressure of the circles steady and even while using a bit more firmness on his heels, where the skin is usually much tougher.

- Massage his toes by pulling on them, gently rotating, wiggling, and pulling each toe until you reach its tip. Then slide your thumb and index finger back to the base of the toe.

- Hold his foot with one hand, forming a cradle behind his heel. Put the index finger of your other hand between each toe, moving your finger toward the base and then back toward the end of the toes. Repeat this move two or three times between all toes.

- Finally, add Fireworks cinnamon-flavored lotion between the toes and blow on them. Your lover should be relaxed, open, and oh-so-stimulated. Your turn! (By the way, you can also give *yourself* this foot massage, so maybe you should add it to your self-pleasure routine.)

Finger Fun

Here's something that may drive him wild: Treat each of his fingers as though it were a penis. Turn over his hand, kissing the palm with your tongue and lips. Then stroke one of his fingers as though it were a penis and put it into your mouth, sucking first gently, then harder. Gently nibble the top of the finger—not too hard, just so he feels the extra pressure. Repeat with the next finger, and the next, and the next, until you've pleasured all ten. Alternately, stroke each finger, then suck each finger, then lightly nibble each finger. Either way, his hands will be alive with pleasure. And if his feet are really nice and clean, you might drive him even more wild by following the same routine with the soles of his feet and each of his toes. If he likes this as much as I think he will, remind him, "Turnabout is fair play!"

Feathers and Fur

Believe it or not, a long, fluffy feather can be one of your most exciting sex toys. We sell the Rainbow Feather Tickler, a set of soft feathers in rainbow colors attached to a handheld wand for the ultimate in sensual touch. Or you can browse a crafts store for colors and styles that either of you might like. A big, clean blush brush also works pretty well. I encourage you to use these feathery toys in your own creative ways. But here's one way you might "tickle his fancy":

Blindfold your partner with a silk scarf and help him lie down on a bed or couch. Tantalize him all over from head to toe, beginning lightly on his face and gliding the feather gently down his chest, arms, tummy, thigh, and calf. Then work your way back up the other calf and thigh. Pay close attention to his responses and linger anywhere he seems to be enjoying himself. (Again, this will give you lots of good ideas for places to kiss and caress later on.) Feel free to stop and linger anyplace you like—except his penis. In this game, waiting is half the fun! When you've had enough—or when he has—flutter the feather between his testicles and on the tip of his penis. You can move on to intercourse from there or ask him to "feather" you.

By the way, some people don't enjoy being blindfolded—or tickled. Make sure your guy is genuinely enjoying this experience; after all, you don't want to torture him! Likewise, make sure if you say "stop," he knows you mean stop. Or if you prefer, have a code word like "soup" or "Tuesday" that really means stop, so you can say "oh, no!" more playfully and teasingly.

For a fun variation on the feather play, try this game with a piece of faux fur. And then remember that later on in your foreplay, you can tickle your guy's nipples, scrotum, perineum, buttocks, and penis with your feather or stroke these tender areas with the fur.

The "Art" of Foreplay

Here at Passion Parties, we sell body finger paints and Glitter Glo, an iridescent body paint that comes in Glowing Blue, Glittering Green, Hot Pink, and Brilliant Yellow, all of which glow in dim light. Have fun painting yourselves or each other. Draw circles around areas where you'd like attention, or paint arrows onto your bodies to indicate where the "target area" should be. Write "tonight" in a provocative place or express yourself in words you wouldn't normally use. You can write with your fingers or use a soft, sensual brush.

Edible Excellence

Edible sexual products are just what they sound like—deliciously flavored oils and lotions and puddings that are made to be licked and nibbled and otherwise eaten off your body or his. Just placing some edible massage cream or lubricant in a place where you'd like him to linger helps make foreplay last longer and gives you the attention you desire. You might encourage him to "sweeten himself up," or perhaps you would like to put the flavors where you want your tongue to go. For both of you, the chest or breast, stomach, knees (front and back), thighs, and groin areas are perennial favorites, but keep exploring to find all your individual preferences as well. Strawberry Passion Mist edible spray is a long-standing top seller at Passion Parties. Just spray it on any body part where either you or he doesn't normally like to linger—and then linger!

NO SUGAR IN YOUR BOWL

You should never put any products that contain sugar in or around your vagina, including real dairy whipped cream, chocolate syrup, honey, maraschino cherries, or any other items that are not specially made for sex play. You could give yourself a yeast infection, and what can make you feel less sexy than that? Always check labels to make sure edible products are sugar-free and especially made for sex play. (Of course, all Passion Parties edible lubricants fit this description, so it's fine to put them anywhere in your genital area, including in your vagina, as long as they have been identified as edible. Note, however, that edible massage lotions and dusting powders are not vagina-friendly.)

I hope you all remember the game I taught you in Chapter 2. If not, turn back to pages 66–67 and try out this approach to foreplay or create your own variation. And don't forget about Nipple Nibblers, the tingly fruit-flavored stimulating balm that either of you can put on your nipples for a double thrill. First it feels good to have it there, and then it feels good to have your partner nibble it off.

The Joy of Stripping

Lots of guys have stripper fantasies and lots of women do, too. See if you enjoy doing your own private striptease for your special guy. It might prove to be incredibly arousing for both of you. And you can learn some new moves by watching the *Striptease for Real Women* DVD—a striptease lesson for women who want to learn to dance for themselves and their partners.

THE *Passion Diva's Guide* TO "UNDRESS FOR SUCCESS"

CREATE A CHARACTER

This isn't absolutely necessary, but it might make the whole experience more fun for both of you. You can use clothing, makeup, and high heels to turn yourself into a "good girl," a "show girl," or anything in between. If you want to start slower and tease longer, add extra layers—gloves, hats, scarves, and those perennial favorites, stockings and garters.

SET THE MOOD

Choose the music you'll enjoy dancing to, with slow, rhythmic drumming to help you keep the beat. You want music that will turn him on, but make sure it turns you on, too. Replace white bulbs with red or pink ones, or use scarves to create sexy lighting. Candles might add a romantic touch, or perhaps you'd like something a bit more raunchy, tacky, or fun: maybe a lava lamp or a disco ball. (Check on eBay!)

Take It Slow

The pleasure is in the *tease* as much as the strip, so find ways to take your time taking it off. Buttons and clasps will delay and tantalize. You can also stroke yourself with the items you remove, especially gloves, scarves, garters, and stockings. He might enjoy being teased with these items, as well. For extra teasing action, forbid him to touch you until *you* give the signal. Keep the dance totally under your control. Part of the fun for both of you is in making him want you and making him wait.

Use Your Eyes

Some couples find it exciting when the stripper keeps her gaze fixed on her lover's eyes. Others like it better when she seems to ignore him. He's watching, her but she's looking elsewhere. Play with different effects and maybe talk about what you each like the next day or that afternoon. You can also discuss whether you prefer talking or no talking. This might be a fun time to try out an accent or another "sexy" voice that is quite different from your everyday tone. Some couples like it

UNDRESSING *HIM* FOR SUCCESS

One of the greatest pleasures in lovemaking can be slowly, carefully, tenderly, and seductively undressing your guy. You can take off his clothes without touching him or vary the garment removal with attention to the newly naked area. Some men like being tantalized by being kissed or blown on through their clothes, especially around the nipples and groin. They love to feel the warmth of your breath through the fabric, and then to have you remove the fabric. Experiment with ways to undress your guy, and, as always, encourage him to do the same with you.

when the woman gives the man orders, asking him to pick up her garments or telling him to stay back. Have fun finding out the roles you like to play. (And for more on fantasy play in general, see Chapter 9.)

LUBRICANTS AND STIMULANTS

Now, ladies, I hope you remember what we learned in Chapter 4: *Wetter is better.* Especially as you work your way down to foreplay involving both your genitals and his, you want to be well-lubricated—not just once, but several times. I like the approach of sex therapist Marty Klein, Ph.D., author of *Ask Me Anything:* "Lubrication is not an event. It's a process." Some skeptics view the time it takes to apply lubricants as a series of interruptions. Not at all. These brief interludes are arousing break-times that invite lovers to savor one another.

As we saw in Chapter 4, the whole process of applying lube can be an erotic experience. Warm the lubricant in your hand—unless he asks you, don't just pour it on straight from the container—and apply it with a loving caress. Encourage him to lubricate your clitoris, labia, and vaginal opening, while you concentrate on his penis and scrotum. Both of you should attend carefully to each other's nipples, which are exquisitely sensitive to touch once they've been aroused—and never more so than after they've been dabbed with a few drops of lubricant.

You can also use stimulating gels that, as we saw in Chapter 4, can add a delicious tingling sensation to your erogenous zones. Passion Parties' Nipple Nibblers is a flavored balm that will feel tingly and exciting on your nipples—or his. It comes in four flavors—strawberry, watermelon, raspberry, and mandarin orange—so that both of you can enjoy nibbling it off!

Another fun variation is a warming lotion, which can literally help heat things up! Passion Parties Fireworks is a flavored lotion that feels warm when massaged on the body. It's available in ten different flavors, and if you blow on them, they get even warmer. Feel the heat!

Final Foreplay

As you've probably noticed by now, I've organized this chapter from least to most intense, suggesting ways you can craft your own foreplay experience so that it builds slowly and steadily to maximum arousal for you both. Of course, not every sexual encounter has to be a leisurely experience in fine dining. Sometimes you just want some quick and easy fast food! And you and your partner will have your own styles and preferences, so you can pick and choose among all the options I've laid out for you here. (Not to mention the creative foreplay ideas you and he will come up with on your own!)

However, by the time you get close to intercourse and your pleasure and arousal build, it's likely that you'll be focusing most of your attention on the genital area. We'll talk about kissing in this area in Chapter 8, but in the meantime, here are four terrific ideas for ways that he can stimulate you, followed by a blow-by-blow description of ways that you can stimulate him.

THE *Passion Diva's Guide* TO
"FINAL FOREPLAY"—FOR YOU

The C-Spot Teaser

Have your guy go around your clitoris very gently, softly, and rhythmically with one lubricated finger. Encourage him to watch you for responses and vary accordingly. You can also teach him some of your favorite self-pleasuring techniques.

The G-Spot Warm-Up

Encourage your partner to lubricate his index finger, insert it into your vagina, and find your G-spot by making a "come-hither" motion with his finger. He can also gently rotate his finger back and forth across this sensitive area—as always, watching you for responses. Eventually, he may want to insert his middle finger as well.

THE A-SPOT WARM-UP

Even if you're not planning on anal sex, you may find this arousing. Have your guy put a condom on a well-lubricated index finger and swirl his finger around the edges of your anal rim. He should make tiny circles moving just the first third of his finger. Just a gentle caress is all you want—no insertion. (For more involved anal sex play, see Chapter 9.)

USING A TOPICAL STIMULANT

If you're using a clitoral stimulant, you or your partner should massage it for several minutes on the top, around the sides, and underneath the hood of your clitoris. This extra boost to your sensitivity may well help you to climax more quickly, fully, and intensely.

THE *Passion Diva's Guide* TO
"FINAL FOREPLAY"—FOR HIM

BETWEEN THE BREASTS

Many couples enjoy pressing the woman's breasts together and inserting the guy's penis between them. Of course, you'll want to be sure this sexy passage is well lubricated with some Vanilla or Pear Embrace Sensual Lubricant.

STIMULATING GELS

What's good for the goose is most definitely good for the gander! For one to two minutes, massage some Pure Satisfaction UniSEX Enhancement Gel around the head of your guy's penis and also into his meatus—that little slit at the tip. That will stimulate some increased blood flow, leading to faster and stronger orgasms and enhanced sensitivity.

GETTING FRIENDLIER

You can bring your guy to a whole new level of enjoyment if you play gently—that's always the operative word—with his scrotum and his testicles. Because this is such a vulnerable, intimate area, always check in with your partner, either verbally or nonverbally, to see how he likes to be handled here. Because the testicles are so susceptible to injury, some guys get anxious when their scrotum is fondled, but it's such a sensitive, erogenous zone that it's a shame to neglect it altogether. Encourage him to relax as you try out some of these intensely exciting ideas:

- Explore the contours of each testicle, one at a time. Gently tug them—*very* gently. Try rolling them with both hands, and maybe gently bounce them on your open palm.

- Cup his scrotum with your hand and apply light and gentle squeezes as you kiss his lips or chest.

- Place your hand around the base of his testicles, where your thumb and middle finger touch to form an "O." The goal here is not to squeeze, but to apply a light pressure that makes the testicles within more defined. Using your other hand, run your fingers lightly across the scrotum with light, "barely there" touches.

FORESKIN FOREPLAY

This is a very sensitive area for most guys—think of it like the hood of your clitoris—and like your clitoral hood, it's as sensitive as the tissue of your eyelids or the inner lining of your lips. As we saw in Chapter 3, the foreskin protects the head of the penis while keeping it soft and moist, and it's loaded with thousands of nerve endings, so don't neglect it, but do be gentle. When you're stroking your guy's (uncircumcised) penis, his foreskin can glide up and down along the shaft with each stroking motion, but be careful—the skin is thin and delicate and can tear easily. Never grip too hard or try to stretch it too fast or too far. Start pleasing him slowly to avoid sensory overload, but if your guy likes attention here, you might gently roll the foreskin back or stroke it (it will retract on its own during arousal, but you can give it some attention ahead of time). And of course, use plenty of lube. Your partner may especially appreciate something like RomantaTherapy Sensual Warming Lubricant, applied with a gentle stroking motion.

STIMULATING HIS PENIS

The casual term for this act is a "hand job," which you can do either to help your guy achieve an erection or to bring him fully to climax. Make sure your hands are clean and your nails are trim, and of course, take off all rings and bracelets.

Fill your palms with water-based lubricant (Revelation works very well) and allow it to warm in your hands. If he's not yet fully erect, massage the tip of his penis gently in one palm while wrapping your other hand around the base of his shaft firmly but not too tightly. Most guys like a combination of circular and up-and-down motions, but see what your man prefers.

When he's firmly erect, wrap your fingers around the middle of his shaft—not as gently, perhaps, as you'd want him to touch you, but not squeezing too tightly either. Most men like you to grasp the shaft of their penis about as firmly as you'd take hold of a frying pan handle. (You need to be far more tender with the sensitive tip, but the shaft enjoys a bit of pressure!) Move your well-lubricated hand up and down in a slow, rhythmic, and steady motion, adding more lube as necessary, adding a little twist at the top so the center of your palm travels over the head. Change your speed and pressure as his arousal grows, and don't forget the corona (the ridge where the head meets the shaft) or the frenulum (the V-spot on the underside of his penis that is richly endowed with nerves). Don't neglect his testicles, either: gently cup them with your other hand, and occasionally tug—very gently—for a pleasant surprise.

You can also gently fondle your guy's testicles with the help of a fla-vored massage cream such as Passion Parties Crèmesicle, which comes in orange and strawberry flavors. You can also try Passion Parties Fire-works edible body lotion, Sweet Sensations edible gel (infused with a tingly spearmint oil), and D'Lickious edible oral gel, especially if you'd like to have oral sex or simply to kiss him occasionally.

For an enjoyable double whammy, use both hands simultaneously. Form a ring with one thumb and forefinger at the base of his shaft and gently stroke upward, while simultaneously fondling his testicles with your other hand. You can also work both hands down the shaft, one after another, in a gentle twisting motion. As he gets close to orgasm, continue stroking his shaft with one hand and gently massage the nerve-packed stretch of skin between his anus and testicles with the middle fingers of your other hand.

Some men also enjoy a hand job in which you wrap his penis in something furry or silky and stroke him through the material. Pick something washable, in case you've already been using lubricant.

For a terrific approach to hand jobs—what we call the "Hand Job of Happiness"—check out the possibilities in the next section.

THE *Passion Diva's Guide* TO
"THE HAND JOB OF HAPPINESS"

PREPARE YOUR SPACE

Gather your favorite massage essentials and prepare your space with candles and music. Invite your partner to lie on his back.

LUBRICATE AND STIMULATE

Warm your hands by rubbing them briskly together as you gather up your warm, radiant energy. Lubricate your hands generously, and then lubricate his shaft as well, perhaps with some Revelation or UltraGlide. Using both hands, slowly start alternating back and forth in a stroking pattern you develop according to what he likes. Be creative and communicate with each other. Now try one of the following hand-job moves—and watch his happiness grow:

- **Hail to the Chief.** Place both of your hands side by side against his shaft like a pair of bookends. Then lift your hands up and down.

- **Endless Love.** Let his penis "penetrate" into your fist on each stroke. Before the head of his penis pops out of your hand, bring the other hand up for the next penetration. This way it seems to him as though he's penetrating deeper and deeper into an infinite vagina. Keep the stimulation for best results, but vary the speed as he likes.

- **The Reverse Swirl.** Use your open palm to swirl around the head of his penis, the way your tongue might lick an ice cream cone. This sensitizes the head and makes it grow larger. Now reverse the direction for extra pleasure.

- **The Open Door.** Turn the head of his penis as though you were trying to open a doorknob coated with grease. The penis doesn't actually move, but your hand does. Now try "turning" the other way. Keep going until he's satisfied.

- **The Ménage à Trois.** Insert his shaft into the Passion Parties' Gigi masturbation sleeve—a sleeve that fits around the penis as snugly as a vagina. Make sure the sleeve is well lubricated and fits him properly. Continue to move the sleeve in slow and steady up-and-down motions until he's ready to climax. Then pull Gigi up all the way over the erect penis, creating a vacuum effect, and his ejaculation will be "swallowed" by Gigi. We'll talk more about Gigi—and how to use it for oral sex—in Chapter 8.

Double Your Pleasure

In addition to the "one-at-a-time" techniques I've just described, you and your guy can also pleasure yourselves side by side, or pleasure each other simultaneously. Here's where all the self-pleasuring techniques you learned in Chapter 4 will really come in handy, because you can show your guy what turns you on, either by demonstrating directly or by telling him what you'd like.

Although many of us are used to thinking of self-pleasuring as a private act, it's a wonderful thing to share with your partner if both of you are into it. Lots of men enjoy watching their partners stimulate themselves, and if your guy has trouble bringing you to orgasm, why not stimulate yourself while he watches? It's a way of both sharing something you love and ensuring your own pleasure.

If your favorite way of coming to climax involves using a vibrator or other sex toy, make sure your partner isn't getting the impression that you prefer a mechanical object to him. Introduce your vibrator into your sex play slowly and tactfully. Maybe leave it on the pillow with a little note, saying, "May I join you?" Help your guy see that you value his kisses and caresses, and that you love touching him as well as being touched by him. If you see your toy as an addition to the whole package, rather than as a substitute for *his* package, you can help him to see things that way, too.

Vicky, a Passion Consultant in Utah, told me a story that illustrates this very well:

> My husband asked if I would let him watch me masturbate, and I of course said, "No!" But one afternoon he came home from work early. I was totally engrossed in my afternoon activity with my vibrator and didn't hear him come in. So, just at the point of climax, he slides into the bed with this huge grin on his face! I was very embarrassed because to me it was a private moment. But he joined in and that made it okay. Now we love adding mutual self-pleasuring and toys to our bedroom play.

I heard a similar story from Leanna, a Passion Consultant based in Vermont. She told me that she'd been secretly playing with toys for almost a year, but whenever she mentioned the possibility of using a toy to her husband, he said he wasn't interested. I suggested that Leanna find a more creative way of working the toy into their sex play. "First," I told her, "start with a bubble bath, and really pamper him. Then use a Vibrating Bath Ball to wash his back. As you move it around to his chest and stomach, accidentally let it slip down. I'll bet he'll want you to keep it there." And he did!

"We splashed water all over the bathroom, and it took a while to clean it up, but who cares!" Leanna told me. "It was the beginning of our love triangle: Him, me, and vibrator makes three!"

SIX WAYS TO RUN THE CLOCK ON YOUR "ONE-MINUTE MAN"

We at Passion Parties have heard so many stories about guys who don't engage in enough foreplay that we've come up with our own nickname for the problem: "The One Minute Man."

If your guy tends to get right down to business, here are six quick ways you can slow things down:

1. Caress his penis and then whisper in his ear something you would like him to do to you. Repeat those two steps as many times as you need to. As long as that caress is happening, he'll be willing, ready, and able.

2. Caress his penis and then guide him to do something you would like. Same deal—he'll like the way your hands are speaking for you!

3. Ask him to perform oral sex on you and offer to return the favor. Maybe it would never occur to him to make these stops along the road to intercourse, but now you've made it clearly worth his while. It's your choice whether you want either version of oral sex to continue throughout climax or to stop a bit earlier.

4. Ask him to perform another act you enjoy—and offer to "trade it" for something you know he likes. He'll get the "turnabout is

fair play" principle, and you can even encourage him to initiate these kinds of sexual bargains, which ideally are fun for both parties.

5. While he's still engaged in his own version of foreplay, murmur, "I'm enjoying this *so much*. What can we do to make it last a little longer?" Maybe he never realized that you wanted more time before penetration, or maybe he just never had the incentive to think about what else he might do. But now he does.

6. While he's still engaged, murmur, "I'm enjoying this *so much*. And now I have a new idea. . . ." and introduce a toy. You might begin with C-rings (see page 225), which are clearly designed to give him pleasure. Or you could show him all the ways a bullet vibrator might stimulate the two of you (see page 132). Or you could introduce him to the delights of stimulating *you* with a Magic Mushroom—a two-inch-long pink plastic mushroom designed to vibrate just inside your vaginal canal and to stimulate that whole area, including your labia and clitoris. If he needs a bit more encouragement, you might say, "After a few minutes of the Mushroom, I'll be so ready for you!"

Patience Plus Passion: An Unbeatable Combination

So now that we've learned how to prepare for passion, the rest of this book will be devoted to intercourse, oral sex, and other exciting varieties of sex play, including shared fantasies, restraint, and anal sex. But before we leave the topic of foreplay, I want to remind you one last time just how important it is to be patient with your guy and to assume the best as you experiment and find the foreplay rituals and routines that work for both of you.

Our Passion Consultant Bridget, who's based in Delaware, told me an extraordinary story along these lines. "The guy in my life is really great, but he is a 'techie' and relates to things from the perspective of logic," she told me. "Being romantic doesn't come naturally, although he always tries. When it came to foreplay, though, he just didn't get it.

He thought that by rushing in, he was showing me that he wanted me so much he just couldn't wait."

Bridget took to heart the Passion Diva principles, and so one day she had a long talk with her boyfriend, explaining how she wanted him to set the mood. She suggested he bring gifts or chocolate and whisper sweet talk. Then, she told him she wanted him to slowly disrobe her and really take his time. She was pleased by how closely he listened, and she felt hopeful and excited that good things would follow.

The next night, her partner surprised her by bringing home a laptop computer she'd been asking for. He told her all its features and said it had a game package with all sorts of fun games to play. "Great," Bridget thought. "He got the gift idea!"

Later, when they crawled into bed, he whispered, "I love you." "Yes!" Bridget thought. "He got the sweet talk idea!"

Slowly, her boyfriend pulled up Bridget's nightgown. By now she was thinking, "Okay, nice and slow, just the way we talked about. I really think he's got it!" Then, boom! He rolled on top of her just the way he always had. For a moment, Bridget was in despair.

But she remembered that practice makes pleasure, and patience helps, too. So she said, "Oh, honey, you know I'm not sleepy yet. Before we get all lovey-dovey, why don't we go play one of those games on the new computer?"

Her boyfriend looked at her as though she had gone crazy. "You can't play the games until the computer is set up," he said.

"Exactly," she replied. "And you can't play games with this human computer until you get it set up either."

The next night, Bridget's boyfriend picked up a bottle of Sensual Warming Lubricant that she had left on the pillow for him. He rubbed it in the right place for about thirty seconds. "It wasn't *exactly* what I had in mind," Bridget concluded. "But it sure was a good start!"

I think so, too! To my mind, Bridget had done a fabulous job with all her Passion Diva principles, especially #9—*Your most important sex toy is your tongue (and we're talking about* talking!*)*. So if you're getting the kind of foreplay you want from your partner, terrific. But if you're not—or if you think it could be better—start that communication process and don't stop till both of you are 100 percent satisfied. Your Passion Diva—and your partner—deserve nothing less.

In Your Passion Pantry

- **Super Deluxe Smitten.** This jelly vinyl mitt features more than 100 soft, stimulating pleasure points outside and in, making your massage a soothing, sensual, and eventually a sexual experience for both of you. Try it in the shower or tub with some Romanta-Therapy Luxurious Bath & Shower Gel.
- **Strawberry Passion Mist.** Spray some of this lickable mist anywhere you'd like some extra attention and invite your lover to linger longer.
- **Nipple Nibblers.** Flavored as strawberry, watermelon, raspberry, or mandarin orange, this beeswax-based balm will condition your tender nipple tissues while encouraging your man to—well, nibble.
- **Feather Tickler.** Add tickling touch to your play time. Use feather ticklers with Passion Parties Passion Powders to ensure that no part of your body—or his body—misses out on the fun.
- **Silky Sheets.** Scented with musk, pear, plumeria, or botanical breeze, this sensual spray will make your sheets smell lovely and feel silky. Spray this delightful product between your bedding a few minutes before retiring and then ventilate the sheets for a few minutes so they'll be thoroughly dry.
- **RomantaTherapy White Chocolate Passion Pudding.** This delicious, chocolaty pudding can add fun and flavor to your foreplay without staining the sheets. If you like food *and* sex, why choose? Have fun sensuously applying this pudding with your hands—and then slowly licking it off.

- **Fireworks.** Choose the flavor that suits your fancy or buy a Fireworks Sampler with all ten flavors: cherry, cinnamon, hot fudge, passion fruit, peppermint, piña colada, raspberry, strawberry, vanilla, and watermelon. Apply this lotion generously, then blow on the area and feel the heat.
- **Crèmesicle Edible Massage Cream.** Flavored in strawberry and orange, this is a cream you can rub on slowly, leaving your skin soft, smooth, and delicious. Try it with a Super Deluxe Smitten for even more sensual pleasure.
- **Tingling Tootsies Herbal Foot Cream.** This delicately scented lotion is flavored with tingly mint to stimulate one of your body's most powerful erogenous zones. You can also use it for pedicures!

Part

III

Passionate Partners

Even though I've been helping women access their Passion Divas for many years, it never ceases to amaze me how much that process can change their lives. Tracy, for example, was a young woman living in Virginia who had graduated college about five years ago and had been dating casually. Tracy had always found it difficult to take her relationships "to the next level," partly because she found the prospect of sex so intimidating.

"I love the kissing and all that part of it," she told her Passion Consultant, Sue Ellen. "But once we get past 'second base,' it just stops working for me." She blushed and looked at the floor. "Maybe there's something wrong with me."

Sue Ellen was one of our most dedicated Passion Consultants, and she made up her mind right then and there that she would not let Tracy leave her party until Tracy had everything she needed to turn this situation around. Even though Tracy had been using a vibrator for years and enjoyed reaching orgasm that way, she had never realized how important foreplay, lubrication, and clitoral stimulation were to her ability to enjoy actual intercourse. For Tracy, self-pleasure and intercourse were two completely different categories, and it had never occurred to her that what satisfied her privately might become part of what she did with a partner.

"But I could never bring a vibrator into the bedroom if a guy was there," she told Sue Ellen, half-horrified, half-intrigued. "Could I?"

Sue Ellen also discovered that Tracy had only heard of one position for making love—the missionary position, with the guy on top—which Tracy had never enjoyed. "I just don't like all that weight on me," Tracy told Sue Ellen. "Does that make me some kind of freak?"

Sue Ellen was able to reassure Tracy that all of her responses were perfectly normal and that she did indeed have more options. She told Tracy about a couple of other positions: spooning, where the man enters the woman from behind while either he or she stimulates her clitoris, and the "woman on top" position, in which the woman straddles the man, so that she has a lot more control over how penetration and intercourse proceed. She reminded Tracy that another option she might enjoy was having a man perform oral sex on her, so that she could fully concentrate on the clitoral stimulation. And she explained to Tracy that lots of women bring toys into the bedroom as part of their relationships with their partners and that most men *want* to give their partners pleasure and are open to all sorts of sexual practices, as long as they're introduced in the right way.

Tracy was astonished. She took Sue Ellen's advice and bought some Pure Satisfaction UniSEX Enhancement Gel and a Pleasure Curve vibrator, both of which would provide additional clitoral stimulation during intercourse. She also purchased some Piña Colada Tasty Tease. "Knowing that I taste good down there might make it easier for me to suggest, you know," she told Sue Ellen. She even asked Sue Ellen if there were any other sexual positions she might try. (If you'd like to hear more about these yourself, don't worry—I'll tell you everything you need to know in Chapter 7.)

A few weeks later, Sue Ellen got a call. Tracy had found some great new ways of incorporating Sue Ellen's advice into her current relationship. And she was astonished at what a difference it made. "I've just never felt this close to a guy—any guy," Tracy told Sue Ellen. "It's like this whole other level of trust. I can't believe it. Knowing I can ask him to do the things I like, and feeling so good about having intercourse. I just never had any idea that sex could be this good."

Another woman who turned her sex life around with a little help from Passion Parties was Daniela, who had been married for twelve years and was now in her mid-forties. "We had a good thing going when we started out," she told Lila, her Passion Consultant in central Missouri. "But after all this time, you know, we've kind of run out of moves."

Lila herself had been married for more than twenty years, so she knew exactly what Daniela was talking about. "Look," she told Daniela, "you can't expect your sex life to run on automatic pilot. You've got to mix it up a little. Add some new things and surprise each other. Isn't there anything you've always wanted to try but have just never brought up before?"

Daniela started to smile. "Well," she admitted. "I did always have this fantasy . . ." She didn't want to go into the details, but before the night was over, Lila had sold Daniela the Frisky French maid's costume, a long feather tickler, a soft silken blindfold, and some fur-covered gentle breakaway restraints. Lila also suggested that Daniela consider the Progressor, a vibrating jelly silicone ring that fits around a man's penis and gives him an extraordinary boost of pleasure during sex. The Progressor comes with an encased Bullet, so Daniela would be stimulated both by the vibrating ring in her vaginal opening and by the Bullet against her clitoris.

Lila didn't hear from Daniela for a while, and she began to wonder if she'd offended Daniela by encouraging her to expand her sexual repertoire. Then she got an e-mail that said simply, "We have *never* laughed so much . . . made love for so long . . . had such a good time . . . or felt so close. THANK YOU, THANK YOU, THANK YOU."

I loved hearing both these stories, because they reminded me all over again about the ways that connecting to your Passion Diva is not only good for you but good for your partner and your relationship. Making your sex life better can sometimes seem a bit daunting, whether you're trying to get comfortable in a new relationship or looking to spice up a long-term one. The basic tools you need in either situation are the same: a knowledge of what's possible, the willingness to go for it, and, as Daniela discovered, a sense of humor! Sometimes the best sex play is just that—*play*. After all, we adults need toys, too!

So in the next three chapters, I'll walk you through everything you need to know about how to make your partnership more sexually ful-filling, whether we're talking about intercourse (Chapter 7), oral sex (Chapter 8), or the more adventurous realms of fantasy, gentle restraint, and anal sex play (Chapter 9). If you're more comfortable sticking with the basics, you'll find some wonderful tips and techniques that will help them work better for you. And if you'd like to be a bit more adventurous, just read on through Chapter 9. Either way, your partnership is about to become a whole lot more passionate.

—◌⟩ 7 ⟨◌—

The Main Event

So now you've connected to your Passion Diva and learned how to let her speak. You've had a sexy anatomy lesson, found out all about self-pleasuring, learned how to bring the right woman to the bedroom, and discovered many new delightful ways of preparing for passion. Now it's time to move on to the pinnacle of passion: sexual intercourse.

Many of you lucky Passion Divas are already enjoying intercourse. You may always or frequently be having orgasms while you're having intercourse, or you may simply enjoy the sensation of your partner inside you, savoring the feelings of closeness, trust, and togetherness. For you, this chapter will offer some tips and techniques that can make sex even better for both you and your partner.

And for those of you who aren't having such a good time in the bedroom, this chapter will talk you through some of the problems you might be facing and offer some very doable solutions. Because, ladies, here's the good news: When intercourse doesn't work well between two people who otherwise like and are attracted to each other, there is almost always something you can do about it. After all, men's and women's body parts come in a wide variety of shapes and sizes, and sometimes it takes a little patience and some good communication to get the right fit between you and your partner. And sometimes the solution is even simpler than that. Here are some of the most common reasons why women don't enjoy intercourse. And before you even look at the list, I want you to remember—for every single one of the problems I'm going to list, there is a perfectly good solution.

If you're not enjoying intercourse, perhaps . . .

- **You need more foreplay before penetration.** After all, 75 percent of us need direct clitoral stimulation to reach an orgasm, and most women are getting an average of twenty minutes less foreplay than they would like. Simply extending the time you engage in foreplay before starting intercourse can make an enormous difference to your sexual pleasure. Check back with Chapter 6 for some ideas about how to make your foreplay longer and more satisfying.

- **You need more lubrication.** As we saw in Chapter 3, lots of women of all ages aren't producing enough of their own natural lubrication to enable the sex act to work smoothly and to heighten their feelings. So just adding some of your favorite lubricant—perhaps some Watermelon Lickety Lube or RomantaTherapy Sensual Warming Lubricant—can make a huge difference. For extra-special pleasure, make sure you lubricate both his penis and your vagina. They'll make magic when they come together.

- **You would prefer a different sexual position or a variation on the sexual position(s) that you and your partner currently use.** Maybe, like Tracy, you don't yet know about all the possible positions in which intercourse might occur. Well, read on. In a moment, I'll talk you through the basics and variations of the top-ten sexual positions for intercourse.

- **You'd like some additional clitoral stimulation during intercourse.** This problem, too, is easily solved. All you need is to ask your partner to accommodate you, either with his hands or with one of the many wonderful toys we've developed for that purpose, such as the Pleasure Curve, an elongated Bullet-type vibrator specially designed to stimulate your clitoris while your partner is inside you. It can easily slide between you during intercourse, unobtrusively, to give you that desired clitoral buzz.

- **Your partner is having sexual problems or isn't the right size or shape for you.** If this is your concern, no worries. I'll talk you through the possible problems and the available solutions at the end of this chapter. Or if you're feeling urgent, turn to page 229 and find out how to fix whatever's been bothering you.

If you're one of the Passion Divas who already enjoys intercourse with your partner and everything it brings, there's plenty in this chapter to surprise and delight you. In addition to my tips and techniques on the top-ten sexual positions, I'll also tell you about some nifty adult toys that can spice things up in the bedroom—vibrators, C-rings, and other devices that can intensify your pleasure and his in remarkable ways.

So let's get started!

THE *Passion Diva's Guide* TO THE
TOP-TEN SEXUAL POSITIONS

Anyone who has watched even a mild sex scene in the movies or on TV knows by now that there are lots of different ways that men and women can come together. What we don't always know is how many ways each position can be made to work better for us and for our partners, too. Here are some tips and techniques that will greatly enhance each of the top-ten sexual positions for both of you. Maybe they'll even inspire you to come up with some variations of your own!

1. MISSIONARY

Sometimes, you just can't beat the classics! This is the way that many of us first learned how to make love: The woman on her back with the man lying on top of her, the so-called missionary position. This setup offers lots of possibilities for romance: You can look into each other's eyes, you can kiss each other, you can touch each other's faces and stroke each other's hair. One possible disadvantage of the missionary is that some women have difficulty getting enough clitoral stimulation— the key, as we know, to most female orgasms. Other women find that the man lying on top of them offers too much clitoral stimulation, as his weight presses down upon their genital area. In this position, often, the man seems to control the act of penetration— its rhythm, its depth, how close or far apart your bodies are between thrusts—and that can be either an advantage or a disadvantage, depending on you, your guy, and your mood of that evening.

Here are some pleasing variations on the missionary position that both of you may enjoy:

- Rub each other's chest with massage oil as part of foreplay or even during lovemaking. The slickness of the oil will add an exciting, sensual tingle to bodily contact. For extra pleasure, use Romanta-Therapy Sensual Massage Oil, which is infused with the sexy plumeria fragrance.

- He can lift his upper body slightly and rest on his elbows so that your faces—and your pubic bones—line up a little better. That way, his pubic bone is more likely to rest on your clitoris and might give you the stimulation you need to reach orgasm during intercourse.

- Work together on creating a joint rhythm, rather than each of you going on your own version of "up and down." Finding a rhythm together means you're more likely to get the clitoral stimulation you need.

- Take advantage of your closeness and intimacy. In this position, your hearts are very near to one another, and it's easy to whisper words into your lover's ear. He can kiss your breasts, neck, ears, forehead—

any part of you within his reach—and a little passion fruit Fireworks in the spots you want attended to may remind him to shower you with tender kisses.

- You can wrap your legs around your partner to bring the two of you closer together. This variation also helps you to position your hips, so that you can lift them up and down in unison with your partner. Move up and down together to facilitate your clitoris being rubbed. Also, the higher you lift your hips, the deeper he can penetrate.

- For a similar effect, pull your knees up to chest level as he penetrates you below. He'll be able to go deeper, and you may be able to get more clitoral stimulation as well. Although many women love the weight of a man on top of them, some women find it oppressive. This variation means that he's penetrating you without resting on top of you.

- Another variation has you putting your legs on your partner's shoulders as he remains on top—a position sometimes called "the anvil." This version of the missionary gives you a lot more control over how your G-spot is stimulated, as you rotate your hips and subtly shift your position to place the thrusting man at the perfect angle.

- Lie on your back with a pillow or two under your bottom. Have him kneel in order to enter you. The pillows come in handy because they lift you up and leave his hands free to caress your breasts and stimulate your nipples, perhaps with a bit of Lickety Lube. His groin is well-angled to stimulate your clitoris, and his penis can reach your G-spot. You can also massage your own clitoris by hand or with a vibrator such as the Pleasure Curve. Or you can fondle his testicles with your hands, because in this position they're so easy to reach. Lubricate your palms with Revelation Lubricant and give him an extra thrill.

• Finally, consider varying your rhythm so that you receive extra stimulation and he's able to last longer. For example, four shallow and two deep thrusts—repeated several times—gives both of you a lovely varied sensation that can prolong the ecstasy for both of you.

2. WOMAN SITTING ON TOP

To many women, this comes as an *aha!*—he doesn't *always* have to be on top! Sometimes, you can be up there, and while you'll have to work harder, you do have a bit more control. In this position, your guy lies flat on his back while you face him and straddle his groin, gently guiding his shaft into your vagina. You control both the speed and depth of penetration, and both of you have your hands free for caresses. You can even look into each other's eyes. And if you're in your third trimester of pregnancy, this is definitely the position for you—all stimulation, no weight! Pregnant or not, consider putting a pillow under each knee to give your body more support.

You may have to experiment with the angle of your body and the style of your movements—short and shallow will help to keep him from slipping out. Actually, chances are good that he *will* slip out, maybe even more than once. So don't worry; just guide him back in once again. You can also vary your motions between up and down, rocking back and forth, or a circular movement. Consider some of these fun variations:

• Lean forward so that your chests are touching. Kiss his lips, face, forehead, and neck. With just a little effort, he can kiss your breasts and nipples. Inspire him with a bit of Nipple Nibbler in a luscious mandarin orange flavor.

• Lean back, resting your weight on your outstretched arms. Now his shaft will angle away from his body instead of upward, so be gentle. Use a rocking motion or a very short up-and-down motion.

THE PLEASURES OF BEING ON TOP

Some women enjoy fantasizing in this position. They imagine they're riding an enormous stallion bareback through open grassy fields or that they're on a super-charged Harley, racing down the highway at full speed.

Some women, too, enjoy wearing their sexiest lingerie when they're "up there"—after all, they're fully displayed!

- Try it with your back to him—the so-called "reverse cowgirl," giving him a perfect view of and access to your bottom for caressing, squeezing, and other sexy moves. You can stimulate his scrotum and inner thighs with your hands, maybe aided by some Cherry Lickety Lube or UltraGlide Gel. If you're into a bit of anal play, he can insert a lubricated finger (with a condom on it) into your anus or, with his bare hand, massage your perineum. (For more ideas on combining anal toys with this position, see Chapter 9.)

3. Woman Lying on Top

This is sometimes called "the clasping position": You lie directly on top of him and he penetrates you with your legs closed. As we'll see later on, this is a good option if you find his penis a bit large for you, since your closed legs prevent his shaft from going in too deeply. As with any position that allows for shallower rather than deeper penetration, your G-spot will get more action and your clitoris might, too. Once again, you and your partner can gaze into each other's eyes, experiencing the intimacy and closeness of your two hearts beating so close.

4. Lying Face-to-Face

Many women love this position. It's like cuddling and sex at the same time. Your guy puts his arms around you in a tender embrace, and then he penetrates you. But because you're both on your side, you've got better access to clitoral stimulation as his pubic bone rubs against you, and you've also got more control over how much pressure you get and when.

In a variation of this position, known as "the T," your partner lies on his side while you remain on your back at a right angle to him, your knees bent over his thighs. Your two bodies form a T while your heads are far apart. The T leaves your hands free to stimulate your clitoris with massage, using Pure Satisfaction UniSEX Enhancement Gel, Nipple Nibblers, or perhaps a Pleasure Curve, while his hands are free to caress your nipples, maybe with some Watermelon Nipple Nibblers or Spice Lubricating Massage Lotion.

5. Spooning with the Man Behind

What a lovely image: two spoons fitting together snugly as they lie side by side in the drawer. For you and your partner, that translates into him lying behind you, reaching around to caress your breasts or your clitoris as he enters you from behind.

In the variation known as "the scissors," he holds up your top leg during intercourse for easier access. Either way, if your thighs and buttocks like lots of stimulation, this is the position for you.

6. You Seated, Him Standing

Sit on the edge of a bed or couch, facing your guy. He comes into you, leaning on his arms.

If you're feeling adventurous, try this on a washing machine, the hood of a car, or any other creative location!

7. Standing Face-to-Face

Now, I'm all for these upright positions, but I do want to warn you that they require a bit more fitness and stamina than the ones where you lie back on a nice, soft bed. Remember how I told you that movement would make you sexier? Here's your chance to find out!

For close face-to-face contact, look at your guy while you lift one leg up and curl it around behind him to give him access to your vagina. He can hold your leg up to help support your weight, or if you're flexible enough, you can even extend your leg across the plane of his chest to rest against his shoulder.

If your guy is strong enough, he can penetrate you while he carries you. Wrap your legs around his waist. He can also lean against a wall to support the weight.

Another adventurous option is to have you lie flat on the ground on your back with pillows below your head and upper back. Your guy faces you, he lifts you by the waist, penetrates you, and then stands up, pulling you along with him. (Your feet will be up around his shoulders, and you'll be resting on your upper back and shoulders in a very sexy shoulder stand.) The great advantage of this position is that it allows him to penetrate you very deeply.

8. STANDING WITH THE MAN BEHIND

This one requires some energy, but perhaps not *quite* as much as the last one. Stand in front of your guy, both of you facing the same direction as he penetrates you from behind. This is a terrific position because it lets you both touch and caress each other. If you're a lot shorter than he is, you may want to stand on a stool, cushion, or—for the *very* naughty—high heels. Some people like to have the woman facing a wall, so that you've both got that hard surface to press against.

9. DOGGIE STYLE

You're on your hands and knees, and he kneels behind you and enters you from the rear, his penis stimulating your front vaginal wall for some extra G-spot action. In this position, you or your partner can also stimulate your clitoris with a hand or vibrator. (Try a Bullet or a Pleasure Curve. The elongated handle of the Pleasure Curve makes it easier to hold on to.) This is a great position for fantasizing because you're not face-to-face, although if you like, you can position a mirror so that you can see each other. This is also a nice position for men who like to see the curves of your bottom. If you enjoy a bit of anal play, your guy can easily insert a lubricated finger, covered in a condom, into your anus. This position is good for pregnant women, too, by the way, since once again, there's no weight resting on you.

And oh, the variations! Adjust the angle at which he penetrates you, or vary the ways you move and the depth of penetration. Always support yourself with both hands, though, to keep your spine moving and undulating.

10. WHEELBARROW

This is the position in which the man can penetrate the most deeply, so if that's something you both enjoy, see if you can try the Wheelbarrow. You lie on your stomach, holding yourself comfortably with your head resting on your crossed arms. The idea is for them to form a kind of pillow that supports your head so you don't have to crook your neck too much. Feel free to add a pillow or two under your arms. Or you can lean over the edge of the bed with your guy standing behind you. Then your partner takes hold of one or both of your legs—help him by lifting your legs up to his waiting grasp—and he enters you from behind.

You can also kneel on the bed on all fours, with your partner also kneeling, and lift one of your legs. He then holds your leg in the air and enters you from behind, again, giving you a lot of G-spot action. You're still free to move your hips in this position, and you can raise your leg higher or lower depending on how it affects your G-spot, while he—holding your legs—has good control of his part of the lovemaking.

Yet another variation is to rest on a hassock or footstool so that you're a bit higher—but make sure the stool doesn't slip!

PARDON MY QUEEF

Sometimes, air gets caught in your vagina and then makes a little sound as it's released. You might even have heard this in yoga class, and you may well hear it during lovemaking. It's called a queef, though some southerners have been known to refer to it as a "cootie-poot." It kind of sounds like passing gas, but it's only the natural release of air that builds up when he thrusts in and out.

When you feel the air building up inside you, resist the tendency to bear down, which will only make your queef sound louder. Instead, when he's pulling out, squeeze down. This will reduce the chances of queefing, and he gets a nice sensation into the bargain. Doggie style seems to create the most queefing, probably because in that position your partner is pumping the most air into you, though it can also happen during oral sex. No big deal, though if you're a bit embarrassed, try saying, "Oh my goodness, you made me queef!" as though it were a triumph of your partner's amazing technique.

Your guy can also hold your thighs rather than your feet, giving you more support but less freedom of movement.

Again, if you like, put a mirror in front of yourself so the two of you can have eye contact and you can see the action, too!

By the way, tell your partner to bend his knees to protect his back. And you might practice undulating your pelvis in a soft movement to prepare for these positions.

Let's Play: Using Toys During Intercourse

Toys can be another wonderful way to enhance the pleasure, intimacy, and variety of your sex life. You can incorporate pretty much any toy into your lovemaking, so this is a terrific opportunity for you and your partner to get creative. You've already seen how you can use either the Bullet or the Pleasure Curve to stimulate your clitoris—or to have your partner do so—while he is inside you. The Magic Mushroom can also double your pleasure during intercourse, since you can use it either for clitoral stimulation or for vibrating either his or your perineum. Besides vibrators, there's a whole other category of toy you and your partner should know about. A c-ring (short for "cock ring") is a circular device that wraps around the penis, testicles, or both. By applying light pressure to the surface blood vessels, a c-ring gently slows the flow of blood out of the penis, keeping the penis engorged, which allows your partner to prolong his erection. When used around the shaft and scrotum, a c-ring applies pressure to the perineum, which is also a pleasurable way to delay ejaculation. C-rings can be made from a variety of materials, but the best type of c-ring for couples is made from hygienic silicone or another comfortable, stretchy material. Plus, you can get vibrating c-rings and c-rings with clitoral or labial stimulators to excite you both.

Because c-rings restrict blood flow in a highly sensitive part of the male anatomy, some caution should be exercised when using one. They should fit snugly, but if they cause any discomfort or discoloration or if they leave marks on the skin, they're too tight.

Either you or your partner can put a stretchy c-ring on his penis—just make sure he's erect. And, if you're using a condom, put it on first. Then, simply stretch the ring with the index and ring fingers of both hands, bringing it underneath and behind the shaft of the penis (or the scrotum if you're more advanced—whichever your partner prefers) and then over the top to rest against his body. Allow the tension to bind the area securely so the c-ring doesn't snap—ouch! (If you encourage your partner to shave the area around the base of the penis and scrotum, it will keep the c-ring from pulling his hair when he puts it on and takes it off.) You might want to apply lubrication first if you're using a particularly snug c-ring, but for most stretchy rings, put the ring on first and the lube after—otherwise, the ring might slip off.

You'll apply the c-ring at the base of his shaft if you're using one of the larger rings: Ring of Ecstasy, Happy Heart, or the Lilac Elephant. If you want to get fancy, try the smaller Magic Rings, which are about the size of a fat rubber band. They come in sets of two—you can add one ring

**WHY YOU AND YOUR PARTNER
WILL LOVE C-RINGS**

C-rings can give a man . . .

• a harder erection
• a longer-lasting erection
• a delayed ejaculation
• more satisfying orgasms

under the head or halfway up the shaft, or, if you've got two sets of Magic Rings, you can even have a three-ring penis with rings in all three places.

The two of you can experiment with different c-rings—for example, textured rings might offer more stimulation to your vaginal walls, while others stimulate your clitoris. And don't forget the vibrating c-rings of the animal kingdom: The Butterfly Ring of Ecstasy comes with two little antennae that can be turned one way to tickle your clitoris and another way to tease his scrotum. Try it both ways so you each get a turn! Or check out the Turtle Ring of Ecstasy: His little round head covers more territory and gives a firmer vibration, slow and steady, that each of you will want to sample. Here's a more complete guide to all the different c-rings you have to choose from:

YOUR *Passion Diva's Guide* TO C-RINGS

• **Nonvibrating rings.** The Happy Heart, Intimacy Enhancer, and Magic Rings don't vibrate, but they are enhanced with clitoral and vaginal "nubs," which should give you some additional pleasure while keeping him hard and intensifying his sensations. The added stimulation is ideal for women who need a little extra clitoral pressure to climax.

• **Basic vibrating rings.** Our Rings of Ecstasy add a consistent, hands-free vibration directly on your clitoris. During penetration, the Ring

"DO I LOOK LIKE I NEED SEX TOYS?"

If you're thinking about introducing toys into your sex play, be tactful. Although plenty of guys are into sex toys—or would be if a woman suggested using them—other men may feel threatened, anxious, or worried that you prefer the equipment you can buy to, well, *his* equipment. Check out page 65 in Chapter 2 for some more suggestions about how to help your guy get used to the idea of adult toys.

of Ecstasy will vibrate gently against you, making the experience that much more pleasurable for both of you.

- **C-rings with clitoral and labial stimulators.** The Progressor, Thrill Ring, and Lilac Elephant all offer adjustable levels of vibration, so that your partner has the teasing power at his fingertips to drive you completely wild. The jelly nubs around the base of the c-ring give added sensation to your labia.

- **C-rings with clitoral and testicular stimulators.** Our Twin Rabbit and Dual Wabbit not only stimulate your clitoris, they also provide a pleasurable buzzing sensation against his testicles, giving him even more intense pleasure.

- **Enhanced c-rings.** You can find c-rings with even more enhancements, such as the Ultimate Pleaser, which besides the c-ring offers a sheath that adds girth and a removable bullet. Inside the sheath are several nubbly pleasure nodes to further intensify your partner's pleasure. The outside of the sheath is ribbed, which enhances your pleasure.

Afterward, the Afterglow

Once you've finished the act of intercourse, even if you're both completely satisfied, it's likely that the two of you may have somewhat different reactions. After a man has an orgasm, his penis becomes flaccid again in about one minute. His penis may also be extremely sensitive, which means he may not want to be touched there, though some men enjoy continued contact and may remain inside you for several minutes. Many men feel exhausted after intercourse—at least for a few minutes—and often fall asleep, sometimes even while they're still inside you.

You, on the other hand, may still feel turned on even if you have an orgasm. That's because your vagina and clitoris can remain swelled and pleasantly sensitive for up to fifteen minutes after orgasm. And if you didn't have an orgasm, they might remain "full" for two to six hours. So you may be feeling cozy and cuddly or even stimulated by all the blood still rushing through your open vessels. For some women, it's a similar sensation to drinking a cup of coffee! You may want some kind of clitoral and/or vaginal contact even though you're also satisfied.

For lots of couples, it can be hard to negotiate these differences in the "after-time," especially after the early glow of dating has worn off. Here are a few suggestions for finding some middle ground:

- Tell him how great it was.
- Share some water or juice to replenish all the fluids you've lost. (Avoid alcohol, though, since you're already both dehydrated.)
- Chat about pleasant topics—nothing difficult or demanding.
- Kiss him and caress him gently.
- Snuggle—but avoid that "invisible circle," the twelve inches around his penis, as he may want to be held without having contact in that super-sensitive place. Cuddle up to his chest and let

SNUGGLE TIME

If you like to cuddle afterward but you also feel the need to clean yourself up after sex, here's an idea: Keep some Baby Wipes by your bed. That idea came from one of our best Passion Consultants, a young mother in Minnesota.

him drape his arm around your shoulders, but keep your bottom half angled away from his groin area to make him feel more secure. If you still feel like more contact, you might arrange yourself so that you're straddling his thigh. That way you can come down more slowly while he protects his sensitive area.

When Sex Isn't Working Smoothly

Sometimes, even for the most experienced among us, sex just doesn't go smoothly. Here are some of the main issues that arise:

- He's too big for you.
- He's too small for you.
- His penis is bent.
- He has difficulty achieving an erection (erectile dysfunction, or e.d.).
- He has difficulty maintaining an erection (premature ejaculation).
- He has difficulty achieving orgasm.

Fortunately, there are many excellent approaches and products that can help you tackle these problems as they come up. We'll get to those in a minute, but first, here's a quick overview for how to cope with bedroom stumbling blocks.

THE *Passion Diva's Guide* TO
COPING WITH INTERCOURSE OBSTACLES

IN THE SHORT TERM (UP TO SIX WEEKS)

- Don't take any concern too seriously—everyone has problems occasionally.
- Consider that the problem is due to the short-term use of drugs or alcohol, or possibly a prescription medication.

- Find alternatives to intercourse—making out, hand jobs, oral sex play.
- Try to find out more about what's going on—if he's under stress, facing a major life change, or concerned about some aspect of your relationship.

IN THE MIDDLE TERM (UP TO 6 MONTHS)

- Make sure there's no medical problem, such as high blood pressure, diabetes, obesity, depression.
- Consider that the problem may be caused by drugs, alcohol, or cigarettes—or by prescription medication.
- Invite your partner to share any concerns he may have about your relationship.

IN THE LONG TERM (MORE THAN 6 MONTHS)

- Make absolutely sure there's no medical problem that needs to be addressed.
- Consider speaking together with a counselor about any relationship problems that may be at issue.
- Raise the possibility that your partner may need private therapy or counseling to work out whatever is bothering him.
- Be open to the possibility of working with a sex therapist who can specifically address the sexual portion of the problems and suggest concrete, workable solutions the two of you can undertake together.

IN GENERAL

- Be aware of your own needs. How can they be met, regardless of your partner's difficulties? Consider self-pleasure, hand jobs, oral sex, and sex toys as ways to find satisfaction solo or with your partner.

- Try not to take anything personally. Most sexual difficulties don't have anything to do with the degree of attraction a man might feel for you or with your sexual experience or abilities.
- Get the support you need—from friends, family, or possibly your own therapist or counselor. Sexual difficulties can be very trying, even if you know you shouldn't take them personally.
- Don't shut your partner out. Find ways to stay connected emotionally, touch each other affectionately, and remain open and alive to each other. Remember, this is a trying time for him, too.

When He's Too Big for You

The average size of an erect male penis is five to seven inches—but we believe averages don't matter when it comes to sexuality. All that matters is what works for you and your partner, so if you're feeling any discomfort stemming from your partner's size, then the two of you may want to take some steps to help your sex life work better. Here are some options you might try:

- **More lubrication.** From a product like Slip 'n Slide or UltraGlide; from taking more time with foreplay; or both.

- **Relaxation.** Anticipating discomfort before sex can cause your vaginal muscles to tense, adding to discomfort for both of you.

- **Slowing down.** If he enters you more slowly and slows down the rhythm of his thrusting, you may have a better experience.

- **Choosing different positions.** Choose one that keeps his thrusting shallow and/or gives you more control over how deeply he thrusts. For example, you might remain on top or have him stand or kneel, remaining perfectly still after he enters you, while you perform a back-and-forth motion, controlling the depth. During the missionary, keep your thighs closer together, since the farther apart your legs are spread, the deeper he can go.

- **Create a "bumper" with Gigi, the male masturbation sleeve.** For example, if your partner has a ten-inch penis and you're only comfortable with seven inches, cut the Gigi into a three-inch length. Use lubricant to help him slide the Gigi over his shaft so that it rests at the base of his penis. You can then have sex as you normally would, with Gigi preventing the additional length of his penis from entering your vagina. If he's wearing a condom, it should go on first, then the Gigi.

When He's Too Small for You

Even if your guy is relatively small, this may not necessarily be an issue for either of you. For many women, the penis is not what brings them to orgasm. His tongue and fingers, perhaps supplemented by toys, may be more important. But if you are feeling less than satisfied, you do have some alternatives:

- **Ribbed or nubby girth extenders.** These can fit over his penis while offering additional stimulation to your vaginal walls. Consider the Hot Rod Enhancer, a three-inch-long silicone sleeve that slips over the shaft of the penis to add girth to the erection. Your partner will enjoy the pleasantly tight grasp around his shaft while you appreciate the extra girth and the ribbing that will stimulate you with each movement; or the Ultimate Pleaser, a penile covering made of realistic FutureFlesh, which simulates the feeling of skin. It's also ribbed on the outside, plus it includes a removable bullet and a stretchy c-ring.

- **Ribbed or nubby penis sleeves.** These are open-ended jelly silicone sleeves that fit over your partner's penis surrounded by ticklers or bumps specially designed to enhance your sensation during intercourse. Consider the Tickling Trio or the Pineapple Pleasure Sleeve.

- **Strap-On Hollow PPA.** This realistically detailed penile prosthetic attachment is a hollow, soft vinyl shaft that's about 6½ inches long and 1¾ inches diameter, with an attached, stretchable harness that holds the PPA securely in place over your partner's penis.

When His Penis Is Bent

Lots of men have penises that curve up, down, or to one side. Also known as congenital penile curvature, this condition might be caused by a hardened plaque or growth; result from urethral stricture, a narrowing or obstruction in the urethra; or be associated with an injury to an erect penis. No problem unless it hurts or interferes with urination or intercourse. If your guy is concerned about a bent penis, he might consult a doctor and perhaps a urologist. (If your man's penis is normally straight and suddenly it becomes bent, he should definitely check it out with a doctor.)

However, some men do have a sense of inadequacy about their unusual organ, which might affect the way they relate to you sexually. He may experience some difficulty penetrating your vagina or have some difficulties becoming erect. I suggest finding as many different ways to be comfortable sexually as possible. Discover the positions for intercourse that work for you both; explore the possibilities of hand jobs and oral sex. And, as always, keep the affection, romance, and good communication flowing. Honest, loving communication can go a long way toward easing the difficulties in any situation.

When He Has Difficulty Achieving an Erection

Erectile dysfunction used to be known as "impotence," and the very word suggests how shameful and anxiety provoking most men found it—a loss of their power. We now understand that erectile dysfunction can affect men of any age or Viagra wouldn't be the billion-dollar seller that it is! Smoking, drinking, stress, and environmental toxins can all contribute to e.d., as can any number of medical conditions, including diabetes, heart disease, high blood pressure, obesity, depression, and a number of prescription medications. So encourage your guy to talk to a doctor, who will conduct a physical examination and possibly order laboratory tests for urinalysis, testosterone, or other screenings.

In some cases—though relatively few—the problem is psychological. Basically, if your man is waking up with erections but not able to perform with you, it's a psychological problem. Anxiety, phobias, or doubts about sexual performance may be at issue, or perhaps the problem is stress: financial problems, difficulties at work, or conflicts with his family. Another source of stress is the prospect of a major life change, including a new job, a new home, a new baby, or a significant change in your relationship. He may also be exhausted, so that his body is simply too tired to maintain an erection. Or his response represents a lack of sexual desire, which could stem from relationship issues such as arguing or from conflicts he feels about being involved with you. If it's

KEGEL EXERCISES: NOT JUST FOR WOMEN

Male Kegel exercises can help your guy achieve and maintain an erection, as well as helping to prevent or overcome premature ejaculation. Kegels can also help prolong lovemaking and may intensify his orgasm. And if your partner practices his Kegels once a day, he'll see results in two to four weeks. So here's how your partner can do his Kegels:

- First, he needs to find his PC muscle. He can either try to stop the flow of urine midstream—the muscle he uses is his PC muscle. Or when he has an erection, if he can make his penis "jump," the PC muscle is at work.
- Then, have him flex and release this muscle, in sets of ten, several times a day. He'll be surprised at what a difference it makes—and so will you.

a new relationship, he may be scared by how strong his feelings are for you or how attracted he is; he may be scared of losing you or worried about disappointing you. His inability to get an erection may be his way of avoiding failure by "walking away first."

If your guy only has occasional problems with e.d., you may not need to worry. But if the problem persists, or if you're concerned, consider seeing a counselor or sex therapist who can help the two of you work through the issue. Meanwhile, encourage your partner to practice a healthy lifestyle: no smoking, regular exercise, a healthy diet, limited alcohol consumption, and at least seven hours of sleep a night, preferably eight. Suggest that he find more effective ways to manage stress, perhaps through meditation, yoga, or martial arts practice. If you can, reestabish intimacy. Talk about what's going on with him in an open, nonjudgmental way. Also consider making love without sex for a few weeks, focusing on other aspects of your physical and emotional relationship.

When He Has Difficulty Maintaining an Erection (Premature Ejaculation)

There is no exact definition for premature ejaculation: basically, it's defined as ejaculating "before you want to," whether that's two seconds, two minutes, or two hours after intercourse has begun. If your partner isn't staying hard long enough for the two of you to be satisfied, then he's suffering from premature ejaculation.

As it happens, premature ejaculation is the number-one sexual problem in young men, but once again, there's no age limit. This condition is quite common. According to a recent survey by researchers at the University of Chicago, about one-third of men from age eighteen to fifty-nine are troubled by rapid, premature ejaculation. There are a variety of causes, including a style of masturbation in which the guy has trained himself to ejaculate quickly; a pattern of rushing into non-sensual sex, which can affect his ability to make it last when he really

HOW HE CAN LEARN EJACULATORY
CONTROL ON HIS OWN

- He could set aside thirty to sixty minutes several times a week to masturbate.
- He can undress and explore his body, allowing himself to enjoy pleasure on other parts of his body, not just his penis. He should make sure to touch his inner thighs and scrotum.
- Then he can begin stroking his penis gently, focusing on how it feels as he varies the grip and plays with the sensitive areas of his penis.
- He should pay special attention to the sensations he feels as he approaches his climax. When he feels close, he should stop stroking the sensitive areas but continue stimulating himself. When the urge subsides, he should begin masturbating again. He can repeat this cycle as many times as needed for up to fifteen minutes from when he began stroking. The initial goal is to last at least fifteen minutes before ejaculation, because if he can last fifteen minutes, he has the control to last longer.
- He should begin with a dry hand until he can last fifteen minutes; then he can add lube, which will enhance his sensations.
- If he doesn't get the result he wants within a few months, he might consider seeing a sex therapist, who can help him come up with strategies that are more effective.

wants to; a response to stress and the relief that orgasm can bring; and a reaction to injury or illness, as his body saves its energy for healing. Phobias or anxiety can also prevent men from achieving the deep relaxation they need to control ejaculation. And drugs—especially stimulants—can also cause problems.

Fortunately, the condition is curable. The key is for the guy to learn how to gain more control over when he climaxes, which is actually easier than it sounds. First, of course, your partner should see his doctor to make sure his medical history—or possibly a prescription drug he's taking—is not at fault. The doctor may prescribe for him a medication that delays ejaculation. But if there's no medical issue, here are some other things he can do:

- **Breathe deeply** to promote deep relaxation.

- **Focus** on his sexual experience, rather than tuning it out, and learn the exact feeling he has when he reaches the point when ejaculation is inevitable.

- **Be patient,** because it could take months to master ejaculatory control.

- **Use a c-ring,** which can help him hold an erection longer.

Meanwhile, what can you do when you're faced with this problem?

- **Talk to him.** Encourage him to join you in a counseling session with a sex therapist if this is truly interfering with your sexual satisfaction. Try to find a neutral time to bring up the topic, though, rather than right after sex.

- **Help him relax.** Instead of going right to foreplay or lovemaking, give him a sensual massage to loosen him up.

- **Ask for more foreplay.** See if you can reach the same heightened state of arousal as he. Accept, though, that there will be times when he finishes before you, so encourage him to continue making love to you via other methods, such as oral sex or manual stimulation. Or have him use a vibrator or the Strap-On Hollow PPA.

- **Accept your limits.** You can be loving and understanding, but you can't fix this problem for him; he needs to help himself.

Meanwhile, consider using some Stay Hard, a prolong cream that contains benzocaine desensitizer to reduce sensitivity and is intended to help your guy stay hard longer. Apply a very small portion to the head of the penis and see how it affects your sex life. Although Stay Hard is vagina friendly, I recommend that you use a very small amount and allow a few minutes for it to "sink in." Otherwise, the cream may numb your vaginal lips, reducing *your* sensitivity.

When He Has Difficulty Achieving Orgasm

He gets hard and stays hard, but he doesn't seem to be able to reach an orgasm. This can be such a frustrating problem for both partners. Possible sources of the problem include:

- A masturbation style in which a guy develops a pattern and inadvertently trains himself to ejaculate only in that way.
- Having sex immediately after intercourse, which may give the guy trouble ejaculating the second time, especially as he gets older.
- Aging in general, which makes the nervous system lose some of its excitability. Aging can also create a loss of pelvic muscle tone, so male Kegels can help here.
- Genital, prostate, or neurological problems.
- Drugs, including pain relievers, blood-pressure medications, antidepressants, anti-anxiety medications, and other prescription and illegal drugs.
- Stress, distraction, and depression.
- Fears of making you pregnant, even if you're using birth control. You might try using a thin condom even if you're using other birth-control methods such as the Pill; sometimes seeing and feeling a form of birth control can help overcome a guy's mental concern.
- The attitude that sex is something you do for a woman, even if you're not interested.

If your guy cannot masturbate to orgasm, most sex therapists recommend seeing a urologist. If he can achieve orgasm on his own but not with you—or not consistently with you—then he might try the following strategy:

- **Become comfortable with other aspects of sex,** focusing on the total experience rather than only the ejaculation.

- **Communicate with his partner** about what pleases him.

- **Move his hips, not his hands,** when he masturbates, so that his activity is more similar to the activity of intercourse. This may bring him closer to climax and help him recognize when ejaculation is imminent.

- **Use c-rings to help intensify sensations in his penis,** making it easier for him to climax. However, he should avoid Stay Hard cream, which will only make orgasm more elusive by lessening his sensations.

As for what can you do for him:

- **Experiment with different sexual positions,** especially those with the man on top, so that he can control the movements.

- **Explore various erogenous zones on his body,** including his feet. Check out the Tantra Tootsie massage in Chapter 6.

- **Stimulate him** by lightly licking the sensitive underside of his penis below the head. For more about oral sex, see Chapter 8.

- **Massage his perineum** and perhaps his anus.

- **Find out about his fantasies** and participate in any that you're comfortable with.

- **Make it an aural experience** with sexy talk and moans; tell him how good everything feels.

- **Accept your limits.** Again, you can be loving and understanding, but you can't fix this problem for him; he needs to help himself.

- **Be self-loving and find the support you need.** It can be demoralizing to have a guy failing to climax, so you need to do what you can to feel sexy, desirable, and loved. Ask your guy for sexual attention and affection, or turn to friends and family for affirmation that you're fabulous. Try hard not to take it personally. Even if a relationship concern is at issue, it still says more about him than it does about you.

As we've seen, sexual intercourse can be a satisfying, intimate, and joyous experience. But there's one other type of sexual pleasure that can be just as wonderful—oral sex. So let's move on to Chapter 8, where you'll find everything you need to know about performing oral sex on him and having him perform this highly pleasurable act on you.

⟳ *In Your Passion Pantry* ⟳

- **Fresh & Frisky.** This soothing liquid intensifies touch, while the cooling sensation encourages additional natural lubrication. When you spray this scented product on your labia and around the vaginal opening, the witch hazel, aloe vera, and other ingredients excite your sensitive genital skin and make sensual caresses feel extra-special.
- **UltraGlide Gel.** This extra-thick lubricant accommodates those marathon lovemaking sessions, so apply some to your favorite vibrator, dildo, or body part, and let the good times roll.
- **UltraGlide.** This lubricant is almost identical to a woman's natural moisture. Its super-silky texture makes sexual intercourse an even greater pleasure and can easily be reactivated during sex with water or saliva.

- **Magic Mushroom.** Check out this mushroom-shaped mini-vibrator whose nonintimidating size and flexible material is great for first-time users.
- **Pleasure Curve.** A vibrator whose smooth, flat surface nestles against your clitoris while you're having intercourse, or you can use it as a G-spot stimulator. For extra pleasure, flip it over and tickle him behind his scrotum.
- **Ring of Ecstasy.** This super-soft, stretchy silicone vibrating c-ring provides the ultimate satisfaction for both partners, with both erection enhancement and clitoral stimulation. You can buy it with either a turtle-, butterfly-, or heart-shaped clitoral stimulator, and it includes a removable, reusable, one-touch vibrating mini-bullet.
- **The Progressor.** Take your lovemaking to the next level with this ultra-powerful, high-tech vibrating c-ring. Just slip the Progressor over an erection to experience six extraordinary levels of vibration, pulsation, and escalation. The super-stretchy jelly silicone hugs his penis for constant stimulation, while the nub-studded pouch can be worn one way for clitoral stimulation, the other to pleasure his scrotum. It also comes with a removable bullet.
- **Loving Spoon.** The concave tip design and slim spiral surface are designed to exhilarate your labia while its clitoral stimulator provides firm action. The bendable shaft allows for customized shaping to suit every woman's needs.

~ 8 ~

Oral Sex

All right, ladies, now we're getting into an area of sexual activity that is subject to an enormous amount of intense feelings and often tension between couples. You can bet that when each woman is alone and speaking in confidence with her Passion Consultant, the comments fly fast and furious when the topic of oral sex comes up:

"He always wants me to do that for him—but I'm sooooo not into it!"

"When we do it, it makes me gag!"

"I don't mind doing it so much. I just really hate the taste."

"It's the swallowing I can't stand."

And yet, as many women will tell you, oral sex is also a kind of sex play that can bring deep joy, intimacy, and extraordinary pleasure. These comments also come out in confidence at Passion Parties:

"Actually, I like kissing my husband's penis and feeling him get harder and harder. I feel like the sexiest woman alive when I can do that for him."

"I really enjoy doing it. It's like the ultimate expression of trust."

"It's like having a big popsicle in my mouth."

"I didn't like it so much at first, but now I think it's kind of fun. And he's *so* into it and is so happy when we do it. I like knowing I can make him that happy."

For these women, oral sex means a chance to feel sexy, powerful, and generous, even while they're having a little fun of their own. So if you're one of those happy Passion Divas who is already enjoying both types of oral sex—you performing it on him (fellatio) and him performing it on you (cunnilingus)—then you can read on to learn about some new ways to make oral sex even more fun and satisfying. And if you're one of the many Passion Divas out there who thinks that oral sex isn't her thing or wonders why it's never been as fun as everyone else makes it out to be, I'd like you to make me a promise: Hold off on making any firm judgments about this kind of sex until you've read this chapter. The suggestions, tips, and techniques included here just might change your mind and open up a whole new world of possibilities!

Oral Sex on Him: Your Basic How-To

When women say they don't enjoy oral sex, they usually give one of four reasons: They don't like the idea of a man's sex organ being shoved into their mouth; they feel as though they're gagging; they don't like the taste; and they don't want to have to swallow the man's semen when he ejaculates. All of these concerns are perfectly understandable. The good news is, there's a way to address each and every one of them. There are approaches that can make oral sex manageable, gag-free, and even tasty!

There are two basic versions of oral sex: "all the way" and "on the way." If you're going "all the way," you're basically bringing your guy to climax through some combination of foreplay and oral sex. Even if this is the kind of oral sex you're having, however, you don't have to swallow. You can stop just before your guy climaxes and allow him to ejaculate into the air or onto the sheets. You can also bring your guy to climax through oral sex by using some combination of mouth and hands, for example, holding his tip in your mouth as you massage his penis with your hands, without ever taking his penis completely into your mouth. Finally, you can "go all the way" using Gigi, the male masturbation sleeve exclusively designed for Passion Parties. I'll explain a bit more about these alternatives later on.

If you're having oral sex "on the way," you're basically using it as a form of foreplay on the way to some type of sexual intercourse. Oral sex "on the way" can be far less elaborate. It might be just a tender kiss on the tip of his penis. Or you might spend a few minutes licking him and caressing him with your tongue before going on to other foreplay activities. You might also alternate back and forth between oral sex and other foreplay: pleasuring each other with your hands, kissing each other's mouth and body, using toys, and so on. And of course, you might also engage in a long session of oral sex, stop just before your guy climaxes, and then switch from oral sex to intercourse.

So take a look at the Passion Diva's Guide to Oral Sex, and then use it as you and your partner see fit. You can work your way through every step, pick and choose, or stop just before you get to the end. As with all your bedroom activities, the choice is up to you.

THE *Passion Diva's Guide* TO ORAL SEX—ON HIM

1. **Get comfortable.** Position yourself so that your upper body and shoulders can move easily with you. If you have long hair, tie it back in a ponytail. Your hair won't get in the way, and he'll be able to see you better.

2. **Add some edible lubrication.** Like most other sexual contact, slippery is better. Saliva works, but you can't always get things— or keep things—as moist as you would like. So keep a lube handy, and for extra oral pleasure, go for some flavored Lickety Lube or Embrace and savor the fabulous tastes. (I'll tell you a lot more about how to make oral sex more tasty further on.)

3. **Tantalize and tease.** Touch him lightly at first. Softly kiss the tip of his penis and gently caress it with your fingertips. Slowly move your light kisses from the tip of his penis down to the base. You don't have to follow a specific pattern. Randomly move your lips

until you've touched him all around. You can also use your tongue to lick up and down the shaft and around the head, as though you were eating an ice cream cone. The frenulum, the ultra-sensitive skin that forms a V on the underside of the penis between the head and the shaft, is very responsive to pressure and sensation, and simply focusing on this one spot, even if you never take the whole penis in your mouth, is already a huge treat for many guys. Gently tease it with your tongue; the softer underside of your tongue is good for this, too.

4. **Stimulate his scrotum.** Using just your tongue, locate the back of his scrotal sack where the scrotum attaches to his groin. Slowly drag the tip of your tongue from this sack along the back of his scrotum, then along the bottom, and around to the front, continuing along the underside of his shaft. When you reach the tip of his penis, you can lick or kiss the area or fully take the head of his penis into your mouth and suck. You can repeat this technique a few times in a row or randomly add it into your oral foreplay to mix things up a little. You can also encircle the base of his scrotum with your free hand while you're kissing his shaft. The combination of sensations will intensify his feeling in both areas.

5. **Take him in your mouth.** Using one hand, grip the base of his penis with your hand—gently but firmly, the way you'd hold a frying pan handle. Open your mouth and take his penis in as far as you feel comfortable. Close your lips around his shaft and

THE HUMMER

No, it's not a new vocal styling or even a new car or truck. It's a version of oral sex in which you take the guy into your throat and then hum, almost as though you were "gargling him." The gentle, penetrating vibrations of your humming is guaranteed to leave him begging for more.

experiment with different tongue movements. You don't want your teeth to touch the shaft, so curve your lips around your teeth to prevent any inconvenient contact. Now, slowly move your head away from his body and apply a little sucking as you move your mouth. When the head of his penis reaches the back of your teeth, glide his penis back into your mouth. Gradually increase the speed of this in/out motion. Feel free to vary between slow sucking and fast sucking. It all feels good. You can also swirl your tongue around his penis as you hold it in your mouth, which provides a sensation that most men love.

6. **Use your hands.** Your mouth isn't the only factor in great oral sex. With the hand that's gripping the base of his penis you can give him some additional sensations by moving your hand up and down in rhythm with the movements of your mouth, giving him the feeling of "full coverage." Your saliva will work like a lubricant so that his overall sensation is of warm, wet pleasure. You can also use two hands to do this or use your free hand to gently fondle or caress his testicles or to place pressure on his perineum (which can help some men with explosive orgasms restrain themselves). And while you're stroking his shaft, don't forget the scrotum. Kiss, lick, or tickle it, varying the amounts of pressure to keep things interesting. Try attending to the sensitive foreskin, too. Although it retracts on its own as your guy becomes aroused, you can certainly give him some much-appreciated attention with your lips and tongue. Try licking or kissing this area very softly, or stroking it with your lips. Or roll it back *very* gently with your hands, and then kiss it and the area you've exposed. Some sweet strawberry Lickety Lube will make it a tasty experience for you and an intensely pleasurable one for him.

7. **Change it up.** Experiment with different speeds, grips, and motions. You'll be able to tell what gets him going by his reactions. If your jaw gets tired, you can occasionally take him completely out of your mouth to give yourself a little breather, but

make sure your hand is still moving in an up-and-down motion, and use your tongue to continue pleasuring the tip.

8. **Be enthusiastic.** Let him know you're enjoying yourself by making little sighs and noises of pleasure or by letting him hear you suck and slurp. The vibrations from these sounds will only enhance the other sensations you deliver. Here's what guys know: Enthusiasm makes the difference between good and outstanding oral sex.

9. **Communicate.** Sometimes it's a turn-on to ask him if he likes what you're doing or what he wants you to do next. Look up into his eyes and smile every now and then. And if you don't feel like talking—after all, your mouth is busy with other things!—find ways to communicate with him through sound and gesture and maybe ask him later what he might enjoy.

Making Oral Sex a Tasty Treat

Unwrap a hard candy or take a mouthful of another one of your favorite treats, and spend just a moment savoring the delicious tastes melting on your tongue and spreading throughout your mouth. Then ask yourself, "If I knew about a product that would make oral sex taste as good as candy or dessert, would I be more willing to add it to my romance agenda?"

If the answer is yes, you're in luck! Passion Parties sells a full line of gels, lotions, and other edibles that taste simply delicious—and can turn routine oral sex into a tasty treat. Tanya of Raleigh, North Carolina, is one Passion Consultant who has made the most of Passion Parties' line of edibles and gels. "My husband and I have struck a win-win deal," she told me. "He gives me massages, and in return I treat him to a great time of oral sex using my favorite mint-flavored oral gel, Passion Parties' Edible D'Lickious."

Just as I don't want you to be a one-lube woman, I don't want you to be a one-edible woman, either. I want you to know about all the different textures, tastes, and sensory possibilities in the full range of edibles that are available to you and your partner, to help you both taste delicious to each other and to enhance all the possibilities in your sexual play. So here's what's on the menu:

POWDERS

Edible powders are a tasty and safe way to excite your senses and turn dessert into a sexual activity. The powders are finely textured, the same consistency as powdered sugar, and come in many flavors, including white chocolate, cotton candy, and chocolate raspberry. They are perfect to be licked or kissed off.

Application: Anywhere on the body, except directly in the vagina. Use a feather, Feather Snapper, or sprinkle with your fingertips.

GELS

Edible gels can turn oral loving into a tasty thrill for both parties. A tiny bit will keep your lover quivering in anticipation and the great taste will keep you eager to please. One of our products, D'Lickious, comes in mint or cinnamon flavor—the mint provides a tingling, cooling sensation while the cinnamon makes you both feel warmer. Another product, Sweet Sensations, is infused with tingling spearmint oil. Gels come in different consistencies, so experiment to find out which one is right for you: For example, Sweet Sensations is a bit thicker, while D'Lickious has a refreshing feel.

Application: Apply a small amount to your tongue or any body part before oral sex. Not safe for use in the vagina.

CREAMS

Edible creams offer a pleasing taste and are completely safe to ingest. The texture is silky smooth, and they are perfect to be licked or kissed off. Try our own Tasty Tease: Our available flavors include mint, piña colada, and strawberry.

Application: Creams can be used anywhere on the body except inside the vagina. Apply with your fingers.

Tip: Try them on your nipples for extra pleasure all around!

PUDDINGS

The name of these products says it all . . . mmmm! Puddings are tasty, safe, and edible treats that have the consistency of a traditional, consumable pudding and offer an additional advantage over powders in that you and your partner get to experience the visual treat of the erotic, creamy texture. We carry our own Passion Pudding that comes in white chocolate flavor and won't stain the bedding, so you can relax knowing that your fun tonight won't result in extra chores in the morning.

Application: Apply wherever you want your partner to linger, except directly inside the vagina.

LUBRICANTS

Edible lubricants are specifically designed to supplement your own natural lubrication while providing delicious tastes to enhance the experience of oral sex. Look for a water-based and water-soluble lubricant, such as our own Embrace or Lickety Lube, which are condom- and toy-compatible, as well as vagina-friendly and wash away easily with water. Lickety Lube comes in four delicious flavors—cherry, piña colada, strawberry, and watermelon—and can be enjoyed even when another lubricant has already been applied.

Application: Apply just a small amount to the desired body part.

MASSAGE EDIBLES

Some massage lotions and oils can also provide a fun and tasty experience. Our Creamsicle Edible Massage Cream comes in strawberry or orange flavor and allows you to tantalize your lover while ingredients such as vitamin E and shea butter moisturize the skin. Another option, flavored massage oils, offers long-lasting lubrication to extend foreplay. To remove any massage edibles, simply take a sexy shower together!

Application: Spread evenly over skin with hands for a sensual and yummy massage.

Tip: For some added texture, apply these products with a Super Deluxe Smitten (see page 207).

OTHER BODY TREATS

At Passion Parties, we never stop with just the basics! Some other fun edibles include:

Body Finger Paints: Exactly what they sound like—colored body paints that come in a variety of flavors and look like icing, but go on smooth, like a lotion. These are mostly decorative, but still safe to taste and ingest. Use them to write sexy messages or specific directions on your body!

Fireworks: This flavored stimulant is not a gel or a lotion, but something in between. Perfect to be kissed or licked off, Fireworks offers a lovely heated sensation, especially on a man's penis. You can blow on any area where it has been applied with your warm breath and feel the product heat up on your skin.

Passion Mist: This strawberry-flavored liquid spray can be used wherever you want your lover to linger, except directly in the vagina. A quick spritz makes you scrumptiously delicious. For an added treat, have some fresh strawberries on hand and treat your lover to a strawberry feast.

Reflex Action: It's No Gag

Now, what about those of you who are concerned about gagging when you hold his penis in your mouth?

First, let me reassure you—the gag reflex is perfectly normal, and we all have it, although each of us has it to a different degree. The reflex is there to protect your throat, and like most bodily responses, it has both

DIETARY DELIGHTS

Okay, now here's a little-known secret that could change your whole relationship to oral sex: Your partner's fluids taste different *depending on what he eats*. And, as a matter of fact, your own vaginal fluids are flavored by what you eat, too. (The other major factor in how fluids taste is genetics, but that's an area you probably won't be able to influence.) So if you want to ensure that your "late-night snack" tastes good, here are the foods you two should add—and avoid—for a few days before the big event:

Foods to Add	Items to Avoid
Bananas	Asparagus
Blueberries	Broccoli
Dark chocolate	Cauliflower
Honey	Chinese, Mexican, and Indian food
Mangos	Cigars and cigarettes
Maple syrup	Coffee
Orange juice	Cumin
Papayas	Curry powder
Peaches	Garlic
Pineapples	Hot pepper
Raspberries	Leeks
Strawberries	Onions
	Red Meat
	Turnips

a physical and a psychological aspect. That means that if you're feeling anxious and vulnerable, or if you view oral sex as an unpleasant experience you wish you could avoid, your throat may be more likely to constrict and your breathing to become shallow, making it still more likely for the act to trigger your gag reflex.

On the other hand, if you think of oral sex as a delicious, delightful experience—and one where you remain in control—you're more likely to avoid gagging or gasping. So the secret to overcoming the gag reflex is making sure that you're always in control of how much you take into your mouth—and that you *know* you're in control. That way, you'll never have any reason to gag, and you'll be able to kiss, suck, and lick your partner in ways that pleasure you both.

THE *Passion Diva's Guide* TO GAG-FREE ORAL SEX

EXPERIMENT

Find out for yourself just how much you feel comfortable holding in your mouth. Try using a pickle, carrot, or banana—whatever tastes good to you—and gently insert it as far as feels good to you. Play around a bit—suck, nibble, lick. Experiment with the different sensations in your own mouth. Do you enjoy any of these moves? And when you're controlling the thrust, how far *are* you comfortable with? Whatever you come up with, that's your limit. And now that you know it, you can make sure that you and your partner never exceed it. Just that sense of knowing what to expect and what works for you will give you a sense of control. For extra bonus points, conduct your next round of experiments on your partner, so that both of you know exactly how much you can take and so you can trust him even more to stay within the bounds you set.

BREATHE

Gagging often occurs when a person feels she can't catch her breath or can't breathe as deeply as she'd like. So if you'd like to get more comfortable performing oral sex, practice breathing through your nose. Close your mouth and draw the breath in through your nostrils. Here's the part that will really help: Pull the breath down through your chest and deep into your diaphragm—the area just behind your tummy. Hold the breath there for a moment, then gently and slowly release it back up through your diaphragm, lungs, and nostrils. The trick is to make sure you're breathing deeply, not shallowly, so that you feel absolutely confident of getting all the air you need. Practice for a few minutes each day until you feel completely comfortable relying on nose breathing. An added bonus: All that deep breathing will help relax you. And the more relaxed you feel, the more pleasure your body can receive.

Don't "Go All the Way"

While lots of guys love oral sex, they're not necessarily committed to climaxing that way. They'll often be just as happy with the oral stimulation, especially if it's followed by penetration. If you can find a pleasurable way of licking, sucking, or caressing with your tongue—or perhaps using a combination of tongue and hands—you can pleasure your man in a way that you find comfortable, too, especially if he's tasting of Sweet Sensations or D'Lickious. Then, when you either get tired of performing oral sex or when you think your guy is about to ejaculate, slip him out of your mouth and into your vagina. Some men love it when oral sex is followed by intercourse with their partner on top, so that they continue to feel receptive and cared-for. Others enjoy rolling over and thrusting into their partner. You and your guy can experiment to find routines that work for you. You can also help your man understand that you'll enjoy oral sex a lot more—and be a lot more willing to perform it—if he commits to letting you know when he's about to climax. "Otherwise, honey, the next time, I'll be so nervous, I won't be able to keep myself from stopping a whole lot sooner."

Focus on the Frenulum

Your guy may think he'll only be satisfied if you take his whole penis into your mouth, but here's another Passion Diva secret: Most guys are pretty happy with attention just to the tip and the frenulum, that V-spot on the underside of his penis. If you don't want his shaft in your mouth, what about licking the tip of his penis and taking it into your mouth? When you feel him getting more excited, hold the tip *very* gently in the palm of your hand—it's a very sensitive area, especially if

FINDING THE RIGHT SPOT

Passion Consultant Regina, who also works as a sales rep in Chicago, told me an inspiring story about one of the guests at her party—a story that illustrates the crucial importance of good communication with our partners.

"This was a woman who'd been married for a year," Regina told me. "But she was frustrated because she'd been married for an entire year and still wasn't able to bring him to orgasm with oral sex. I suggested that she ask him casually where the sensitive parts of his penis were. They were still pretty much in their newlywed phase, so he was more than happy to show her right then and there.

"Well, she started out sucking as usual, moving her mouth over his shaft in a forward-and-back motion. And as usual, she wasn't making much headway. But then she had an idea. She closed her mouth around the head of his penis and maybe an inch of his shaft and firmly pressed her tongue on the underside of his penis where the head comes together. She gripped his shaft firmly with her hand and began to stroke him. Her mouth moved back and forth in rhythm with her hand, but the key point, she told me, is that she never stopped applying pressure on that one spot with her tongue.

"Soon, she told me, he climaxed. And ever since, this technique ensured that she could bring him to orgasm any time they wanted her to." I love this story as a beautiful reminder of how a little experimenting and communicating can really open things up for a couple—with often delightful results.

your guy hasn't been circumcised—and then use the tip of your tongue to tickle his frenulum. If you like, you can even cover the frenulum with your tongue without actually taking the whole penis in your mouth. Maybe use some Sweet Sensations or D'Lickious either in tingling mint or delightful cinnamon. Your guy will thank you for it!

USE YOUR HANDS

Here's another "compromise" version of oral sex that may end up feeling terrifically satisfying for both of you: Take your guy's sensitive tip into your mouth, licking and kissing as you please, but instead of taking the shaft in your mouth, use your hands. Lubricants like Lickety Lube strawberry or piña colada will keep him feeling warm and slippery all the way down. The idea is to create the sensation of a vagina by giving him complete coverage. You can move your hands and mouth up and down at the same time, and when your mouth needs a break, use your top hand to swivel over the top of his penis in a gentle juicing motion while you keep the up-and-down movement going with your lower hand. (Check out "The Hand Job of Happiness" in Chapter 6 and combine it with some oral attention to his tip if you'd like to take this idea further.)

Oral Sex Play: Use Your Toys to Give Him Pleasure

There are so many ways that your adult toys can enhance oral sex— here are just a few to get you started. I encourage you to let your own imagination run free and to invite your partner to think of some great new ways to play.

- A Bullet with multiple levels of vibration can add a nice buzz to the party. Start it at its lowest setting and place it along his perineum while you are engaged in oral sex. And to enhance both your pleasure and his, try placing a velvety smooth vibrator like Velvet Pleasure next to your cheek while you're kissing and fondling his penis and scrotum. He'll enjoy both your mouth and the vibrator for twice the satisfaction.

- A small personal massager like the Honey Bunny can add a light, tickling vibration during oral sex if you place it below his penis, near the base and above the scrotum. The Honey Bunny is a bullet vibrator encased in a rabbit-shaped silicone sleeve, so step one is to let the bunny's ears tease and tickle your guy. If you'd like to get more direct, step two might be to press the bunny's face gently into this sensitive area. And if you'd like to create the same effect in the shower, try a Waterproof Finger Fun personal massager. It's got a ring to fit on your finger so you don't actually have to hold it.

- We can't leave the subject of toys without mentioning the c-ring! Apply one to his erect penis before you continue with oral sex: It will make his shaft and scrotum far more sensitive to the loving caresses of your mouth and hands. Magic Rings, a super-stretchy pair of jelly c-rings, are small enough not to get in the way of your mouth. You can use just one on his shaft or two for his shaft and his scrotum.

THE *Passion Diva's Guide* TO GIGI

- **Step one.** Lubricate Gigi and also his shaft with a small amount of edible lubricant. Some fun choices might be Lickety Lube watermelon, Embrace Sensual Lubricant vanilla, or perhaps Gigi's own personal lube, Slip 'n Slide.

- **Step two.** Slowly slide Gigi onto his erect penis so that it completely rests against the base of his shaft, leaving the head exposed for your mouth and tongue to stimulate.

- **Step three.** With your mouth wrapped around the head of your guy's penis, slide Gigi back and forth along his shaft. Vary the speed and pay attention to his reaction. If you feel as though you need guidance, place his hand over yours so he can help you find the speed he likes best.

- **Step four.** As the Gigi gets closer to your mouth, suck and/or lick; as the Gigi travels toward the base, release. For variety, do the opposite—suck as Gigi moves away from your mouth and release as you move it closer.

WARM AND COZY

Of course, you'd never use Gigi without lots of lubricant. For extra pleasure, though, consider using a special warming lubricant to make Gigi feel even more lifelike. RomantaTherapy Sensual Warming Lubricant is an excellent choice.

- **Step five.** If you choose, you can slide Gigi all the way forward so it completely covers the head.

- **Step six.** When he gets close to climax, you can decide whether to let Gigi "swallow" for you. If you prefer not to swallow, keep repeating Step Five, and just before he ejaculates, pull the Gigi up over the head of the penis creating a sensual vacuum effect. The semen will go straight into Gigi, and your guy will get every last bit of stimulation when he ejaculates.

Oral Sex on You: A Basic How-To for Him

As with oral sex on guys, oral sex on women provokes a lot of different responses at our Passion Parties. Some women just don't feel comfortable with it:

"Oh, I can never relax when he's doing that. It just makes me uncomfortable."

"I worry about whether he'll like the taste, and even if I've taken a shower, I always worry that there's a smell."

"Well, I love it when a guy kisses me down there, but I've been with one or two guys who made it pretty clear that they didn't like it. Sometimes I even got the feeling that they thought less of me for wanting it."

But for every woman who expresses reserve, there is another who professes pure enthusiasm—and then some: "Wow. For me, oral sex is one of the best things we do. It took me a while to show my guy what I like, but now he's really got it down ... and am I glad about it!"

I think oral sex for women is such a wonderful source of pleasure and such a terrific way to build intimacy with your partner that I want to encourage each and every one of you to at least consider overcoming any barriers you might face in enjoying this wonderful experience. I know some of us were raised to believe that Good Girls don't enjoy oral sex, and that some of us have encountered men who had negative attitudes about this delightful practice. All the more reason to tap into your Passion Diva's courage and sensuality, so that you can find your own way to make it a part of your bedroom repertoire.

If freshness or taste is a concern of yours, there are a few simple things you can do to relieve your worries. Of course, regular bathing or showers is pretty much all that you need to guarantee freshness, and many guys genuinely enjoy the slightly salty taste of a clean vagina. But you can also create a new taste for yourself through diet (see page 251) or with Fresh & Frisky spray, Fresh & Frisky Feminine Wipes, or Tasty Tease in three luscious flavors—mint, piña colada, and strawberry. Or try one of the many other sprays, gels, and flavored lubricants offered by Passion Parties and other companies.

Meanwhile, the more you know what you want your guy to do, the better your chances of having a good experience. So read through the tips in this chapter and bring your favorite discoveries from self-pleasuring into the mix as well. As always, you need to let your partner know what you want. Talk to him about your likes and dislikes or simply respond—with words or sounds—as he proceeds. Shift your hips to guide his lips or use your hands to gently guide his head. And if you're shy about letting him know that you'd like oral sex in the first place—or about giving him more details—let me tell him for you. Put a pretty Post-it by the places in this book that describe activities you'd enjoy and add a word or two; perhaps something like, *This looks like fun. Would you like to try it?*

As with oral sex for men, you can use your own oral-sex experience either as an end in itself (something that brings you to orgasm) or as part of foreplay (something that makes the final act of sexual intercourse even more enjoyable). Since you're more likely than your guy to have more than one climax in the same lovemaking session, you can always go for "all of the above"—an orgasm from oral sex and then another one while you're having intercourse. The possibilities are endless!

Finally, don't forget how lubes and gels can enhance the experience for both of you. As Idaho Passion Consultant Beth told me:

> My sweetie wasn't big on a lot of foreplay. I love to have a man perform oral sex on me, but he was always ready to dive right in, and I needed a little time to get warmed up. One night I told him that I had applied some Lickety Lube all over my clitoris and vagina, and that he had to tell me what the flavor was before he went any further. By the time he figured out whether it was cherry or strawberry, I was ready for him!

THE VAGINA MONOLOGUES:
LEARNING TO LOVE OUR BODIES

We've all grown up with so many negative myths about our bodies that even the most confident woman can feel hesitant and shy about oral sex. Even if she's a tigress in the bedroom in every other way, a woman can find it difficult to overcome these attitudes. That's why I'm so happy to see the nationwide—and worldwide—popularity of Eve Ensler's play *The Vagina Monologues*, which offers such a positive, joyous way of looking at our sexual selves. If you're struggling with negative feelings about your most intimate area, consider seeing a production or even reading the published version of this wonderful play, which is all based on interviews that Ensler did with women in America and around the world, asking them to share their thoughts, feelings, and experiences with their vaginas. You'll realize that you're far from alone in your struggles and frustrations, and that there's a whole world of Passion Divas out there, ready to support you in your joy.

So take a look at the Passion Diva's Guide to Oral Sex—On You, and once again, pick and choose and vary in any way that works for you and your partner. A fabulous experience is in store for you both.

THE *Passion Diva's Guide* TO ORAL SEX—ON YOU

- **Make sure you're both comfortable.** Slide a pillow under your hips or move to the end of the bed so he can kneel on the floor.

- **Encourage him to get there slowly.** Lots of women like their guy to work their way down to that "sweet spot"—kissing your breasts, tummy, thighs, letting the anticipation build, waiting until you are tingling with desire. Help your guy find your rhythm by cuing him with words or sounds.

- **Use plenty of lube.** You can use a clear lubricant with no taste or add some Lickety Lube in cherry or watermelon to make his experience more tasty.

- **Help him work from the outside in.** Encourage him to nibble on your *labia majora*—your outer lips—but he should only use *his* lips, never his teeth! Then he can work his tongue in between the *labia majora* and the *labia minora* (inner lips), kissing and caressing. And remind him not to neglect the clitoris! Then have him slip inside your vaginal opening with his finger or tongue. Some women like it when their guy gently inserts a finger or two while using his tongue to provide clitoral stimulation a few inches above.

- **Invite him to be gentle with your clitoris.** Because your clitoris is so full of nerve endings, it's exquisitely sensitive, which makes it very receptive to oral pleasure but which often requires a slow and gentle approach. Some women like a very direct contact on and around the clitoris. Others like to work up to that kind of intensity.

- **Be playful and creative.** He might tease the underside of your clitoris with light, quick strokes of the tongue. Or he could combine licking with finger or palm massage on your inner thighs, your perineum, or your buttocks. Invite him to pleasure your lips and vagina with his lips and tongue while the tip of his nose stimulates your clitoris. And encourage him to vary the intensity and speed of his kissing and caressing, especially in response to your words and sounds.

- **Communicate.** Let him know what you like and how you feel about what he's doing. The more enthusiastic and responsive you are, the more he'll enjoy it, too—and the more he'll learn about what works for you. And as always, feel free to talk outside of bed about what you might like on your next night of passion.

Oral Sex Play: Using Toys to Give You Pleasure

Once you and your partner have mastered the basics of oral sex on you, the two of you may want to add some toys to mix things up a little. Brianna, a Passion Consultant and human resources worker in Oregon, told me about a guest who found that toys were the key to making oral sex play work for her and her husband. "He's very sweet and affectionate, but to be honest, I like to keep things going several minutes longer than he does," Brianna's guest told her. "Now that we've got the Mini Tongue, we have this great new routine. He starts off using his tongue, gives me all the stimulation I need with the

CAN YOU SPELL "MISSISSIPPI"?

Are you looking for a thirty-second way to tell him how to give you oral pleasure? Suggest that he slide his tongue over your clitoris and labia and spell out the names of one of the fifty states. Or pick just a few states—preferably the ones with lots of "s's"!

Mini, and then, when I'm close to finishing, he switches back to his own tongue. I love the personal contact. It makes us both feel very close—but this way no one gets tired, and no one gets frustrated. It's perfect!"

THE *Passion Diva's Guide* TO
USING TOYS FOR YOUR PLEASURE

- **Bullet.** This little vibrator can be used to provide stimulation to the clitoris while your partner focuses his attention on your labia and vagina.

- **Vibrators.** A vibrator designed without a clitoral stimulator, such as Pink Passion, can be used for penetration while he caresses your clitoris with his tongue. The Pink Passion is a jelly vibe with pleasurable ridges for you and a simple twist control base for him. For oral pleasure in the shower, try using the Spa Mate for penetration—a waterproof jelly vibe with nubs at the base to stimulate your labia.

- **G-spot vibrators.** For a double whammy in ultimate oral sex, try using a G-spot vibe like the Nubby G. The combination of simultaneous G-spot and clitoral stimulation from his tongue or fingers might just give you the best oral sex orgasm ever. The Nubby G vibes are specifically designed with a curve to apply just the right pressure to your G-spot.

- **Mini Tongue.** Let's face it, oral sex can be tiring, and it can also be frustrating when your partner must slow down or take a break just when you're on the brink of orgasm. Or maybe some nights he's too tired for oral sex. Now you've got a great alternative: Let the Mini Tongue do the licking for him. It looks like a tongue, moves like a tongue, and even feels like a tongue, with just one difference—it never needs a break! Made from a super-soft silicone for an amazingly real feel, the Mini Tongue has three speeds and comes with a bullet for extra stimulation elsewhere. You can also try the Disco Mini Tongue, which lights up as it wiggles, swirls, and licks. This one also comes with a bullet, but instead of being soft like a real tongue, it's made from a hard plastic material for a different type of sensation.

69: The Magic Number!

If both you and your partner enjoy oral sex, there's one more way you can pleasure each other. Curl into what is known as the "69" position—lying beside each other, each of you with your mouth upon the other's genitals—and perform oral sex on each other. While some couples find this a challenge—it can be hard to concentrate on giving pleasure while you're receiving so much of it, and vice versa—other couples consider it the ultimate in mutual trust and generosity. It's certainly something to try at least once!

THE *Passion Diva's Guide* TO 69

- **The basic position.** The classic position for 69 has you and your partner lying on your sides, facing each other. This is a nice arrangement, because you're both sharing equally in the creation of the experience—neither of you is controlling the action. And both of you have your hands free to caress breasts or chests, nipples, tummy, back, thighs.

- **The straddle.** You can also try the position with your guy lying on his back, his knees raised, while you straddle his face. Support your weight with your knees, then bend down and take his penis into your mouth. In this position, your vagina is directly over his face. He has the chance to wrap his arms around your thighs and use his hands to play with your bottom, while your hands are free to stroke his shaft or play with his scrotum. As the one on top, you can play a bit—move your vagina directly onto his mouth, or hover it over his face so he can use his hands to stimulate you.

- **On your back.** Yet another pleasurable variation has you on your back, your knees raised and your legs apart. Use a pillow to lift and support your head, while he straddles your head and leans his face in between your legs. In this setup, he's got the most access to your clitoris, since he's completely free to move. And you've got his penis right at your lips, with your hands free to stroke his shaft, apply pressure to his anus or perineum, or gently stroke and squeeze his scrotum. Since from this position you can't control the penetration, make sure you can let him know if you feel overwhelmed by his shaft in your mouth and can't maneuver to a comfortable position on your own—maybe pat his thigh three times or signal him in some other way.

- **Toys for 69.** In this variation of oral sex, you can use all the toys you'd normally enjoy during cunnilingus or fellatio: the Pulsing Orbiter, Velvet Pleasure, Bullets with a variety of sleeves, and hard cylinder vibrators for vaginal and clitoral stimulation. You can even use the Love Swing for creative 69: Sit in the seat with your feet on the ground as your partner stands behind you. Lean back until his shaft and testicles are available for your oral stimulation, and then once you've achieved this, have him bend over to perform oral sex on you.

If you feel that the use of toys and the swing is turning the whole encounter into a "three-ring circus," just stop, come up for air, and start over. The main thing is to have fun and enjoy each other.

So now you have a great idea of the sexual basics: foreplay, intercourse, and oral sex. Have I left you wanting more? Move on to Chapter 9 for some Great Adventures, including fantasy play, restraints, and anal sex. If you've ever been curious about any of these activities, all you have to do is turn the page.

~ⓢ In Your Passion Pantry ⓢ~

- **Gigi.** If you'd like a different approach to oral sex, try this masturbation sleeve; modeled after a real vagina, it quickly becomes as warm and soft as the real thing and is lined with ribbing for extra pleasure. Slip 'n Slide Lubricant keeps everything moving smoothly.

- **Lickety Lube.** Flavored in cherry, piña colada, strawberry, and watermelon, this crystal-clear lubricant is water-based, delicious, and works well with toys and condoms.

- **Tasty Tease.** In its three flavors—mint, piña colada, and strawberry—this silky-smooth cream will help calm your gag reflexes, encourage your lover to linger longer, and inspire some delicious, enthusiastic oral sex.

- **D'Lickious.** Tasting of warm cinnamon or tingly mint, this edible gel masks natural body taste with great flavor.

- **Sweet Sensations Edible Gel.** Another great product for oral lovemaking, this refreshing, edible gel is infused with tingling spearmint oil to excite the senses and delight the taste buds.

- **Breath mints and candies.** Freshen up your oral sex play with Altoids or other strong breath fresheners. Just be careful not to swallow them during your excitement! And check out Pop Rocks exploding candy, whose fizzy effect creates a bubbling sensation for both partners.

- **Mini Tongue.** This little vibrator looks like a tongue, acts like a tongue, and provides endless hours of lifelike oral stimulation.

⤙ 9 ⤚

Great Adventures

When I think of great adventures in the bedroom, I always remember the story I heard from Harriet, a beautician and Passion Consultant in Kentucky. She was sitting in the confidential ordering room when in walked her last guest, Vera, a matronly woman in her early sixties. Dressed in a floral-print dress with a lacy collar, Vera was the picture of traditional southern charm. She looked so prim and proper, in fact, that Harriet had been a bit concerned about offending her during some of the more descriptive portions of her presentation. And to be sure, Vera hadn't said a word or even betrayed the hint of a smile. She simply sat and listened, looking more and more uncomfortable each time Harriet introduced a new item.

Now, as Vera entered the room, Harriet couldn't help wondering what in the world this elderly woman would order. Some body lotion? Perhaps some bath salts? Harriet noticed that there was no ring on Vera's finger, so maybe she was there to buy something for a favorite niece.

Before Harriet could even ask what she wanted, she said, "Tell me, dear, I'm a bit concerned, because you never once mentioned anal beads. Do you really not carry any tush toys at all? The company that makes the ones my boyfriend and I usually use has just gone out of business."

"Well, if I needed any reminding," Harriet told me later, "that one

266

incident would have reminded me good and proper: *Never* make assumptions about *anybody.* What people do behind closed doors—you just never know!"

Indeed, you don't. And I'd like to extend Harriet's lesson to all of you out there who are reading this book: Not only do you not know what your neighbors are doing, but you may not even know what you yourself might be capable of. Perhaps you're already being quite adventurous in the bedroom and would like a few more ideas; or maybe you've always wondered about a particular sexual activity and have never quite dared to do it; or perhaps this moment is the very first time you've ever thought about going beyond intercourse, hand jobs, and oral sex. Whatever your situation, I encourage you to let your Passion Diva run free. Read through this chapter, see what might appeal to you—if not today, maybe one day—and allow yourself to be open to any thoughts, feelings, or images that come to mind. Great adventures come in many varieties—and at least some of them happen in the bedroom!

Pushing the Boundaries—and Feeling Safe

This chapter is all about pushing the boundaries, but it's also about finding ways to be comfortable while doing so. In my opinion, a sexual relationship is the highest form of trust between two people. So in a long-standing sexual relationship, one built on a deep foundation of trust, you and your partner may choose to experiment a bit. You may even find that pushing on some boundaries together deepens your connection.

But you can't push on the boundaries unless you have a clear, reliable set of rules and principles. It sounds contradictory, but it's true: When you know what you *can* count on, then you can feel free to experiment a bit with the rest. So consider these guidelines as you and your partner prepare to take your sexual experience together to a whole new level:

YOUR *Passion Diva's Guide*LINES
FOR ADVENTUROUS SEX

- **Be adventurous.** Remember Passion Diva Principle #8—*Your most important sex organ is your brain.* Allow yourself to think "outside the box," to imagine new possibilities, to tap into your secret desires and fantasies. You don't have to act on anything you imagine; you don't even have to tell anyone; and you certainly don't have to do anything you're not comfortable with. But as with so many other aspects of sex, being adventurous is a state of mind, the willingness to replace "Eeeeuw!" with "Why not?" If there's an activity you genuinely don't want to do, of course, say no. But before you say no, ask yourself if you're saying it because you really mean it, or because you just can't imagine yourself as the kind of person who does something that wild and crazy. If it's the latter, maybe reconsider. Maybe you've got a whole other Passion Diva in there who's never yet been invited to come out—and now's her chance.

- **Be generous.** Again, I don't want you to do anything that makes you feel bad about who you are, and I certainly don't want you to feel pressured by your partner or anybody else. But consider if there's any way to say, "Yes, just this once," or "I'll do it, but if I hate it, I'm going to stop, even if we're right in the middle of it," or "I'll do *that* for you if you do *this* for me." Being generous with your partner about his sexual desires and fantasies is a gift based on trust, commitment, and faith in his love for you. So if those qualities are present in your relationship, see if there's a way for you to maintain your integrity and still be generous.

- **Take it in steps.** Just because you're being adventurous and generous doesn't mean you've turned into a different person overnight. As the saying goes, "Start low and go slow." Throughout this chapter, I'll lay out each activity in steps, so you can ease your way into this new type of sex play. If your partner cares for you and is trustworthy enough to share your adventure, he'll respect your need to go slowly. And if you're the one who's initiating the new adventure, then you do the same for him. It may take longer to get there, but the enhanced trust and the additional pleasure will definitely make that extra time worth your while.

- **Be honest with yourself.** Being adventurous means being willing to give something a try, and being generous means doing something nice for another person. But neither of those wonderful qualities means you have to lie to yourself about what you're enjoying or what *you* really want. Maybe trying a new adventure will work for you, and you'll be just as into this new activity as your partner. But maybe you won't like it as much as he does, and maybe you'll never like it. Being honest with yourself will help you decide how to balance your own needs, limits, and desires with your partner's. So what if you like something that your partner doesn't like—even something that he thinks is freaky? Be honest with yourself about that, too. That's *your* Passion Diva in there; you don't have to apologize for her to anybody.

- **Remember you have the power to say no at any time**. And I do mean *any* time, up to and including the very last moment of whatever act you choose. If you don't like what's happening, you have the right to stop it. And if you don't trust your partner to respect that right, don't engage in the adventure. Only by knowing that you have the power to say *no* can you really enjoy your power to say *yes*.

- **Commit to good communication before, during, and after.** I know it can be hard to speak honestly about how a sexual activity made you feel. But if you and your partner aren't communicating on that

A SIMPLE FANTASY . . .

Sometimes the best fantasies are the simplest. Passion Consultant Micki in Nebraska told us about a guest who learned to fulfill her husband's fantasy of "taking him in a rage of passion." "Normally, I have trouble initiating sex," Micki's guest explained, "and my husband sometimes feels as if I don't want him, which isn't the case at all." Micki helped her guest pick out some toys to use with her husband, and then the woman got the idea of using them on her own. "They helped me understand my own body and the joys of masturbation," she told Micki. "This in turn increased my sex drive. I now am able to sincerely initiate sex more often with a real hunger and enthusiasm for the act itself—which is a huge turn-on for my husband."

level, maybe the two of you aren't yet ready for the kind of adventurous sex play described in this chapter. On the other hand, if you are able to be honest about how these activities affect you, and to listen without judgment about how they affect him, these shared adventures can deepen your trust and connection, no matter how the sex itself turns out.

Exploring Your Fantasies

Throughout this book, I've encouraged you to let your fantasies run free while reminding you that fantasy is often a very private matter. No matter what you think about in daily life, your fantasies while self-pleasuring or during sex with your partner are your business and your business only.

Having said that, let's also remember that some fantasies are fun to talk about, and some are fun to act out. As long as you and your partner understand that fantasies don't represent what you *really* want and approach them without judgment, you can become immeasurably closer by sharing them—or at least some of them!

YOUR *Passion Diva's Guide* TO
SHARING FANTASIES WITH YOUR PARTNER

NOTE: You don't have to follow each and every one of these steps—feel free to skip ahead! However, never neglect Step Four, choosing a password. Having a password is crucial every time you engage in a sexual adventure that involves fantasy, role-playing, or restraints.

- **Step one: Talk about it.** Pick a safe, intimate time when you've got plenty of privacy and no pressures, and start talking about your fantasies with your partner. You might choose a nonsexual setting—driving in the car, or taking a long walk together—so that it's clear to both of you that this is merely a "what-if" kind of conversation, not something that you're necessarily going to act on right then. Or you might bring the conversation up during the afterglow, when you're both feeling sexually confident and comfortable in your relationship and when it's clear that you're saying, "Maybe someday . . ." instead of "How about now?"

- **Step two: Start small.** Pick something that is easy to fulfill, something you could actually do without much risk or effort. For example, you might say, "Someday, honey, I'd like to have you come home, and I'd answer the door wearing nothing but a trench coat with maybe some garters underneath. How would you feel about that?" Or you could simply ask your partner, "Haven't you always wanted a French maid?"

- **Step three: Talk it through.** If it seems too daunting to jump right in, talk about what it might be like if you did act out your fantasy. You might want to have this conversation in a private place so that if either of you gets turned on, you can translate those feelings into lovemaking, whether directly related to your fantasy or not. To start the conversation, you might say, "So there I am, in nothing but my garters. And when you see me, you say? . . ." Let your partner imagine the scene and help create it with you, in words first and perhaps in actions later. Or you might say, "Suppose you did have a French maid. What's the first thing you'd ask her to do? . . . Okay, so there I am, with my little feather duster, tickling you in that very private place, and then you say? . . ." When the fantasy becomes a shared scenario, it may be easier for the two of you to enact it. Likewise, if you feel shy about enacting your partner's fantasies, encourage him to talk them through with you so that you, too, can get used to the idea.

- **Step four: Choose a password.** This step is crucial if you ever intend to get beyond the "what if" stage. A password, also called a "safe word," is a word that will stop whatever activity is proceeding—immediately and without question. That's in order to prevent confusion between the fantasy character, whose protests and objections may be part of the game, and your real selves, who may genuinely want to stop. For example, suppose your password is "flamingo." You and your partner are enacting a scenario in which he asks the French maid to take off her uniform. As the maid, you might say, "Oh, no, m'sieu! I could never do that! Please don't ask me again!" That's all part of the fun, and your partner can continue to play the part of the evil aristocrat who threatens you with dire punishments if you refuse. But if you say, "Flamingo," he knows to drop the role-playing and say, "Honey, what's wrong?" Obviously, you want to choose a password that will never come up in the fantasy you're acting out, a word completely unrelated to any possible scenario, so that there's no chance of a mistake: The password means *"Stop immediately."* Period.

- **Step five: Act it out.** Now that you've talked through your ideas and agreed upon your password, you're ready to act out your fantasy. Here, too, be encouraging and nonjudgmental. It may take a while for you both to get into the spirit of the game, but the more room

SOME COMMON FANTASY SCENARIOS

Our Passion Consultants have heard it all! I asked them to let me in on the most common fantasy scenarios they heard about at their parties, and here's what they shared with me:

Fantasies for You and Your Partner

- answering the door naked
- propositioning your husband in an elevator or bar as though he were a stranger
- wrapping yourself up in cellophane and ribbon, and giving yourself to your guy as a birthday present
- going out with no underwear
- revealing to your guy that you've got something sexy on underneath a more conservative exterior
- pole dancing . . . in your bedroom

Fantasies Involving Characters

- boss and secretary
- captain and first mate
- Cleopatra and Anthony
- damsel in distress and knight in shining armor
- doctor and nurse
- flight attendant and passenger
- housewife and mailman or delivery guy
- movie star/rock star and fan or bodyguard
- pilot and flight attendant
- pilot and passenger
- police officer and speeding driver
- lady and gardener
- lady and pool boy
- rich person and driver
- two strangers

you give each other to just have fun, the more pleasure both of you will have. Ideally, you'll choose a fantasy that turns both of you on or at least intrigues you, although it's fine to occasionally act out a fantasy that only one of you is really attached to. Whatever scenario you choose, personalize it, make it your own. Find the parts of yourself that you don't normally get to express—the flirty little maid, the sultry stripper, the seductive movie star. Try out new voices, gestures, personalities. Go back to the part of yourself you knew as a kid playing dress-up or "Princess" or acting out your favorite TV shows, and encourage your guy to do the same. (Yes, guys play "pretend," too, even if it's more often video games or reenactments of *their* favorite TV shows.)

- **Step six: Use props and costumes.** Of course, you can always just *imagine* the physical details of your encounter. But if a French maid's costume, a flight captain's hat, or a movie star's feather boa turns either of you on, why not take your fantasies a step further and *really* play dress-up? Creating more elaborate fantasies may actually free both of you to take your pleasure a step further. Our most consistent seller is Fishnet Fantasy Hosiery, a body stocking that can be worn under clothes for all-day excitement and that can transform you into the Passion Diva temptress that you are. Or you could purchase Passion Parties' Frisky French Maid costume or our Naughty Nurse costume. Or maybe create your own costumes from things you find in the craft shop, thrift shop, and discount store. Just like when you were a kid, dressing up can be half the fun. And then for adult play, *un*dressing is the other half!

Further into Fantasy

Here are some role-play suggestions that you and your partner might enjoy or that might give you some ideas for your own personal fantasies. Have fun, and remember that you'll enjoy this type of fantasy more if you follow these principles:

MAKE THREE AGREEMENTS

1. Attitude—You agree to keep it playful.
2. Attention—You agree to give each other undivided attention.
3. A Game—You agree to play all out, have fun, and do your best.

MAKE THREE COMMITMENTS

1. Presentation—You are committed to look the part, dress the part, and act the part.
2. Preparation—You are committed to take the time to plan ahead a little, to be creative, and, where necessary, to add drama and staging.
3. Password—You commit to honor the password.

Backyard Explorers

You'll be enacting this fantasy in your very own backyard, so make sure you've got the privacy you need, as well as the supplies that will keep you comfortable in any weather: tent, camping gear, blankets, and pillows. If it's cold out, get some coats and blankets to pad your "love tent," since you're going to get naked in there! And don't forget the picnic basket and champagne so you and your partner can share the food and drink that will put you in the mood.

The situation: You are in a remote, perhaps dangerous place, far from any shelter. You have to share your tent and your provisions for the night with a stranger.

Sexy Dancers

Ever wondered what it would be like to dance seductively for a stranger or to have a stranger dance for you? Well, now's your chance to find out in the privacy of your own bedroom. Whichever one of you is the dancer should craft an enticing costume—perhaps a veiled seductress for you, a cowboy or construction worker for him. Remember that the fun of the costume is in taking off various pieces and teasing your partner with them. Whichever one of you is the dancer might also want to shave or trim around your genitals for added visual pleasure. You can also use some type of lotion or oil that leaves your skin looking moist, or maybe even paint yourself with body glitter. See pages 194–97 in Chapter 6 for some more ideas.

The situation: You are a private dancer whose customer is behind a two-way mirror, so that he can see you but you can't see him. Position a mirror behind you so that you can be seen from both the front and the back. Then undress slowly, dance sensually, and arouse yourself using your own hands while your partner sips champagne and watches. (Or you watch and have him dance.) For an added thrill, have the dancer be blindfolded. Take advantage of these tips for sensual dancing:

- Use slow movements.
- Arch your back, legs, and limbs.
- Let each piece of clothing that you remove fall very slowly to the floor.
- Touch yourself softly and sigh.
- Wet your lips and moan.
- Say "yes" . . . slowly . . . deeply . . . repeatedly.
- Arouse your nipples with cold champagne.
- At the dance's conclusion, wrap your body around the viewer like a snake.
- Grind your hips into the viewer's and rock your pelvis.

By the way, if you'd like some extra pointers, you can always order a copy of the DVD *Striptease for Real Women*. It's a guide for women who are interested in doing a striptease only for themselves and for their partners.

Going Bold with Blindfolds

If you and your partner really trust each other, playing with blindfolds can be an extraordinary turn-on. When you can't see, you really are at the mercy of your partner, and that sense of completely abandoning yourself to his care can be very exciting for some women. (Or vice versa, if he is the one in the blindfold.) If you're the one who can see, you get to experience the thrill of having the other person "at your mercy," knowing that he has placed himself totally in your hands. (And again, that goes for him, too, when it's his turn to enjoy the "power" role.)

Besides the elements of power, helplessness, and trust, the blind-folded person will begin to notice that his or her other senses are sharpened and that the whole experience creates a new alertness. Often, in a long-term relationship, sex can become a bit routine. Well, there's nothing routine about being blindfolded: You have no idea what's going to happen next, where you're going to be touched, or even what you're going to be touched with. Introduce feathers and faux fur into your sex play for new sensations (we sell several different types of feathers, including a Feather Snapper, which has a soft feather with lit-tle leather snappers hidden in the center, for an enticing mixture of naughty and nice), or try stimulating your partner's taste buds with strawberries, chocolate, pineapple, mango—all eaten "in the dark." Wave a stick of sandalwood incense beneath his nose or give him a whiff of your favorite perfume. See if he can identify the tastes of edible gels and puddings as he licks them off the body parts you guide him to. The possibilities are endless—and again, you can always reverse roles.

Of course, to honor your vulnerability and trust, you'll want to set some ground rules with your partner before engaging in this kind of sex play. The most important rule is that the blindfolded person should be able to stop the play and have the blindfold removed at any point, just by saying *Stop* or, to be extra safe, using your password. Sometimes, when people are being tickled, they cry out "Stop!" or "No!" without really meaning it, but a password always means *Stop immediately*. Knowing that you're safe and that you can trust your partner will enable you to surrender completely to the experience of the blindfold and allow your senses to awaken.

Gentle Restraints

If you like the interplay of power, control, trust, and vulnerability, take it a step further with some gentle restraints. Use a simple silk scarf, or for even greater ease, try our Private Pleasures Set, which includes plush furry breakaway cuffs and a pink satin blindfold. In some cases, the fun is simply in the power—knowing, for example, that you can stimulate and excite your partner, but he can't touch you. It may be even more thrilling to combine restraint with fantasy, acting out an elaborate scenario that turns you both on.

Lee, a Passion Consultant from Maryland, told me about one guest who loved our furry handcuffs with quick release. "She thought it was kind of naughty," Lee told me, "but that's just what made it so exciting for her. She told me that the handcuffs spiced up the sex, sure, but they also introduced a new level of trust. Most important to her was the way her guy treated her with great respect before, during, and after their 'close encounter.'"

REMOTE-CONTROLLED PLEASURE

The remote-control vibrator is a Bullet vibrator that's controlled via a powerbox that works up to twenty feet away—a terrific device for some spicy couples' fun and games. If you and your guy enjoy the idea of him giving you some long-distance pleasure when you least expect it—at a party, say, or when you're out to dinner—you might enjoy this adult toy. This toy might also add some pleasure to your play with blindfolds or even with restraints. And of course, you can always find ways for him to wear it, too!

As you can see, communication—and your password—are paramount. It's crucial that both of you know how to stop the sex play at any point, and that you feel comfortable sharing any feelings that the experience brings up. If either one of you lacks experience with this kind of activity, I urge you to take things very slowly indeed, so that you can process and release any unexpected emotions that emerge. Of course, if all that emerges is sexual pleasure—well, then, let the games continue!

Anal Sex

In a recent survey of 100,000 *Playboy* readers, 47 percent of men and 61 percent of women admitted to having tried some variation of anal sex play. This should come as no surprise to anyone who remembers that many years ago famed sex researcher Dr. Alfred Kinsey also announced that the anal region seemed to be a sexy area for about half of the population. So whether you find the idea of anal sex play a turn-on or a turn-off, you've got a substantial number of people on your side.

Let's start with the bare facts. The anus is richly endowed with sensitive nerve endings, all interconnected with your pelvic muscles. Whether you know it or not, your anal muscles also contract rhythmically during orgasm, just as your PC muscles do (and his, as well). So the chances are good that at least *some* kind of stimulation in this area may feel good to you. The question is what kind and how much?

For men, the area is even more likely to be pleasurable because of its proximity to the prostate. His prostate is like your G-spot—both of them often enjoy a little stimulation—but just as your G-spot can be best reached through the vagina, his prostate can be best reached through the anus. That's why guys often appreciate some attention back there, especially during sex.

Guys may be turned on by *your* anal region for a whole variety of reasons. Just as many men find it sexy to see and feel breasts, they are also turned on by buttocks. A man may also like the idea of the nice, tight way an anus fits around his penis, or he may enjoy the thought of simply sliding his penis between your buttocks without actually entering you.

On the other hand, for many women, the very idea of anal sex is a turn-off. We've been socialized to associate that area with dirt and "unmentionables." And unlike the vagina, the anus isn't really made to receive something as large as a penis. Anal penetration can be painful even for people who also find it pleasurable, especially if you don't use enough lubrication (the anus, unlike the vagina, doesn't produce any lubricant of its own).

So the first thing to get straight is the difference between anal sex play—sexual activity that involves the area around your anus—and actual anal penetration. You may like neither, only one, or both, and so might your guy. To make things even more interesting, either one of you may enjoy doing things to the other that you don't enjoy having done to yourself, and either of you might enjoy receiving attention that you don't enjoy giving.

DON'T FORGET THE LUBE!

The main reason anal sex can be painful—for both the inserter and the recipient—is a lack of lubrication. Unlike the vagina, the anal canal produces no natural lubrication, plus it's a smaller, tighter opening. So use lubricants liberally in and around the anus as well as on anything that enters it, whether that be a finger, a penis, or a sex toy, and replenish your lubricants frequently during anal sex.

Some anal lubricants contain desensitizers—lidocaine and/or benzocaine—to help reduce discomfort. But discomfort is the body's way of saying that something is wrong, and the use of desensitizing products turns off your body's own warning system and thus increases your risk of injury. Be careful with any product that contains a desensitizer, and use it very sparingly indeed. Personally, I feel that you should be fully aware of what's happening in your body at all times. But if you'd like something to "take the edge off," these products are available to you.

To help you sort out all the possible options, let's take things step by step. (You can also buy the very useful CD *Anal Foreplay*, to teach you more of the ins and outs.) That way, you'll know exactly what your choices are, and then you can decide.

YOUR *Passion Diva's Guide* TO ANAL SEX PLAY

Remember, lots of bacteria tend to collect around the anus, so anything that goes in or around this area, including the rim, needs to be sheathed in a condom. That goes for fingers, penises, and sex toys. And before any of those items can go anywhere else—especially into a mouth, against a clitoris, or into a vagina—you have to take off the condom and clean the item, with soap and water for body parts or with special cleanser for sex toys. I recommend buying special sex toys for anal use only.

- **Rimming.** This is the mildest version of anal sex play, so if you're not familiar with anal activities, start here. As the name suggests, rimming involves playing with your rim—the sensitive outer edges of your anal opening. Your partner might lubricate his condom-clad fingers and gently push in around the edge of your opening, using a circular motion. You might enjoy him bearing down slightly for more pressure and massaging your perineum, using a finger on his other hand. Another fun choice is for him to hold a bullet against your anal opening during oral sex, which a lot of women say gives them an extra-strong orgasm. You can also try all of these moves on him. Just remember never to insert a bullet into an anus—it's too difficult to get it out and could get lost. I'll tell you about some sex toys you *can* insert a little further on.

- **Fingers.** One of the best anal sex toys you can find is the one you both already own: your fingers. Let him use the tip of his finger to tickle your anus, and if that feels good, invite him to slip a very well-lubricated pinky or forefinger into your anus during foreplay, oral sex, or intercourse. (Again, those fingers should be wearing condoms.) Revelation and UltraGlide Gel are terrific lubes for this kind of sex play. And find out if your guy likes this kind of finger play as well. Many men particularly appreciate anal stimulation when they're receiving oral sex—the combination of penile and prostate stimulation for them is like clitoris plus G-spot for us.

- **Bring him into the fold.** If your guy is turned on by your backside and you're not happy about anal penetration, invite him to have intercourse within the crease between your buttocks. You may enjoy the stimulation to your anal region and your perineum without any of the hassles of anal penetration. Good positions for "crease intercourse" are you on your stomach or you on hands and knees, doggie style. Prepare your crease with plenty of lube—Revelation and Slip 'n Slide are good choices—and then invite him to guide his penis into your crease and then have him squeeze your cheeks together as his pleasure requires. Or, if you're good at squeezing your cheeks yourself, he can hold his penis in place with one hand or move it up and down within the crease, reaching his other hand around to your clitoris, which he can stimulate either with his fingers or with a vibrator such as a Bullet or Pleasure Curve.

Now that you've explored anal sex play, you and your partner may be interested in trying to "go all the way." I'll explain how you might try this, step by step, but first, let me remind you, this is a practice that

WHAT IF I GET "STRETCHED OUT"?

Although many people fear that anal sex will make their bowels weak and uncontrollable, you have nothing to worry about. Though over time your body may learn to accommodate your partner's penis more comfortably, this is not caused by stretching—rather, it is caused by you learning how to relax your muscles.

requires lots of respect and good communication. And, frankly, anal sex is going to hurt, at least initially. So if either of you feels pain—you from his penis, him from a tush toy—be prepared to stop. It's not possible to insert a penis into your anus without some initial discomfort that can be pretty intense, so it's your call whether you are interested enough in this sexual activity to put up with the pain that will probably be involved, at least at first. If you continue, you will eventually learn to relax and control the sphincter muscles and be able to accommodate your partner's penis more easily. Even so, if either of you is inserting *any* item into your anus—either sex toy or penis—you'll need to be sensitive to the difference between this "to be expected" initial pain and a more intense pain that indicates either too great a strain on the anal muscles or that something is tearing your anal tissue. More lubrication or greater relaxation may help. You may decide that the pain isn't worth it, or that this isn't an activity that you want to continue. As with all aspects of sexual activity, the final choice of what you will and won't do should always be up to you.

YOUR *Passion Diva's Guide* TO ANAL PENETRATION

- **Step one: Relax.** This is the key to enjoying anal sex. Feeling tense, wary, or unwilling means your muscles tighten up. Feeling relaxed and open means you'll be relaxed and open. Encourage your partner to help relax you with the kind of foreplay you most enjoy and perhaps a massage. Have him apply a very slippery lubricant such as Revelation or UltraGlide Gel in your anal area as he engages gently in some rimming and finger play. Breathe deeply (see the suggestions for deep breathing on page 252) and visualize the pleasure you expect. Put yourself into an open, receptive frame of mind for maximum pleasure.

- **Step two: Apply lubrication.** You've heard about this step before, but it bears repeating. Both your anal area and the item to be inserted—toy or penis—should be well lubricated, ideally with a long-lasting, very slippery lubricant such as Revelation. Often petroleum-based lubricants such as Vaseline or baby oil are recommended for anal play; however, petroleum will destroy a condom (always recommended for anal sex). The choice here is about safe sex. If you use a condom, stick with Revelation, and stay both safe *and* slippery. By the way, if you two try RomantaTherapy Sensual Warming Lubricant, your guy will be stimulated both from the slippery sensation and from the warmth; the extra excitement may even cause him to climax sooner.

• **Step three: Start with a tush toy.** Since initial penetration is always the most difficult part of anal sex, why not start with a tush toy to help prepare the way. You can also use any of these tush toys while self-pleasuring or during foreplay. Make sure to use only toys specifically designed for anal use. Another type of sex toy might get stuck inside your rectum. All anal toys should have a topper at the end—a flat round or oval base that prevents the toy from slipping all the way in. Consider one of these choices:

  ~ **Anal plugs,** such as the Playful Plug, are great for the first-time anal explorer. These vinyl toys are very flexible and often feature a secure finger ring for safe play. They have small shafts that are easy to insert and remove. Some shafts widen in the middle for some extra sensation.

  ~ **Anal vibrators,** such as the Disco Mini Tongue, are thinner than a regular vibrator. You can get many different kinds with many different types of action. Sometimes they're called "probes." You can also use the Magic Mushroom for anal sex, because it's got a stopper. Just don't use it for anything else once you've used it for anal sex.

  ~ **Anal beads** are a series of little balls spaced from a half-inch to an inch apart, either connected by a string or encased in plastic. I recommend the encased variety—such as our Love Wand—

because they're a lot easier to clean than the strung-together kind. You insert the beads slowly, then remove them even more slowly. It's the removal part that feels good. Just be sure to remove them very gently. Don't yank them out as if you were starting your lawn mower.

- **Step four: Insert the penis.** After you've gotten used to anal sex play and tush toys, you may feel relaxed and open enough to receive your guy's penis. The same principles apply: He should use a condom and plenty of lube on both his penis and your anus; he should wait till you're aroused, relaxed, and ready; and he should take it very, very slowly, stopping at the first sign of pain. Some women experience a tearing sensation, which may mean your anal tissues are being torn or bruised. Remember, the anal sphincter is a muscle, so the more relaxed you are, the less pain there will be.

Suggest to your guy that he use short, thrusting movements. The less friction, the less chance of pain or discomfort. Since every inch of his penis will be tightly grasped, the typical speed or depth of thrusting during vaginal sex really isn't needed during anal sex. He may not even need to thrust at all. Short, rocking movements may be just as pleasurable for him and more comfortable for you.

You can also use Gigi as a buffer for anal sex. Just cut the sleeve to your desired length. Using plenty of lubrication (again, I recommend the RomantaTherapy Sensual Warming Lubricant), slide Gigi onto his shaft all the way to the base of his penis. With this method, you can relax knowing he's not penetrating too deeply and he still gets the full-coverage experience.

For the most part, your bottom is going to feel "full," which you may experience as a pleasant sensation, especially as the thousands of nerve endings within your anus are stimulated. With an adequate amount of lube and the right frame of mind, anal sex can even be another way for you to experience an intense orgasm. You can use your finger or a

THE OTHER SIDE OF GIGI

Gigi is a great toy that can be used to simulate anal as well as oral sex. Just turn the Gigi inside out, so that the hole on the end is smaller and tighter, resembling an anus. Make sure that everything is well-lubricated: the inside, the opening, and his penis. Then insert his shaft into the Gigi and enjoy simulated anal sex with no pain, anxiety, or discomfort.

vibrator to give yourself clitoral stimulation. I recommend the Pleasure Curve because it's longer and easier to hold than a Bullet. (And if you don't particularly enjoy the anal penetration, focusing on the clitoral pleasure can be a helpful distraction.)

Let's Play: Fun in Your Love Swing

The Love Swing is a device that allows you to perform otherwise difficult positions with ease and comfort. It's a swing with sturdy and padded harnesses that you suspend from the ceiling or a door frame—and it's your doorway to a countless amount of sexual positions, the ultimate couples toy.

The swing can also give you a completely new experience for oral sex, allowing you to focus solely on the pleasure you're receiving. Sit in the Love Swing just as you'd seat yourself on a playground swing. Place one foot in each stirrup so you can keep your legs separated with little or no effort. Have your partner kneel in front of you in between your legs, holding your thighs or buttocks as he pleasures you orally and as you lean back completely—head, neck, and back—while supporting your upper body by holding each side of the swing. It feels like getting oral sex while upside down! Your partner has lots of access to stimulate you with his fingers, a bullet, a vibrator, or some combination of the three.

The Love Swing also offers you numerous options for intercourse. For example, have your partner sit in the swing, his body supported by a strap placed behind his upper back. He can also hold on to the side straps. Straddle him as if you were going to sit on his lap facing him, or, in another variation, face away from him. Either way, you've got the control of the movements while he sits back and enjoys.

Another gift that the Love Swing offers is the chance to have sex while standing without having to maintain all the fitness and flexibility that an unsupported standing-sex position requires. Sit in the swing and support your feet by placing them in the stirrups. As he stands in front of you, facing you, have him pull your body against his and carefully lower you onto his erect shaft. The same technique can also be used for rear entry into your vagina: Instead of facing each other, he approaches you from behind.

For solo pleasure, use your Love Swing for self-pleasuring with a dildo. Use a dildo with a concave bottom that allows you to attach it to a wall like a suction cup. Seat yourself in the swing, but don't put your feet in the stirrups. Keep both feet on the floor and back your body up to the dildo, leaving your hands completely free for clitoral stimulation with your fingers, Bullet, or Finger Massager.

Now your Passion Diva has a full toolkit—from self-pleasure to

FUN WITH FERNS?

One of our Alabama Passion Consultants, Darlene, sold a Love Swing to a Passion Parties hostess. Darlene explained in detail how to use the Love Swing, stressing the need for a strong, sturdy hook driven into the ceiling from which the Love Swing could be suspended. "Remember," Darlene told her customer with a wink, "when you're not using the Love Swing, simply hang a beautiful big fern on the hook, and no one will ever be the wiser." The customer smiled knowingly.

A few months later, the hostess gave another party, and Darlene prepared to return. To her surprise, there were ferns hanging in every room of the house! There were even a few ferns hanging from the giant oak tree out back. The great adventure was certainly in full swing for that happy hostess and her husband.

RomantaTherapy to foreplay and many different types of sex. More important, you've made a deep, lasting connection with your Passion Diva, one that can continue to fill your life with joy and your relationship with intimate, exciting, and delicious sex.

Now it's time for one last treat—our 7-Day Passion Challenge, which will help you apply everything you've learned. The 7-Day Passion Challenge will push you to take your sexual relationship with yourself and your partner to great new heights. Read on to find out more.

—⌐ *In Your Passion Pantry* ⌐—

- **Frisky French Maid Costume.** A classic, ideal for fantasy play. Leave it on, or take it off slowly in a sexy striptease.
- **Fantasy hosiery.** Fishnet Body Stockings are hugely popular and can transform you into a temptress. You can even wear one under your day wear. From the hemline down, you're wearing fishnet hose, but only you and your partner will ever know how far the costume really goes.
- *Striptease for Real Women* **DVD.** If you've ever wanted to know how to do a sensual dance, check out this DVD for some pointers on how to move, dress, and open up to your sensual side.
- **A sexy blindfold.** Don't think pirate-style black. Think pink satin! You can also use a silky, sensuous scarf.
- **Quick-release handcuffs.** Some of them even come in faux fur for a more gentle, playful feel.
- *Anal Foreplay* **CD.** Renowned relationship coach Suzie Johnson offers these wonderful "how-to" tips and techniques for anal foreplay and penetration if you and your guy want to learn more about this popular sexual option.
- **Playful Plug.** This gentle tush toy offers pleasurable sensations for both men and women, with the option of adding a vibrating bullet for some more great vibrations.

- **Disco Mini Tongue**. The slender shape of this narrow-tipped toy makes this mini-tongue ideal for either rimming or penetration. It also comes with a bullet.
- **UltraGlide Gel**. If you're going in for anal play, you'll need a nice, extra-thick lube. UltraGlide is easy to use and lasts a long, long time.
- **Love Wand anal beads**. For an introduction to anal play, you can try inserting one bead at a time into your anus or his. Then pull them out slowly during orgasm for incredible sensations.

$$\sim\!\!\text{co}\ 10\ \text{o}\!\!\sim$$

The 7-Day Passion Challenge

Fun + Passion = Great Sex

The point of all sex, including adventurous sex, is to add fun, passion, and creativity to your relationship. Remember, sex is not rocket science. You don't have to take it so seriously. Laughing and giggling during lovemaking heightens your pleasure and builds the bond between you and your partner. Great sex is not about becoming a sexpert or even the world's greatest lover. It's about the connection and the ability to let go and enjoy everything you do together. Now that you've reached the end of this book and learned all about RomantaTherapy, foreplay, and everything that comes afterward, I invite you to have lots of fun as you take my Passion Challenge below. This is your opportunity to take the information, tips, and ideas in this book and incorporate them into your relationship. The 7-Day Passion Challenge is my challenge to you and aims to pull you and/or your partner up to new sexual heights that will bring you closer together. Not only will you receive all the benefits of your own sexually satisfied journey, but you can also use your experiences to win one of the many incredible prizes we're giving away (go to www.7daypassionchallenge.com for further details):

- FIRST PRIZE: A cruise for two that will allow you and your partner to enjoy your Diva at a romantic destination.

- SECOND PRIZE: A $1,000 Passion Parties gift certificate
- THIRD PRIZE: A $500 Passion Parties Passion Basket of romantic goodies.

The rules of the 7-Day Passion Challenge are *passionately* simple:

STEP 1: Create 10 little pieces of paper and number them 1 through 10. Scramble them up and blindly draw seven. Your Diva will be attracted to the 7 that are right for you.

STEP 2: Refer each day to the Passion Diva Principle in the book that matches the number you drew. Each day allow your Diva to be set free. You and/or your partner must engage in an activity that represents the Passion Diva Principle of the day.

STEP 3: Each day, journal what you learned about yourself and each other from each activity, including which ones made you giggle and which ones turned out to be true passion powerhouses—and why. Here are some suggestions and questions to get you started:

Shine the spotlight on your Diva; notice her feelings, her thoughts, and her manner. What did you observe that was different? What was the most inspiring thing your Diva learned/noticed?

_____

_____

_____

Dare to engage your Diva and remember that awareness and uniqueness can be pointers and opportunity for growth. What was your new awareness and how did it feel? How did people or your partner respond to you?

_____

_____

_____

What new possibilities did you and your Diva discover?

_____

_____

_____

What was your biggest "a-ha" moment?

_____

_____

_____

STEP 4: Share your Passion Diva stories and be eligible to win Passion Parties prizes. Go to http://www.7daypassionchallenge.com, where you'll be asked to share your biggest "a-ha" from this book and how it has helped your relationship. If your Passion Diva were speaking to another woman who was trying to discover her own inner Passion Diva, what would she say? How would you guide another Diva to be the most satisfied, gratified, and exhilarated Diva she could be?

Write your advice in a concise paragraph and read it to the Passion Diva within you, share it with your friends, AND share it at www.7daypassionchallenge.com.

_____

_____

_____

_____

_____

_____

A Final Word

By reading this book you have come slightly (or perhaps a great deal) closer to your Passion Diva. It is not enough to learn. We have to then "become," and we do that by practicing what we have learned. Don't stop with the 7-Day Passion Challenge; join in the mission of women helping women. Give or suggest *The Passion Parties Guide to Great Sex* to another woman; give it as a bridal gift or a birthday present. Help spread the word to Passion Divas to rise up and be counted as we unite and continue to spread passion and joy through the world. The next time you watch another woman carry herself with confidence, shoulders thrown back and strutting, you can say to yourself, "She has her Passion Diva present!"

Passionately yours,

Pat Davis

Acknowledgments

From the conception of this book to its conclusion there have been many people who have believed in it, supported it, and unselfishly given of themselves to make it become a reality. I can't name every single one of you, but know that if you have met me, in some way you have contributed, and I appreciate you.

The opportunity to make my contribution was possible because two men, Bill Clark and Bill Dillingham, believed in me and entrusted me to become their business partner and run with their company, Passion Parties, to heights never thought possible before.

To Joanne Harvie, trusted friend for thirty years and honored business partner, I owe you the deepest gratitude for continually giving your unselfish time, wisdom, love, faith and belief in my vision, the company, and especially this work. Without you, neither Passion Parties nor this book would be what it is.

As I look into the eyes of the Passion Parties Consultants, leaders, and corporate staff, I see the spark of passion and desire to make a difference in the lives of women and their families. I wish to express my profound appreciation for the dedication you give every day to making a difference.

To Passion Parties' Million Dollar Club and Executive Director Council, an amazing collection of our top performers, I owe a deep debt of gratitude for working on the "secret project" for a year behind the scenes. You and your teams are the core of this book. Thanks to all of you for sharing your stories, your experience, your testimonies, your tips and techniques, and for your deep passion and love for this business. Most important, thank you for daily making a difference in the world by empowering women from the bedroom to the bank.

To Claudia Cross, my agent, thank you for all your endeavors in making sure I had the right publisher and your continued confidence in me, Passion Parties, and our mission. Your smile, positive attitude, coaching, and professionalism are a treasure to me.

To Karen Kelly and Rachel Kranz for the many hours you gave in editing this work and helping me find new and more concise ways to express myself.

To Ann Campbell, my amazing Broadway Books editor, your conviction in this project was unshakable. I knew from the first day that I met you that you understood my mission and that I would be safe in your hands to deliver my message. I wish to express my profound appreciation for the patience and wisdom that you have shown me through these many months and for your inspiration when at several points it got shaky. Thank you for your confidence in me and your priceless input in making this work an amazing project.

To the Passion Parties home office team, who gave inspiration and contribution beyond your normal responsibilities—Tony Giovanni, Vice President of Communications and a business associate and friend for over fourteen years; Susan Nicholas, the Senior Editor at Passion Parties; Passion Parties Graphic Artist Anna Phillips; my Executive Assistant Tina Ogas, who supports me daily and works diligently to keep me organized. And in all endeavors you need experts to advise and guide you. Three such experts to whom I owe a deep appreciation are Michael Castleman, leading sex and health writer since 1973—you truly understand women; Suzie Johnson, relationship coach—all the way from expert content contribution to the final edits, your sensuality, knowledge, and passion always shone through; and Dr. Louanne Cole Weston, Ph.D., sex therapist for more than twenty years, whose research, knowledge, and experience have been a cornerstone of Passion Parties training for years. I want to express gratitude to all of you for unselfishly giving of your time and knowledge, and for your belief in this book and in our mission.

Finally, to my family, you all journey with me through many adventures in life and are always willing to love me and believe in me. I am blessed with my son, Matthew, my daughter, Laura, and their partners Audrey and Mike, and my precious grandchildren Megan, Walker, and Mason. Most of all, I am deeply thankful for my good fortune to be married to my loving soul mate, Ollie. After over forty-eight years together, you continue to make me feel special, make me laugh, and you are my most enduring supporter. I relish each night that I fall to sleep holding your hand, the mornings that I wake up to you with excitement that you are there and beside me in all that I do. I love you!

Thank you to those who are reading this book, thank you for being willing to start your journey to meet your Passion Diva. It is a journey worth taking and I wish you joy, happiness, fun, and laughter.